THE FEAR OF THE DEAD IN PRIMITIVE RELIGION

VOL. III

MACMILLAN AND CO., Limited
LONDON · BOMBAY · CALCUTTA · MADRAS
MELBOURNE

THE MACMILLAN COMPANY
NEW YORK · BOSTON · CHICAGO
DALLAS · ATLANTA · SAN FRANCISCO

THE MACMILLAN COMPANY
OF CANADA, LIMITED
TORONTO

THE

FEAR OF THE DEAD
IN PRIMITIVE RELIGION

BY

SIR JAMES GEORGE FRAZER
O.M., F.R.S., F.B.A.

FELLOW OF TRINITY COLLEGE, CAMBRIDGE
ASSOCIATE MEMBER OF THE *INSTITUT DE FRANCE*

VOL. III

MACMILLAN AND CO., LIMITED
ST. MARTIN'S STREET, LONDON
1936

COPYRIGHT

PRINTED IN GREAT BRITAIN
BY R. & R. CLARK, LIMITED, EDINBURGH

PREFACE

THIS volume concludes my study of the Fear of the Dead in Primitive Religion. It forms a sequel to the two volumes of my lectures delivered under the William Wyse Foundation at Trinity College, Cambridge. The subject is the same, and the treatment is continuous. Throughout we are dealing with some of the answers which primitive man has given to the great enigma of death—of death in the widest sense, as the inevitable end, not only of man, but of every living thing. We may smile at some of his answers as childish and absurd, but do we of this generation read the riddle better than he? May it not be that posterity will smile at some of the solutions of the problem to which our contemporaries, with all the resources of modern science at their disposal, cling as tenaciously as does primitive man to his phantasmagoria of the dead? The only lesson we can safely draw from the survey of facts here submitted to the reader is a lesson of humility and hope: a lesson of humility, because it reminds us

how little we know on the subject, which, of all others,
concerns us most nearly ; a lesson of hope, because
it suggests the possibility that others may hereafter
solve the problem which has baffled us.

J. G. FRAZER

13th February 1936

CONTENTS

The fear of the spirits of the dead has led primitive man to take many precautions to keep them at bay. One method commonly and widely adopted is to destroy or desert the house in which the deceased lived and died, and which his spirit will consequently be expected to seek out. Examples from Australia, from the East Indies, from the Straits, Burma, India and Assam, from Lappland, from Africa, and from North, Central and South America.

Stinks are occasionally employed to repel ghosts, as among various Indian tribes of North and South America.

Corpses may be buried in the bed of a stream to prevent the spirits from returning: examples from different parts of Africa. Alaric the Goth was thus buried, and the ashes of the prophet Daniel are reported to have been similarly treated.

The ghost of a dead man may be pegged down into the earth. Examples from India, Cochin-China, and Africa.

By burying the body in certain positions also some people imagine they prevent the return of the spirit. Examples from South America, India, and Siam. For the same purpose a corpse is very often carried out of the house feet foremost, as among some natives of the East Indies, of South America, and of Northern India, as well as among the inhabitants of Germany, Denmark, and Italy.

Sometimes a corpse is blindfolded to blind the spirit. Examples from Australia, Corea and Cambodia. Often a coin is placed on each of the dead person's eyes to blind him, a custom recorded for various parts of the Indian Archipelago and Europe. The masks found covering faces in the ancient royal graves of Mycenae may have had a similar purpose. Such masks for corpses have been employed in different parts of Asia and Europe.

connexion it may be suggested that the legend of Orestes, how he recovered sanity by biting off one of his fingers after murdering his mother, may contain a reminiscence of a drastic mode of appeasing the angry ghost of a murdered person.

Persons who have taken their own life are greatly feared after death, and special precautions are often taken to guard against their spirits. Examples from Africa, India, China, Russia, Indo-China, ancient Greece and modern Europe.

All who have died violently are commonly dreaded after death by primitive man. Thus in India various precautions are taken against the spirits of those slain by tigers. Other examples from Burma, the East Indies, Africa and North America.

A special dread is widely entertained of the spirits of women dying in childbed. This dread is particularly prevalent throughout India and the Malay region to the east. It is also recorded in parts of Africa and among the ancient Mexicans.

The ghosts of dead husbands and wives are commonly deemed very dangerous to their surviving spouses, and special precautions are often taken to guard the widow or widower. Examples from East Indies, India, Kamtchatka, Africa, America and Australia.

Adults who die unmarried or without issue are thought to have missed the crowning blessing of this world, and to be ill at ease in the next, so that their spirits are greatly feared as especially dangerous. Various means are adopted of propitiating them. Commonly this takes the form of a marriage of the dead with another dead person, with a living person, or with some animate or inanimate object. Examples from Fiji, the Indian Archipelago, Africa, India, China and Russia. The ancient Greek custom of placing a pitcher on the tomb of all unmarried people may have originated in this way.

Since the soul of a recently deceased person is supposed to be greatly concerned with the disposal of his mortal remains, the bodies of people who die away from home, and therefore cannot be buried in the usual way, occasion much anxiety to their survivors. Commonly their kinsmen attempt to pacify the spirits of such people by holding

CHAPTER I

PRECAUTIONS AGAINST THE RETURN OF GHOSTS

In a former part of this work[1] I endeavoured to show that a belief in the survival of the human spirit after death has been general, if not universal, among those races of lower culture whom we call savages or barbarians, and whom we may legitimately term primitive in a relative sense, by comparison with civilized nations. We saw that in the opinion of primitive man the spirits of the dead continue to exert a great influence on the life of the survivors both for good and evil. It is thought on the one hand, for example, that they can cause the rain to fall and the fruits of the earth to grow, that they can bless women with offspring, that they can give oracles, and aid their living kinsfolk in war. These are substantial benefits, but on the other hand the spirits of the dead are supposed to be touchy and prone to take offence, and to visit offenders with their displeasure in the shape of many grievous calamities, including sickness and death. Naturally,

[1] *The Fear of the Dead in Primitive Religion*, vol. i. (London, 1933), pp. 1 *sqq.*

therefore, primitive man looks on the spirits of the dead with very mixed feelings. The thought of them is associated in his mind with emotions of hope and fear, of love and hate, of attraction and repulsion. It is not possible for us to measure exactly the force and extent of these diverse and conflicting emotions and to gauge the relative proportion in which they stand to each other ; but it is safe to say that if the fear of the dead has not been the predominant motive in the attitude of primitive man to their spirits it has at least been a very potent agent in moulding the early history of religion. As such, it deserves our serious attention, and forms the subject of this work.

The fear of the spirits of the dead has led primitive man to adopt many precautions for the purpose of keeping these formidable beings at bay and removing them to what he deems a safe distance from him. Thus, for example, he often attempts to drive them away by main force, or to dismiss them peaceably under the safe-conduct of an animal or bird, who is supposed to guide the poor wanderers to that bourne from which no traveller returns ; but in case the spirits should nevertheless attempt to force their way back to the land of the living he sometimes erects barriers of fire or water or more solid materials which he hopes may arrest their progress, and so will leave him in peace. Another mode of preventing the return of the spirits is to render their old home as unattractive as possible in the hope that they will thus be prevented from

attempting to regain it. With this view it has often
been customary to destroy the property of a dead
man in order to spare him the temptation of returning
to take possession of it from its living proprietor.
This destruction of the property of the dead I have
illustrated at some length in a previous volume,[1]
and I now take up the subject at the point where
I broke off.

Some primitive peoples, not content with destroying the property of a dead man, demolish the
dwelling in which the death took place, and flee
from the spot in order to avoid a possible encounter
with the ghost who may be prowling about his
desolate home. Other peoples, without destroying
the house or hut, content themselves with retiring
to a distance from the scene of death, with the same
object of avoiding all possible contact with the
spirit of the deceased.

Thus, to take examples: in the Mara tribe of
Northern Australia, when any person dies, the body
is eaten by the relatives, and the bones deposited
on a platform in a tree. " As soon as any one
dies, the camps are immediately shifted, because the
spirit, of whom they are frightened, haunts its old
camping ground."[2] Among the aborigines of the
Lower Murray River, when a death took place, it
was customary to pull down the wurley or rude
temporary hut of the deceased, because no one would
inhabit the spot where a death had taken place.[3]

[1] The Fear of the Dead in Primitive Religion, vol. ii. pp. 119 sqq.
[2] Baldwin Spencer, Native Tribes
of the Northern Territory of Australia (London, 1914), p. 254.
[3] R. Brough Smyth, The Ab-

An English traveller in New Zealand has described his visit to a Maori village which had been totally deserted on the death of the chief. " Here, though everything was in perfect preservation, not a living soul was to be seen : the village, with its neat houses, built of *raupo*, and its court-yards and provision boxes, was entirely deserted. From the moment the chief was laid beneath the upright canoe, on which was inscribed his name and rank, the whole village became strictly *tapu* or sacred ; and not a native, on pain of death, was permitted to trespass near the spot : the houses were all fastened up, and on most of the doors were inscriptions, denoting that the property of such an one remained there. An utter silence pervaded the place. After ascertaining that no natives were in the vicinity of the forbidden spot, I landed and trod the sacred ground ; and my footsteps were probably the first, since the desertion of the village, that had echoed along its palisaded passages." [1]   Similarly in the Marshall Islands, when a chief dies, his hut is abandoned and allowed to fall into decay, for no one will dare to enter it. [2]

Among some of the natives in the eastern part of British New Guinea, " after a death has taken place in a house it is usual for the house to be deserted and allowed to fall to pieces ; but sometimes it is so nearly new that it is a pity to have to build

origines of Victoria (Melbourne and London, 1878), i. p. xxx.

[1] G. F. Angas, *Savage Life and Scenes in Australia and New*   *Zealand* (London, 1847), i. pp. 278 *sq.*

[2] A. Erdland, *Die Marshall-Insulaner* (Münster, 1914), p. 325.

another, the doorway is closed up and a new doorway made in another wall and the house still used. It seems that the spirit of the dead one will haunt the place, but it can be deceived by this little artifice. As people lie awake at night they will sometimes say they have heard the spirit scratching along the wall trying to find its way into the house."[1] Among the Kai of Northern New Guinea, the house in which a death has taken place is abandoned because the spirit of the deceased is supposed to haunt it.[2] In Misol, a small island to the north-west of New Guinea, when a death has taken place in a house the house is abandoned, and a new one is built elsewhere. The body, wrapped in cloths, is deposited on a scaffold built for it in the forest. From time to time the relations come to inspect the corpse until decomposition is complete. The skeleton is then brought to the place, generally a cave, where the bones of all the dead inhabitants of the village are collected.[3] In the East Indian island of Buru, when a death has taken place in a house, the survivors desert it, and go in search of a dwelling elsewhere.[4]

In the Andaman Islands a dead body is either buried in a grave or deposited on a platform in a tree. When this has been done the men return to the camp, "where the women have been busy packing

[1] H. Newton, *In Far New Guinea* (London, 1914), p. 227.

[2] R. Neuhauss, *Deutsch Neu Guinea* (Berlin, 1911), p. 83.

[3] J. Wanner, "Ethnologische Notizen über die Inseln Timor und Misol", in *Archiv für Anthropologie*. N.F. xii. (1913).

[4] J. G. F. Riedel, *De Sluik— en Kroesharige Rassen tusschen Selebes en Papua* ('s-Gravenhage, 1886), p. 12.

up all belongings. Plumes of shredded palm-leaf stem (*koro*) are put up at the entrance to the camp to show chance visitors that there has been a death. The camp is then deserted, the natives moving to some other camping ground until the period of mourning is over, when they may, if they wish, return to the deserted village. No one goes near the grave again until the period of mourning is over."[1]

Among the Sakai of Perak, a primitive dwarf race of the Malay Peninsula, when a death took place the house was invariably burned down and the settlement deserted, even at the risk of the loss of standing crops.[2] Among the Mantra of Malacca, after a death in the clearing, nothing more was planted there, and when the crop or plants on the ground had been gathered it was abandoned.[3] Among the Benuas of Malacca the house where a person has died is generally deserted and burnt.[4] The Kachins of Burma, who have attained to a higher level of culture than these wild tribes of the Malay Peninsula, do not destroy a house in which a death has taken place, but merely make a pretence of doing so and of building a new house in another place.[5] It is thus with the growth of civilization, superstition yields to economic consideration.

[1] A. R. Brown, *The Andaman Islanders* (Cambridge, 1922), p. 108.

[2] A. Hale, " On the Sakais ", in the *Journal of the Royal Anthropological Institute*, xv. (1886) p. 291; W. W. Skeat and C. O. Blagden, *Pagan Races of the Malay Peninsula* (London, 1906), ii. p. 96.

[3] Skeat and Blagden, *op. cit.* ii. p. 111.

[4] T. J. Newbold, *British Settlements in Malacca* (London, 1839), ii. p. 410.

[5] C. P. Gilhodes, " Mort et funérailles chez les Katchins (Birmanie) ", in *Anthropos*, xii-xiii. p. 431.

The Karens of Burma desert a house in which a death has taken place lest the soul (*Kelah*) of some person remaining in it, especially of one of the children, should be induced to accompany the departed, whose soul (*Kelah*) may thereby the more readily return to a wonted spot and call for a friend's soul. Of this many cases are believed to have occurred.[1]

Some of the Ainus, a primitive tribe of Japan, say that " in years long gone by the ancients used to burn down the hut in which the oldest woman of a family had died. This curious custom was followed, so some of them say, because it was feared that the spirit of the woman would return to the hut after death, and, out of envy, malice, or hatred, bewitch her offspring and sons- and daughters-in-law, together with their whole families, and bring upon them various noxious diseases and many sad calamities. Not only would she render them unprosperous, but she would cause them to be unsuccessful in the hunt, kill all the fresh and salt-water fish, send the people great distress, and render them childless. She would curse the labour of their hands, both in the house, the garden, and the forest ; she would blight all their crops, stop the fountains and springs of drinking water, make life a weary burden, and eventually slay all the people and their children. So vicious and ill-disposed are the departed spirits of old women supposed to be, and

---

[1] Rev. E. B. Cross, " On the Karens ", in the *Journal of the* *American Oriental Society*, iv. (1854) p. 310.

so much power for evil are they said to possess. For this reason, therefore, the ancients used to burn down the hut in which an old woman had lived and died ; the principal idea being that the soul, when it returned from the grave to exercise its diabolical spells, would be unable to find its former residence and the objects of its hatred and fiendish intentions. The soul having been thus cheated of its prey, and its malignant designs frustrated, is supposed to wander about for a time in a towering rage, searching for its former domicile ; but of course to no purpose. Eventually the spirit returns, defeated and dejected, to the grave whence it came, and woe betide the person bold or unlucky enough to venture near the spot.

The custom, however, is now being discontinued ; but customs die hard, and part of this one is still seen to survive. Thus, whenever a woman is getting to be very old and likely to die soon, her children build her a tiny hut somewhere near her old home. When finished, she is sent there to reside, where she is provided with food till she dies. But when she is dead and buried this hut is burned instead of her old house." [1]

Among the Dhanwār, a primitive hill tribe of the Central Provinces of India, when an elder man dies his family usually abandon their hut, because they believe that his spirit haunts it, and would cause the death of anybody who dared to live there.[2]

[1] J. Batchelor, *The Ainus and their Folk-Lore* (London, 1901), pp. 130 *sq.*

[2] R. V. Russell, *The Tribes and Castes of the Central Provinces of India* (London, 1916), ii. 498.

Among the Korwas, another tribe of the Central Provinces of India, when a man dies his hut is broken down, and the family does not inhabit it again.[1] Among the Kurmis, yet another tribe of the Central Provinces of India, " there is a belief that the spirit of the deceased hovers round familiar scenes and places, and on this account, whenever possible, a house in which any one has died is destroyed or deserted."[2]   Among the Savaras, an important hill-tribe of Southern India, on certain days every house in which a death has taken place during the last two years is burned down.   After this the ghost of the deceased (*Kulba*) is supposed to give no more trouble, and does not come to reside in the new hut that is built on the site of the burnt one.[3] In Assam, " if a man dies inside a house, no Hindoo can eat in it afterwards, or reside in it, as it has become impure ; it is generally pulled down and burned, and a new house erected on the same spot. All Assamese when dying are, therefore, invariably brought out to die in the open air on the bare ground, that the building may be preserved ; and also to ensure the happier liberation from the body."[4]   Far from India the Lapps in the north of Europe used to strew with stones the place in the hut where a person had died, and then to remove their dwelling to another site, doubtless to avoid the spirit of the

[1] Russell, *op. cit.* iii. 574.
[2] Russell, *op. cit.* iv. 80 (referring to Gordon, *Indian Folk-Tales*, p. 54).
[3] E. Thurston, *Castes and Tribes of Southern India* (Madras, 1909), vi. 328.
[4] J. Butler, *Travels and Adventure in the Province of Assam* (London, 1855), pp. 258 *sq.*

deceased, which they had apparently sought to pin
down by a weight of stones piled on the place where
he had died.[1]

In Africa the custom of deserting a place in
which a death has occurred is very wide-spread.
Thus, among the Banyankole, a pastoral people of
Uganda, mourning lasts for three or four months.
When it ends the survivors remove to some new
site, and build another kraal. The old place falls
into decay and is soon overgrown and lost to sight.[2]
Sometimes when the heir had had time to build a
new kraal, the old kraal was not only deserted but
broken down and left in its ruins to decay.[3] Among
the Basoga, another people of Uganda, when a death
has taken place the hut of the deceased is deserted,
and never repaired. No one may live in it, though
the chief's house may be built near the site.[4] Similarly among the Bateso, another people of Uganda,
the house in which a death has taken place is deserted
and suffered to fall into decay, and no one attempts
to repair it.[5] Among the Nilotic tribes of Kavirondo
the hut in which a death has taken place is used for
a month. The neighbours then assemble and drink
beer, and break down the hut.[6]

Among the negroes of the Slave Coast the dead

[1] C. Leemius, *de Lapponibus Fin-
marchiae eorumque lingua, vita,
et religione pristina commentatio*
(Copenhagen, 1767), pp. 499 *sq*.

[2] J. Roscoe, *The Northern Bantu*
(Cambridge, 1915), p. 129.

[3] J. Roscoe, *The Banyankole*
(Cambridge, 1923), p. 149.

[4] Roscoe, *The Northern Bantu*,
p. 227.

[5] Roscoe, *The Northern Bantu*,
p. 267.

[6] C. W. Hobley, *Eastern Uganda*
(London, 1902). p. 27 ; Sir H.
Johnston, *The Uganda Protectorate*,
Second Edition (London, 1904), ii.
793.

are buried in the house. The room in which the
dead is buried is no longer used ; but often the roof
is removed and the house abandoned. They burn
the clothing of the deceased, and destroy the objects
which he used in his life.[1]

Among the Ewe-speaking people of Togoland,
nine days after a burial the house of the deceased is
pulled down, and the remains of it are taken outside
of the house and burned.[2] But if the deceased has
died a violent death away from home, whether killed
in war, or drowned in a river, or fallen from a tree in
the forest, nine days after the burial they go to the
place where the misfortune overtook him, dig up
some of the earth from the spot, put it in two little
pots, tie them up with blue stuff, and place the pots
on the grave. When they have done this they break
down the house of the deceased and burn it. Among
these same people when a man has been killed by
the bite of a snake a curious ceremonial is observed.
His friends shoot the body of the deceased and bring
it to a public place in the village, where they bathe
it, ornament it, and smear it with white earth. Then
they pour palm-wine into his mouth, and continue
to fire their muskets for a long time. Nine or eleven
days after they break down the house of the deceased.
But before doing so they take a small pot with a lid
and carry it to the spot where the man was bitten
by the snake. There they dig up some earth, put
it in the pot, and close the pot. The oldest woman

---

[1] P. Bouche, *La Côte des Esclaves
et le Dahomey* (Paris, 1885), p. 214.

[2] J. Spieth, *Die Ewe-Stämme*
(Berlin, 1906), p. 288.

of the family then carries the pot on her head, and
followed by the whole population of the village,
drumming and firing shots, she goes to the grave of
the deceased, on which she places the pot upside
down. The firing continues for a long time, and
the companions of the deceased then break down his
house. Afterwards they entertain the inhabitants of
that quarter of the town, and then they play till
nightfall.[1] The writer who describes this quaint
rite does not explain it ; but we may conjecture that
the soul of the deceased is supposed to be taken up
in the earth dug up at the spot where he was bitten
by the snake, and that having been thus recovered,
the soul is safely bottled up in the pot, and finally
restored to the deceased at his grave.[2] Among the
Bimbians in the valley of the Niger, on the death of
a chief or great man, " more or less of the property
is left in the house, which is abandoned, and allowed
after an interval to go to decay."[3] Among the
Yaunde in the Cameroons, when an unexplained
death has taken place in a hamlet, the inhabitants
abandon it, and shift their abode to a distance, often
to a considerable distance. We are told that the
motive is to avoid the evil magic which has proved
fatal to one of their number ; but we may conjecture
that the true reason is to avoid the ghost of the
deceased.[4] Among the peoples in the district of

---

[1] J. Spieth, *op. cit.* 156–158.
[2] J. Spieth, *op. cit.* p. 760.
[3] W. Allen and T. R. H. Thomson,
*Narrative of the Expedition to the
River Niger in 1841* (London, 1848),

ii. p. 297.
[4] G. Zenker, " Yaunde ", in
*Mitteilungen von Forschungsreis-
enden und Gelehrten aus den
Deutschen Schutzgebieten*, iii. p. 69.

Ogowe, when a chief or other man of importance dies, the custom is to abandon the site where the death took place, and to remove the settlement to another place in the forest. A traveller in West Africa tells us that he often met with the remains of such abandoned settlements in the forest. The old houses are either left to fall into decay or are burned down.[1] Among the Wangata of the Belgian Congo when a death occurs they pull down the house in which the deceased died, fell the banana-trees which overshadowed it, and allow the grass to grow on the site.[2] Among the Baholoholo of the Belgian Congo when a death has taken place all the huts of the deceased are burned.[3] The writer who reports the custom supposes that this is done as a measure of hygiene; but more probably the motive is a fear of the ghost. An old Portuguese writer, Dos Santos, speaking of the Kafirs of South-East Africa, tells us that after a burial they burn the thatched house of the deceased with all it contains, so that no one may possess anything that the dead person made use of in his lifetime, or even touch it, and if it so happens that some one touches anything belonging to the deceased he does not enter his house until he has washed in the river. The ashes of the burnt house with any pieces of wood not quite consumed they put on the top of the grave.[4] With regard to the Barotse, a Bantu tribe of South Africa, we are told

---

[1] O. Lenz, *Skizzen aus Westafrika* (Berlin, 1878), p. 208.

[2] Lieut. Engels, *Les Wangata* (Brussels, 1912), p. 53.

[3] R. Schmitz, *Les Baholoholo* (Brussels, 1912), p. 223.

[4] Dos Santos, in Theal, *Records of South-eastern Africa* (1901), vii. 307.

that death inspires them with a mortal terror, and that among them consequently the hut of the deceased person is almost always abandoned.[1] Livingstone was told that among the Makonde, another South African tribe, when any one died in a village the whole population deserted it, saying that it was a bad spot.[2] Of the Bantu tribes in South Africa generally the attitude to the spirits of the dead has been described as follows by their historian, Dr. McCall Theal. " There was an idea that something connected with death attached to the personal effects of the deceased, on which account whatever had belonged to him that could not be placed in the grave, his clothing, mats, head-rest, etc., was destroyed by fire. The hut in which he had lived was also burned, and no other was allowed to be built on the spot. If he had been the chief, the whole kraal was removed to another site. Those who touched the corpse or any of the dead man's effects were obliged to go through certain ceremonies, and then to bathe in running water before associating again with their companions. Except in cases of persons of rank, however, very few deaths occurred within kraals. As soon as it was seen that any one's end was near, the invalid was carried to a distance and left to die alone, in order to avert the danger of the presence of the dreaded something that could not be explained."[3]

[1] L. Decle, *Three Years in Savage Africa* (London, 1898), p. 76.
[2] D. Livingstone, *Last Journals* (London, 1874), i. 28.

[3] Dr. G. McCall Theal, *Ethnography of South Africa* (London, 1919), p. 76.

With regard to the Bushmen of South Africa we are told by two French missionaries in the first half of nineteenth century that when a man died his hut was broken down, piled over his grave, and burned.[1] At the other extremity of Africa the nomadic Tuaregs of the north, when a death has taken place, always shift their camp, and avoid everything that might recall the memory of the deceased.[2] Among some tribes at the foot of the Atlas Mountains, when a cadi dies, the new cadi never inhabits the castle or house of his predecessor, unless he happens to be a member of the same family. He always builds a new house for himself. A traveller in these regions has described how he saw many such castles falling into ruins after the death of their last occupants.[3]

Similar customs have been observed for similar reasons by the aborigines in many parts of America, both north and south. Thus the Eskimos think that a hut in which a death has taken place is polluted and dangerous, and they will make no use of anything that is in it at the moment when the dying person breathed his last. Hence when a sick person is obviously dying they hasten to remove him to a small temporary hut which after the death can be abandoned without serious loss.[4] Among the

[1] T. Arbousset and F. Daumas, *Relation d'un voyage d'exploration* (Paris, 1842), p. 503.

[2] H. Duveyrier, *Exploration du Sahara : Les Touareg du Nord* (Paris, 1864).

[3] E. Doutté, *En Tribu* (Paris, 1914), p. 247.

[4] C. F. Hall, *Life with the Esquimaux* (London, 1864), pp. 201, 249. Cf. Lecorre, in *Annales de l'Association de la Propagation de la Foi*, vol. xlvii. (1875) p. 121.

Eskimos of Alaska if there are many deaths about the same time, or an epidemic occurs, everything belonging to the dead is destroyed. The house in which a death occurs is always deserted, and usually destroyed. In order to avoid this, they commonly take a sick person out of the house, and put him in a tent to die.[1] Among the Thompson Indians of British Columbia, " the lodge in which an adult person died was burned. The winter house, after a death had taken place in it, was purified with water in which tobacco and juniper had been soaked, and fresh fir-boughs were spread on the floor each morning. Pieces of tobacco and juniper were also placed in various parts of the house. But if two or more deaths occurred in it at the same time, or in immediate succession, then the house was invariably burned. Most of the household utensils of a deceased person were also burned, as well as the bed on which he had died. The place where the deceased had lain when dying was not occupied for some time. Then an adult male slept on it four nights in succession. After that it was considered safe for any one to lie there." [2] From this account we may see that while these Indians invariably burned a summer hut in which a single death had occurred they spared in a similar case the more solid and therefore more valuable winter house, not burning it down until several deaths in it had con-

[1] W. Dall, *Alaska and its Resources* (London, 1870), p. 146.

[2] J Teit, *The Thompson Indians* *of British Columbia* (Memoirs of the American Museum of Natural History, vol. ii. The Jesup North Pacific Expedition), 1900, p. 331.

vinced them of the great danger of allowing it to stand. Among these Indians economic considerations have partially tempered the fear of the spirits of the dead. Yet among them that fear is very serious ; for we are told that " nobody could with impunity take possession of the bow and arrows, long leggings, and moccasins of a dead man. If any one appropriated the first of these, the dead man would come back for them, and in taking them away would also take the soul of the man possessing them, thereby causing his speedy death. If either of the other two were appropriated, the one who took them would be visited by a sickness which would cause his feet and legs to swell enormously. It is not safe, except for a person who has a strong guardian spirit, to smoke out of the pipe of a person who has recently died. The tobacco will burn up in it faster than usual. This is a sign that the deceased wishes the pipe." [1] Among the Cree Indians of Canada, when a death has taken place in a tent, the whole camp is shifted for several miles.[2] Among the Apache-Yumas, an Indian tribe of the United States, if a death occurs in a hut, the hut with everything in it is burnt. " As soon as a death is announced, all the huts in the immediate neighbourhood are deserted, and often burned. . . . They dislike to speak of the dead, but refer to him indirectly, and usually in a whisper." [3]   Among

[1] J. Teit, *op. cit.* p. 331.
[2] C. Leden, " Unter den Indianern Canadas ", in *Zeitschrift für Ethnologie*, xliv. (1912), p. 816.

[3] W. F. Corbusier, " The Apache-Yumas and Apache-Mojavas ", in *The American Antiquary*, vol. vii. p. 338.

the Navahos, another Indian tribe of the United
States, when a death takes place the rafters of the
house are pulled down over the remains and the
place is usually set on fire. After that nothing
would induce a Navaho to touch a piece of the wood,
or even approach the immediate vicinity of the
place ; even years afterwards such places are recog-
nised and avoided, because they are believed to be
haunted by the spirits of the dead. These shades or
spirits of the dead are not necessarily malevolent,
but they are regarded as inclined to resent any
intrusion or the taking of any liberty with them or
their belongings.[1] The Tamarahumare Indians of
Mexico always destroy a house in which a death has
taken place, and they break the baskets and other
household utensils which it contained.[2] The Yuca-
tecs, a Maya people of Mexico, used always to forsake a house in which a death had taken place,
because they greatly feared the spirit of the dead.[3]

The Anabali and other tribes of the Orinoco in
South America have so great a fear of death that
as soon as they have buried one of their number
near where he lived they immediately abandon
their crops, and build a new village at a distance of
twelve or fifteen leagues, and when they are ques-
tioned for their reason for thus abandoning their
crops they answer that since death has entered

[1] C. Mindeleff, " Navaho Houses ",
in the *Seventeenth Annual Report of
the Bureau of American Ethnology*,
1895–1896 (1898), p. 475.
    [2] C. Lumholz, *Unknown Mexico*

(London, 1903), i. p. 384.

    [3] H. H. Bancroft, *Native Races of
the Pacific States of North America*
(London, 1875–1876), ii. 800.

among them they no longer feel secure in that neighbourhood.[1] Among the Jibaros, a wild Indian tribe of Ecuador, when a death took place the dead used to be deposited in the house, which was then abandoned. The dead man was given his spear in his hand, and pots of food were placed around him ; then the door was shut and strongly fastened, and the relations departed.[2] Among the Guarauno Indians, a tribe in the delta of the Orinoco, when a death has taken place the body is placed in the hollowed-out trunk of a tree or in a canoe, wrapped in leaves, and is then left in the house, which is deserted. When several persons die in the village at short intervals, the village is deserted, because, as they assert, "an evil spirit (*gébu*) has passed by, cursing it."[3] Here again we may conjecture that the real evil spirits whom they dread are the ghosts of the departed.

Among the Jaguas, an Indian tribe in the upper valley of the Amazon, when a death has taken place the survivors burn the hut of the deceased and build a new one.[4] In a tribe of Peruvian Indians, whom the German traveller von Tschudi visited, the dead were buried in the huts which they inhabited in life. The relations broke the household utensils of the deceased, deserted the house, and built for themselves a new one in a distant place. But they

[1] P. J. Gumilla, *Histoire de l'Orénoque* (Avignon, 1758), i. 325.

[2] Dr. Rivet,"Les Indiens Jibaros", in *L'Anthropologie*, xviii. (1907) p. 608.

[3] J. Chaffanjon, *L'Orénoque et le Caura* (Paris, 1889), p. 13.

[4] G. Osculati, *Exploratione delle Regioni equatoriali lungo il Napo ed il fiume delle Amazzoni* (Milan, 1850), p. 209.

buried the weapons and agricultural instruments of
their dead kinsman with his body in the grave, because they thought that he would need them in the
spirit land.[1] Among the Conibos, an Indian tribe
visited by the French traveller Castelnau in the
interior of South America, when a death had taken
place and the body of the deceased had been
buried, the relatives used to break all the household vessels of the departed and then set fire to
his house. When the hut was burned down they
spread a thick layer of ashes over the spot, in which
they expected to find traces of the wandering soul
of the deceased.[2] The Tucanos, an Indian tribe
in the valley of the Uaupes, a northern tributary of
the Amazon, always bury their dead in the huts
which they inhabited in life. Then the family
immediately desert the hut and go and build
another, leaving the old one to decay. In a few
years the site of the old house has disappeared, and
is overgrown once more by the forest.[3]

Among the Yuracares, an Indian tribe in the
interior of South America, visited by the French
traveller D'Orbigny, when a death has occurred,
and the relatives have buried the deceased, they
abandon his hut and his fields.[4] The Calchaquis,
an Indian tribe of Brazil to the north of Paraguay,
always burned the hut in which a death had taken

[1] J. J. von Tschudi, *Peru—
Reiseskizzen aus den Jahren 1838–
1842* (St. Gallen, 1846), i. 235.

[2] F. de Castelnau, *Expédition
dans les parties centrales de*
l'Amérique du Sud (Paris, 1850–
1851), ii. 385.

[3] H. A. Coudreau, *La France
équinoxiale* (Paris, 1887), ii. 172.

[4] A. D'Orbigny, *L'Homme Améri-
cain* (Paris, 1839), i. 359.

place, and they buried the deceased with his eyes open, that he might see to find his way to the other world.[1]   The Lengua Indians of Paraguay were wont to burn down the hut in which a death had occurred, and then to destroy and vacate the village, till the eminent English missionary, Mr. Grubb, exacted from them a promise not to follow this ruinous practice.   They thought that the souls of the dead returned to the ruined village, to warm themselves at the fires in the chilly morning air, and that if they found the fires extinct they used to throw the ashes about in a rage.[2]   Mr. Grubb's evidence on this point is confirmed by the testimony of another English missionary, Mr. L. E. Guppy, who spent many years with the English Mission to the Paraguayan Chaco.[3]   Among the Coroados Indians of Brazil when an adult dies they bury him in his hut, and abandon it for another dwelling at a distance, for they fear to be haunted by the spirit of the deceased if they ever visited the place of death.[4]   The Tacunas, another Indian tribe of Brazil, bury their dead in pots in the huts which they inhabited.   Then they set fire to the huts and burn them with all their contents, unless the children of the deceased care to appropriate their father's weapons, which in that case are spared from the flames.[5]

[1] R. Southey, *History of Brazil* (Second Edition, 1822), i. 395.

[2] W. B. Grubb, *An Unknown People in an Unknown Land* (London, 1911), pp. 124, 165, 169.

[3] T. Koch, " Die Lenguas-India-ner in Paraguay ", in *Globus*, lxxvii. (1900) p. 220.

[4] J. B. von Spix und C. F. Ph. von Martius, *Reise in Brasilien* (Munich, 1823–1831), i. 382.

[5] *Ibid.* ii. 1187.

Another mode of avoiding all contact with the dangerous spirits of the dead is to repel them by stinks, for apparently the spirits are credited with a delicate sense of smell which leads them to shun persons and places infected with foul smells. Thus the Algonquin Indians of Canada used to burn stinking substances in order to repel the hovering spirits of the dead, and for the same purpose they sometimes put stinking stuffs on their own heads in order to guard themselves against the approach of the dreaded ghosts. This curious custom was observed and recorded by Jesuit missionaries in the seventeenth century,[1] and it has persisted down at least to the middle of the nineteenth century among the Ojebway Indians, one of whom has described his observations and experiences for us. After mentioning various modes of repelling the dangerous ghosts of the dead, he goes on, " Lest this should not prove effectual, they will also frequently take a deer's tail and, after burning or singeing off all the hair, will rub the necks or faces of the children before they lie down to sleep, thinking that the offensive smell will be another preventive to the spirit's entrance. I well remember when I used to be daubed over with this disagreeable fumigation, and had great faith in it all. Thinking that the soul lingers about the body a long time before it takes its final departure, they use these means to hasten it away."[2]

[1] Relation des Jésuites dans la Nouvelle-France en 1639 (Quebec, 1858), p. 44.

[2] P. Jones, History of the Ojebway Indians (London, N.D.), pp. 99 sq.

The Hidatsa Indians of the United States believe that the ghost of a deceased person lingers near his dwelling for four nights after his death. During this time " those who disliked or feared him and do not wish a visit from his shade, scorch with red-hot coals a pair of moccasins, which they leave at the door of the lodge. The smell of the burning leather, they claim, keeps the ghost out ; but the true friends of the dead man take no such precautions." [1] Of the Pampa del Sacramento Indians of South America it is recorded that when a person is dying and at his last gasp, " the women fall upon him, some close his eyes by force, others his mouth, and they throw upon him whatever comes to hand, and literally kill him while he is dying. Meanwhile others run to put out the candle, and dissipate the smoke, lest the soul not knowing how to get out should be entangled in the roof, and lest it should come back again to the same dwelling they collect all sorts of filth round about it, that the stink may drive it away." [2]

A forcible way of preventing the spirits of the dead from returning to plague the survivors is to divert the water of a stream, bury the corpses in the dry bed of the river, and then allow the water to resume its natural course. The double barrier of earth and water may then be regarded as sufficient to prevent the ghosts from escaping to return and molest living folk. This mode of burial has been

[1] Washington Matthews, *Ethnology and Philology of the Hidatsa Indians* (Washington, 1877).

[2] R. Southey, *History of Brazil,* i. Supplementary Notes, p. xxiv.

adopted in various parts of Africa. It has been reported for the dwarfs of West Africa by Mgr. Le Roy, who was personally acquainted with these primitive folk. He says that among the A-Kôa, when a death has taken place, the elders assemble at midnight to decide on the place of burial, while the women and children are sent away from the camp. When a decision has been reached the elders go a long way into the forest till they come to the stream which has been chosen for the burial. There they divert the current of the stream and dig a deep round hole in its bed, taking care to surround the edges of the hole with little posts to prevent the sand or earth from tumbling in. Then they return to the camp to fetch the corpse. They find it wrapped in rough mats or fig-tree bark. Afterwards at midnight they convey the body silently and secretly to its destined grave in the bed of the stream. There they place it upright, with its face turned to the sky and set a large stone over the head with a ridge of clay to prevent the water from penetrating. Then one of the elders pronounces the last farewell to the departed spirit, bidding it to go away to the happy land. After that they allow the stream to resume its course and to flow over the grave of their kinsman.[1]

A similar custom is reported by Du Chaillu for the Obongo, a tribe of West Africa. " The modes of burial of these savages, as related to me by my Ashango companions, are curious. The most com-

[1] Mgr. Le Roy, " Les Pygmées ", in *Les Missions Catholiques*, vol. xxix. (1897) pp. 238 *sq.*

mon habit is to place the corpse in the interior of a
hollow tree in the forest, filling up the hole with
branches and leaves mixed with earth ; but sometimes they make a hole in the bed of a running
stream, diverting the current for the purpose, and
then, after the grave is covered in, turning back the
rivulet to its former course." [1]

In the Watumbe and Wabemba tribes of Tanganyika it is customary to bury great chiefs in the beds
of rivers, of which the water has been temporarily
diverted to permit of this mode of sepulture. Most
of the great chiefs choose their place of burial during
their lifetime. At the chosen spot when the water
of the river has been diverted they dig the grave in
the dry bed. Two of the wives of the deceased
chief are then lowered into the grave, and placed in
a sitting posture with their legs crossed and firmly
tied. The skeleton of the dead chief is deposited
in their arms, resting on their knees, and with it is
put a vessel of food. They occupy the bottom of
the cavity. Near them on each side are lowered
two young men, one holding the chief's pipe and the
other his fire tongs. The opening is next covered
with a mat. Next they throw into the grave a
number of slaves in proportion to the dignity of the
deceased chief, first killing or stunning them by
blows of a club upon their heads. Then the grave
is filled up and the earth stamped down. Afterwards the other slaves of the chief are forced to walk
over the grave, and each receives the blow of a club

[1] P. B. Du Chaillu, *A Journey to Ashango Land* (London, 1867), p. 321.

on his neck. If he does not succumb under the
blow he is free; but if he succumbs it is because the
chief desires his company, so his body is left to lie
upon the tomb. After that the water of the river is
allowed to resume its course, and to flow over the
remains of the dead chief and his victims. When
that has been done every one runs upstream and
bathes in the river to purify himself; but the last
to arrive is not allowed to enter the river. He is
deemed impure and may not enter the village for a
month. After a month he purifies himself in the
river and may go home.[1]

In his journey across Africa, Commander
Cameron visited the country of the Kirua, and
learned from them the grandiose fashion in which
they used to bury their dead kings. He says, "The
first proceeding is to divert the course of a stream,
and in its bed to dig an enormous pit, the bottom of
which is then covered with living women. At one
end a woman is placed on her hands and knees, and
upon her back the dead chief, covered with his beads
and other treasures, is seated, being supported on
either side by one of his wives, while his second wife
sits at his feet.

"The earth is then shovelled in on them, and all
the women are buried alive, with the exception of
the second wife. To her custom is more merciful
than to her companions, and grants her the privilege
of being killed before the huge grave is filled in.

[1] C. Delhaise, *Notes ethno-* *du Tanganyika*, Second Edition
graphiques sur quelques peuplades (Brussels, 1905), pp. 21-22.

" This being completed, a number of male slaves—sometimes forty or fifty—are slaughtered and their blood poured over the grave ; after which the river is allowed to resume its course.

" Stories were rife that no fewer than a hundred women were buried alive with Bambarré, Kasongo's father ; but let us hope that this may be an exaggeration." [1]

Among the Grebos, a tribe of Liberia, persons who have filled the office of high priest (*Bodia*) are usually buried on an island off Cape Palmas if they have died a natural death ; but if they have died through drinking sassy-wood they must be buried beneath a running stream of water. [2] The drinking of sassy-wood is one form of the poison ordeal, which is very common in Africa as the supreme and infallible test in a charge of sorcery. If the accused vomits the poison he is regarded as innocent ; if he fails to vomit it he is guilty and, should the poison not prove fatal on the spot, he is regularly executed as a convicted sorcerer. [3] Thus we see that a Grebo high priest who dies by drinking an infusion of sassy-wood must always be regarded by the natives as a convicted sorcerer, and his ghost will therefore inevitably be deemed exceedingly dangerous. That, therefore, must be the reason for burying his body, not with his fellow high priests on the island, but under the bed of a running stream,

[1] V. L. Cameron, *Across Africa* (New Edition, 1885), pp. 365–366.
[2] Sir H. Johnston, *Liberia* (London, 1906), vol. ii. p. 1076.
[3] J. G. Frazer, *Folk-Lore in the Old Testament* (London, 1918), vol. iii. pp. 307–401.

in the hope that the double barrier of earth and water will prevent his malignant spirit from molesting living folk by his sorcery as he had done in his lifetime by his black art. In antiquity the Gothic leader Alaric was similarly buried in the bed of a river, which was then allowed to flow over his grave.[1] The object of this burial in his case is not stated. It may have been to prevent his too powerful spirit from roaming at large to the danger of living folk, or it may have been to guard the grave from desecration by the king's enemies.

Curiously enough, the ashes of the prophet Daniel are reported by an Arab geographer to have been subjected to a similar treatment by order of the khalif Omar ben Khattab. Having found in the latest of his conquests the traditional site of the grave of Daniel, and being informed that the natives invoked the name of the prophet for the purpose of obtaining rain, the pious khalif took measures to stop this idolatrous rite for the future. By his order they stopped the course of a river, dug a grave in its dry bed, and there deposited the remains of the prophet in order that for the future no man might know where the ashes of the prophet lay, and so might no longer employ his name in incantations for rain.[2]

A much simpler and less troublesome mode of preventing the return of an unwelcome ghost is to peg his remains down into the earth. This method is adopted by the Oraons of Orissa for all ghosts

[1] Jordanes, *Getica*, c. xxx. § 158.

[2] Módjem el Bouldan, in C. B. de   Meynard, *Dictionnaire geographique, historique, et littéraire de la Perse* (Paris, 1861), p. 327.

except those of their dead ancestors. They imagine
that the wooden pegs prevent the ghosts of the dead
from rising through the earth to molest them.[1] In
Cochin China the troublesome ghost of a stranger
can be confined to his grave by knocking a nail or
other piece of iron into the earth of the grave at the
point where his head reposes.[2] Among the Wa-
wanga in the Baringo district of East Africa when
a sick man in his delirium calls out the name of a
dead relative the friends of the sick man imagine
that his sickness is caused by the ghost of the
deceased. Accordingly, to give a quietus to the
ghost they sometimes drive a stake into the head of
the grave and pour boiling water down after it;
or as an alternative they engage a poor old man to
undertake the dangerous task of digging up the corpse,
after which the bones are burned over a nest of red
ants, and the ashes swept up and thrown into a river.[3]

In order to prevent the return of the spirits of the
dead some peoples bury the bodies in certain positions which they imagine will produce the desired
effect. Among the Chiriguano Indians of the Rio
Pilcomayo in South America when a man has been
killed by a jaguar they bury him head downwards
in the earth to prevent him from turning into a
jaguar after death, and in that form committing
ravages upon the people.[4] When the Ibibio of

[1] S. C. Roy, *Oraon Religion and Customs* (Ranchi, 1928), p. 50.

[2] P. Giran, *Magie et Religion Annamites* (Paris, 1912), pp. 132 *sq.*

[3] Hon. K. R. Dundas, "Notes on the Tribes inhabiting the Baringo District, East Africa Protectorate ", in *Journal of the Royal Anthropological Institute*, xl. (1910) pp. 54 *sq.*

[4] E. Nordenskiöld, *Indianerleben* (Leipzig, 1912), p. 218.

Southern Nigeria wish to prevent the reincarnation
of persons whom they regard as undesirable they
bury the bodies in the grave with their faces downwards, apparently imagining that their spirits will
thus be unable to find their way back to earth. On
the contrary, young people are usually buried lying
on their side, in an attitude of sleep. " Grown men,
on the other hand, are buried lying flat on their
backs, ' so that they may be able to see straight
before them and soon find their way back to earth'."[1]
To prevent the ghost from walking some of the
menial tribes of Northern India bury the dead face
downwards in the grave.[2] We have already seen
that this mode of burial is adopted for the Mehtar,
a caste of sweepers in the Punjab.[3] In Siam the
corpse is very often placed in the coffin face downwards in order that the spirit of the dead may not
be able to find its way back.[4]

For the same purpose a corpse is very often carried
out of the house feet foremost. Apparently the
notion is that in this posture the eyes of the corpse
are turned away from the house and that therefore
the ghost will not be able to see his way back to the
dwelling. Thus for example in Mabuiag, one of the
Torres Straits Islands, a corpse was always carried
out of the camp feet foremost, for otherwise it was
believed the spirit of the dead would return to haunt

[1] P. A. Talbot, *Life in Southern Nigeria* (London, 1923), p. 144.

[2] W. Crooke, *Natives of Northern India* (London, 1907), p. 216.

[3] J. G. Frazer, *Fear of the Dead* (London, 1934), ii. p. 108.

[4] E. Young, *The Kingdom of the Yellow Robe* (London, 1907), p. 346.

and torment the survivors.[1]   The Kiwai Papuans
of British New Guinea, on the other hand, carry
their dead out head foremost, thinking that otherwise their ghosts will return to the village and make
people sick.[2]   Thus the practice of the Kiwai differs
from that of their neighbours, the natives of Mabuiag,
but their intention is the same, namely, to prevent
the return of dangerous ghosts.   The Pehuenches,
a nomadic tribe of Indians in Central Chile, always
carry the dead out of a tent feet foremost, for they
think that otherwise the wandering ghost might
return to its old abode.[3]   In Northern India the
corpse of an orthodox Hindu is always carried out
of the house feet foremost in order that the ghost may
not find its way back to the dwelling.[4]   Similarly in
many parts of Germany people are very careful to
carry out their dead feet foremost, believing that
otherwise their ghosts would return to the house.[5]
In Denmark corpses are always carried out of the
house feet foremost, because it is believed that if
they were carried out head foremost their ghosts
would see their way back to the house and return to
haunt it.[6]   In Italy, also, it is the general practice
to carry a corpse out of the house feet foremost.[7]

[1] A. C. Haddon, in *Reports of
the Cambridge Anthropological Expedition to Torres Straits* (Cambridge,
1904), vol. v. p. 248. Cf. Haddon, in
*Internationales Archiv für Ethno-
graphie*, vol. vi. (1893) p. 152.
[2] J. Landtman, *The Kiwai Papuans of British New Guinea* (London, 1927), p. 257.
[3] E. Poeppig, *Reise in Chile, Peru,
und auf dem Amazonenstrome* (Leip-

zig, 1830–1836), i. 392.
[4] W. Crooke, *Natives of Northern
India*, p. 217.
[5] A. Wuttke, *Der deutsche Volksaberglaube* (Berlin, 1869), § 736.
[6] Dr. H. F. Feilberg, "The Corpse-
Door: A Danish Survival", in *Folk-
Lore*, xxiii. (1907) p. 369.
[7] A. de Gubernatis, *Storia Com-
parata degli Usi Funebri in Italia*,
Second Edition (Milan, 1878), p. 52.

Another way of preventing the spirit of the dead from seeing his way back is to blindfold him by bandages or otherwise. Some of the Australian aborigines in the neighbourhood of Lake Alexandrina place bandages round the eyes of their dead, which they fasten behind.[1] The Bana of the Cameroons tie up the eyes of a corpse and fasten the hands and feet before they carry the body out of the house.[2] In Corea people tie blinkers, or rather blinders, on the eyes of a corpse. These are made of black silk, and are fastened with strings at the back of the head.[3] In Cambodia pieces of gold leaf are placed on the eyes, the mouth, and the nose of the corpse, but are removed when the body has been brought to the funeral pyre.[4] The Warangi and Wambugwe tribes of East Africa, when a death has occurred, kill a goat, extract its fat, and rub it on the eyes of the corpse in order that the ghost of the deceased may not see new-born children and injure them by his evil looks.[5] In the Nicobar Islands they do not indeed blindfold the dead, but " one near of kin gently closes the eyes of the corpse in order to give the appearance of sleep, for not only is the glazed fixed look of death held in fear, but the further benefit is gained of darkening the vision of the departed spirit—believed to be still hovering near—

[1] E. J. Eyre, *Journals of Expeditions of Discovery into Central Australia* (London, 1845), ii. 345.

[2] G. von Hagen, " Die Bana ", in *Baessler-Archiv*, ii. (1912) p. 108.

[3] J. Ross, *History of Corea*, p. 325.

[4] J. Moura, *Le Royaume de Cambodge* (Paris, 1883), i. 360.

[5] A. Baumann, *Durch Massailand zur Nilquelle* (Berlin, 1894), p. 187.

and thereby preventing it from acting malevolently
towards the living."[1]

A common mode of blindfolding a corpse is to
place a coin on each of the dead person's eyes. This
is done by the Dyaks of Borneo immediately after
death, for the avowed purpose of closing the eyes of
the ghost, and so preventing him from seeing and
injuring the surviving kinsfolk on earth.[2] Among
the Galelareese of Halmahera, a large island to the
west of New Guinea, if the eyes of a dead person
are wide open, they say that he is looking round
for a companion, in order to draw him away with
him to the spirit land. Hence they are always careful to weight the eyelids of a corpse, generally with
a *rijks-dollar*, in order to keep them shut.[3] But if
the deceased is suspected of being a were-wolf it is
necessary to strew lime on his eyes and to cover his
head with a pan ; for then, they say, his eyes are
dim and he cannot see to come and visit the survivors with sickness or death.[4] A similar custom
has been practised for similar reasons in various
parts of Europe. For example in the north-east of
Scotland, if the eyes of a corpse did not close, or if
they opened a little after being closed, an old penny
or halfpenny piece was laid on each eye to keep it

[1] E. H. Man, " Notes on the
Nicobarese ", in *The Indian Anti-
quary*, xxviii. (1899) p. 253 ; *id.*
Man, *The Nicobar Islands and their
People* (Guildford, N.D.), p. 130.

[2] F. Grabowsky, " Der Tod, das
Begräbnis, das Tiwah oder Todten-
fest und Ideen über das Jenseits bei
den Dajaken ", in *Internationales*

Archiv für Ethnologie, ii. (1889) p.
178.

[3] M. J. van Baarda, " Fabelen,
verhalen en Overleveringen der
Galelareezen ", in *Bijdragen tot de
Taal- Land- en Volkenkunde van
Nederlandsch-Indië*, xlv. (1895) p.
538.

[4] *Ibid.* p. 541.

closed.[1] A like practice seems to have been observed
in some parts of England, as we learn from the words
put by Dickens in the mouth of Mrs. Gamp: "When
Gamp was summonsed to his long home, and I see
him a-lying in Guy's Hospital with a penny piece
on each eye, and his wooden leg under his left arm,
I thought I should have fainted away. But I bore
up."[2] The custom of placing coins on the eyes of
the dead is recorded also for Russia, Serbia, and
Bulgaria.[3] Modern Jews put potsherds on the eyes of
a corpse.[4] The notion that if the eyes of the dead
be not closed his ghost will return to fetch away
another of the household still exists in Bohemia,
Germany, and England.[5]

On the citadel of Mycenae the royal graves of the
ancient kings were discovered by Dr. Schliemann in
his memorable excavations of the site.[6] In them he
found seven golden masks, five of them covering the
faces of men, and two the faces of children. The

[1] Rev. W. Gregor, *Notes on the Folk-lore of the North-East of Scotland* (London, 1881), p. 207.

[2] Chas. Dickens, *Martin Chuzzlewit*, ch. xix.

[3] W. R. S. Ralston, *Songs of the Russian People*, Second Edition (London, 1872), p. 318; F. S. Krauss, *Volksglaube und religiöser Brauch der Südslaven* (Munster, 1890), p. 140.

[4] J. C. G. Bodenschatz, *Kirkliche Verfassung der heutigen Juden* (Erlangen, 1748), iv. p. 174.

[5] J. V. Grohmann, *Aberglauben und Gebräuche aus Böhmen und Mähren* (Leipzig, 1864), p. 188; G.

Lammert, *Volksmedezin und medezinischer Aberglaube aus Bayern* (Wurzburg, 1869), p. 106; A. Wuttke, *Der deutsche Volksaberglaube*, § 725; T. F. T. Dyer, *English Folk-Lore* (London, 1884), p. 230; A. Schleicher, *Volksthumliches aus Sonnenberg* (Weimar, 1858), p. 52; C. L. Rochholz, *Deutscher Glaube und Brauch* (Berlin, 1867), i. 176. Cf. Witzschel, *Kleine Beiträge zur deutscher Mythologie*, ii. 256; E. Veckenstedt, *Wendische Sagen Märchen, und abergläubische Gebräuche* (Graz, 1880), p. 449.

[6] J. G. Frazer, *Pausanias's Description of Greece* (London, 1898), iii. 107.

masks were clearly portraits of the dead, and the intention with which they were so placed can only be conjectured.   In one of the children's masks holes were cut out for the eyes ; but there were no such holes in the men's masks.   This perhaps suggests an intention of blinding the eyes of dead men, while allowing a dead child to retain its eyesight. The custom of covering the faces of the dead with masks appears to have prevailed widely in the world, and is still practised in some places.   Thus golden masks are regularly placed on the faces of dead kings of Siam and Cambodia ;[1] and among the Shans of Indo-China the face of a dead chief is invariably covered with a mask of gold or silver.[2]   In ancient Mexico masks made of gold or turquoise mosaic or painted wood were placed on the faces of dead kings.[3] Among the Ibibio of Southern Nigeria in olden days the faces of chiefs were regularly covered by wooden masks, conventionalized enough, but carved with a certain dignity.   In modern times the art of carving these funeral masks has much degenerated.   The object of placing them on the faces of dead chiefs is not mentioned by our authority.[4]   The Aleutian Islanders used to put masks on the faces of their dead, and as they wore masks at certain dances as a protection against a dangerous spirit who was supposed to descend into a wooden idol, it seems

[1] Mgr. Pallegoix, *Description du royaume Thai ou Siam* (Paris, 1854), i. 247 ; J. Moura, *Le Royaume du Cambodge* (Paris, 1883), i. 349.
[2] A. S. Colquhoun, *Among the Shans*, p. 279.

[3] F. S. Clavigero, *History of Mexico*, translated by Cullen (London, 1807), p. 324 ; Bancroft, *Native Races of the Pacific States*, ii. 606.
[4] P. A. Talbot, *Life in Southern Nigeria* (London, 1923), p. 147.

possible that their mortuary masks were intended to
guard their dead against some spiritual danger.[1]
The masks placed upon the faces of dead kings may
perhaps have had a similar protective intention.   In
ancient Egypt every mummy had its artificial face ;
and masks made of gold, silver, bronze and terra-
cotta found in Mesopotamia, Phoenicia, the Crimea,
Italy, the valley of the Danube, Gaul and Britain,
appear to testify to the extent to which a similar
custom prevailed both in Western Asia and Europe.[2]
Some people, not content with covering the eyes of
the dead, block up all the other openings of his head,
his ears and mouth, that he may not be able to see,
hear or speak.   The custom seems to be specially
prevalent in the East Indies.   Among the people
who practise it are the Malays, and the Batak and
Achinese of Sumatra.[3]   Such practices seem to
testify to a great fear of the spirits of the dead.
In the Bari tribe of the Nilotic Sudan the rain-maker
is a very important personage, and if he dies a natural
death his corpse is subjected to a special treatment
for the purpose of keeping his precious spirit within
his body and so under the control of his son, who
succeeds him in the office of rain-maker.   To effect
this purpose all the orifices in the dead man's body
are plugged up to prevent the escape of the soul.

[1] W. H. Dall, *Alaska and its
Resources*, p. 389.
[2] O. Benndorf, *Antike Gesichts-
helme und Sepulcralmasken* (Wien,
1878) ; R. Andree, *Ethnographische
Parallelen und Vergleiche*, Neue
Folge (Leipzig, 1889), pp. 120–134.

Cf. J. Abercromby, " Funeral Masks
in Europe ", in *Folklore*, vii. (1896)
pp. 351–366.
[3] Albert Kruijt, *s.v.* " Indonesians " in *Encyclopaedia of Religion
and Ethics* (Edinburgh, 1914), vol.
vii. p. 241.

In the words of Mr. Whitehead, " When the rain-maker is dead, he is plugged, his ears are plugged, his nose is plugged, his eye is plugged, his mouth is plugged, he is plugged, his fingers are plugged. And then he is buried.   It is done thus so that . . . the spirits may not go out, so that the son may manage the father so that he obeys (him), so that the spirits obey the son." [1]

Among the Chuwash, a Turkish tribe on the Volga in Russia, it is the custom to stop up the nose, ears, and mouth of a corpse with silk, in order that on his arrival in the spirit land the deceased may be able to say that he has seen and heard nothing of what is going on on earth in the land of the living. The writer who records this custom does not say that the eyes of the dead are stopped up, but that they are so seems to be implied by the reason which he gives for the practice. [2]

[1] C. G. and B. Z. Seligman, *Pagan Tribes of the Nilotic Sudan* (London, 1932), p. 292.

[2] H. Vámbéry, *Das Türkenvolk* (Leipzig, 1885), p. 462.

CHAPTER II

DECEIVING THE GHOST

THUS far we have seen that primitive man has resorted to many contrivances for the purpose of banishing the dreaded spirits of the dead to a safe distance and keeping them there ; but often it appears that all his contrivances are vain. The spirits of the dead break the bounds which he has attempted to impose upon them and they return to their old haunts to plague and torment the living. But even when they do so our primitive man is by no means at the end of his resources. Trusting to that intellectual weakness which he appears to impute to the spirits of the dead, he fancies that he can outwit them and escape their attention even when they are hovering about him in the air. This he thinks he can do, in the first place, by remaining strictly silent after a death, in the hope of thus avoiding the attention of the ghost.

The custom of observing strict silence after a death for the purpose of eluding the attention of the ghost is particularly prevalent among the peoples of the Indian Archipelago, or Indonesia, as the islands

are now commonly called.   On this subject we may
quote the testimony of the Dutch missionary, Dr.
Albert C. Kruijt, our highest living authority on
the customs and religion of Indonesia.   " The Indonesians assume that, when a person has died, his
soul is angry at renouncing life on earth.   Afterwards it gets used to its new condition, but at first
it is in a mood dangerous for the survivors.   Therefore great care is recommended for the first few days
after a death ; this fear has given rise to the institution of mourning customs.   During the first days
after a death the inhabitants of a village must keep
perfectly quiet.   No noise must be made, dancing
or singing is forbidden, music must not be heard,
rice must not be pounded, nor coconuts thrown
down from the trees, nor shots fired ; in fact, they
go so far as to forbid fishing, sailing on the water,
and carrying goods in the usual way.   The intention is that no sound should meet the ear of the soul
to indicate the way to its home ; people try to
conceal themselves from it.   Such injunctions are
found among all Indonesian peoples." [1]

A remarkable instance of the silence imposed
upon mourners for the sake of eluding the attention
of the ghost is furnished by the practice of some
Australian widows, who are debarred for a certain
time, often for a very long time, from speaking after
the deaths of their husbands.   In the Warramunga
tribe of Central Australia the period of silence

---

[1] A. Kruijt, s.v. "Indonesians", in *Encyclopaedia of Religion and Ethics*
(Edinburgh, 1914), vol. vii. p. 241.

imposed on widows extends from one to two years, and curiously enough it is not confined to widows. His mother, his sisters, his daughters, his mother-in-law or mothers-in-law, must all equally be dumb and for the same protracted period.   More than that, not only his real wife, real mother, real sisters, and real mothers-in-law are subjected to this rule of silence, but a great many more women whom the natives, on the classificatory principle, reckon in these relationships, though we should not do so, are similarly bound over to hold their tongues, it may be for a year, or it may be for two years.   As a consequence it is no uncommon thing in a Warramunga camp to find the majority of women prohibited from speaking.   Even when the period of mourning is over, some women prefer to remain silent and to use only the gesture language, in the practice of which they become remarkably proficient.   Not seldom, when a party of women are in camp, there will be almost perfect silence, and yet a brisk conversation is all the while being conducted among them on their fingers, or rather with their hands and arms, for many of the signs are made by putting the hands or elbows in varying positions.   At Tennant's Creek some years ago there was an old woman who had not opened her mouth, except to eat or drink, for twenty-five years, and who has probably since gone down into the grave without uttering another syllable.   A similar ban of silence is imposed on widows for a shorter or longer period among other Australian tribes, such as the Unmatjera, the Kaitish, the

Arunta, and the Dieri.[1] The motive for this silence imposed upon native Australian widows is not mentioned by our authorities, but we may safely suppose that it is a fear of attracting the attention of the jealous ghosts of their husbands, for a similar rule of silence is imposed on widows in some Indian tribes of North America, and in one of them, the Bella Coola tribe of British Columbia, the reason assigned for it is a fear of the dead husband's ghost, who if she broke silence would come and lay his ghostly hand upon her mouth, and she would die. In this tribe the period of silence imposed upon widows lasts only four days.[2] But in the Nishinam tribe of California the period of silence imposed on widows lasted for several months, sometimes for a year or more.[3] A similar custom for widows is recorded for some parts of Africa. In the Kutu tribe of the Congo widows observe mourning for three lunar months. They shave their heads, strip themselves almost naked, daub their bodies all over with white clay, and pass the whole of the three months in the house without speaking.[4] Among the Sihanaka in Madagascar the observances are similar, but the period of silence is still longer, and

[1] Baldwin Spencer and F. J. Gillen, *The Northern Tribes of Central Australia* (London, 1904), pp. 525 *sq.* and *The Native Tribes of Central Australia* (London, 1899), pp. 500 *sq.*; J. G. Frazer, *Folk-Lore in the Old Testament*, iii. pp. 73-80.

[2] Franz Boas, in Seventh Report of the Committee on the North-West Tribes of Canada, *Report of the British Association for the Advancement of Science, Cardiff Meeting*, 1891, p. 13 (separate reprint).

[3] Stephen Powers, *The Tribes of California* (Washington, 1877), p. 327.

[4] *Notes analytiques sur les collections ethnographiques du Musée du Congo*, tome i. fascicule 2. *Religion* (Brussels, 1906), p. 185.

sometimes for a year. During the whole of that time the widow is stripped of all her ornaments and covered up with a coarse mat, and she is given only a broken spoon and a broken dish to eat out of. She may not wash her face or her hands, but only the tips of her fingers. In this state she remains all day long in the house and may not speak to any one who enters it.[1] We may safely assume that all these observances are intended to render the widow unattractive, and even repulsive, to the jealous ghost of her deceased husband, so that he may not come and annoy her by his unwelcome attentions.[2]

Another case of silence imposed upon the living for the sake of eluding the attention of the dead is the widespread rule which forbids the living to mention the names of the dead for a longer or shorter period after their death, lest the ghost of the deceased should hear and answer to his name. Elsewhere I have cited many examples of this common custom :[3] here it may suffice to illustrate the practice with some instances which I have not quoted in my other work. Thus we are told that the very primitive aborigines of Tasmania had " a fear of pronouncing the name by which a deceased friend was known, as if his shade might thus be offended. To introduce, for any purpose whatever, the name of

---

[1] Rabesikanaka (a native Malagese), " The Sihanaka and their Country ", *The Antananarivo Annual and Madagascar Magazine*, Reprint of the first Four Numbers (Antananarivo, 1885), p. 326.

[2] Elsewhere I have treated more at large the subject of the silence imposed upon widows after the deaths of their husbands. See my *Folk-Lore in the Old Testament*, iii. pp. 71-81.

[3] *The Golden Bough, Taboo*, pp. 349-374.

any one of their deceased relatives called up at once a frown of horror and indignation, from a fear that it would be followed by some dire calamity."[1] A similar custom was observed among the aborigines of New South Wales by one of the earliest voyagers to Australia. He says, "They either bury or burn their dead ; in both cases they commit to the grave or the pile the arms and utensils of the deceased, viz. spears, fishing-tackle, canoes, etc. ; even the very name is consigned to oblivion, which they take care never again to mention : the namesake (*Tomelai*) of the deceased assumes, for a time, the name of *Bourang* ; which appears to be the general appellation for those in such circumstances, and signifies that they are at present destitute of a name, their name-father being dead. This title they retain till they become the namesake of another person."[2] The natives of the Andrawilla tribe on the Diamentina, Herbert, and Eleanor Rivers, in East Central Australia, never mention the names of the dead, believing that their spirits would never rest peacefully if their names were spoken.[3] At Buin, at the extreme south of Bougaineville, in the Solomon Islands, the old names of the dead are not pronounced. The departed are referred to by new names, "names of the

[1] J. Barnard, "Aborigines of Tasmania ", in *Report of the Second Meeting of the Australasian Association for the Advancement of Science* (1890), p. 605.

[2] J. Turnbull, *A Voyage Round the World in 1800–1804*, Second Edition (London, 1813), p. 87.

[3] F. H. Wells, "The Habits, Customs, and Ceremonies of the Aboriginals on the Diamentina, Herbert, and Eleanor Rivers, in East Central Australia ", in *Report of the Fifth Meeting of the Australasian Association for the Advancement of Science* (1893), p. 519.

other world," which were usually chosen by the deceased in their lifetime.[1] In Dobu, at the southeast extremity of New Guinea, one cause of war was the naming of the dead, for as a rule the dead might only be named in mighty oaths, or by a sorcerer as a last resort to save the life of a dying man.[2] The Kiwai Papuans of British New Guinea avoid mentioning the names of the dead, in particular of those who have recently died, and are feared after death. They say that to do so would be a way of calling on the ghost, who might respond to the call, and cause sickness. It would be impolite, also, to mention a name which might renew the sorrow and evoke the lamentations of the kinsfolk of the departed.[3] Among the primitive aborigines of the Andaman Islands the names of the dead are not mentioned during the period of mourning, which lasts several months. If it is necessary to refer to a dead person he is spoken of as " he who is buried by the big rock," or " he who is laid in the fig-tree ", or otherwise mentioning the place of burial. There is no objection to mentioning the name in other connections; for example, if a man were called *Buio*, from the name of a species of *Mucuna*, it is not necessary to avoid the word *buio* when speaking of the plant. Further, if there is

[1] R. Thurnwald, " Im Bismarck-archipel und auf den Salomo-inseln, 1906–1909 ", *Zeitschrift für Ethnologie*, xlii. (Berlin, 1910), p. 129.
[2] W. E. Bromilow, " Some Manners and Customs of the Dobuans of South-East Papua ", in *Report of the Twelfth Meeting of the Australasian Association for the Advancement of Science* (1909), p. 447.

[3] G. Landtman, *The Kiwai Papuans of British New Guinea* (London, 1927), p. 293.

another person alive of the same name as the dead
man it is not necessary to avoid the name in referring
to the living individual.   The custom is that a dead
person must not be spoken of unless it is absolutely
necessary, and then must not be spoken of by name.
After the period of mourning is over the dead person
may again be spoken of by name.[1]

The Yakuts of Siberia never mention the name
of a dead person except allegorically, and allow the
hut in which a death took place to fall into ruins,
believing it to be the habitation of demons.[2]

Among the Malagasy or natives of Madagascar
it is prohibited under the pain of sacrilege to pronounce the names which their dead relations and
chiefs or kings bore in their lifetime.   They fear
that if they were to pronounce their names the
spirits of the dead would hear and return among
them, for they have a great dread of entering into
any direct relations with the spirits of the deceased.
Only a wicked sorcerer plotting the death of somebody would dare to invoke the names of the dead.
Further, among some peoples of Madagascar, such
as the Sakalavas, it is forbidden under the gravest
penalties to use in current language words which
form parts of the names of dead kings, or which
have a similar sound, such words being replaced by
synonyms created for the purpose.[3]

[1] A. R. Brown, *The Andaman
Islanders* (Cambridge, 1922), pp.
111, 121.
[2] M. Sauer, *An Account of a
Geographical and Astronomical Expedition to the Northern Parts of*
Russia in 1785-1794 (London, 1802),
p. 125.
[3] J. Grandidier, " La Mort et les
funérailles à Madagascar ", in
L'Anthropologie, xxiii. (Paris, 1912)
p. 348.

Among the Banyankole, a pastoral people of Southern Uganda, it is a rule never to mention the name of a dead person, " and a child who inherited property from his father was called ' the father of himself ' : thus, if N died leaving a son L who inherited, L was never called the son of N but ' the father of L ', which made it clear to every one that he possessed property inherited from a dead father ".[1] In the same tribe Mr. Roscoe experienced great difficulty in ascertaining the names of dead kings (*Mugabe*), because the name of a dead king is never pronounced after his death, and moreover if it corresponded with some word in ordinary use, that word was dropped out of the language.[2] Among the Barundi, a Bantu tribe of Tanganyika to the west of Lake Victoria-Nyanza, the name of a dead man is never pronounced for fear of attracting his dangerous and mischievous ghost. All persons and things that bear the same name drop it and take new names.[3] For example, after the death of the eldest son of king Kisabo, named Namagongo, the name of the mountain Magongo was changed to Mukidja. Another son of king Kisabo was named *Mafjuguru* which means *spear*. After his death the name for spear was changed from *mafjuguru* to *itschumu*.[4] Among the Bakongo in the valley of the Congo the name of the dead is taboo and never pronounced, " but if it is necessary to refer to the deceased one, they call him ' old what's his name ' (*nkulu nengandi*) or

[1] J. Roscoe, *The Banyankole* (Cambridge, 1923), pp. 151-152.
[2] J. Roscoe, *op. cit.* p. 35.
[3] H. Meyer, *Die Barundi* (Berlin, 1916), p. 114.
[4] Meyer, *op. cit.* p. 186.

' old Peter ' (*nkulu Mpetelo*), or ' of the name of Peter ' (*ejina dia Mpetelo*).   Any photographs of the deceased are torn up, all signs of him removed from the house, and every effort is made to forget him ".[1]   Among the Bechuanas of South Africa the name of a dead person was usually never mentioned after his death, lest his spirit might be offended.[2]   Similarly among the Bushmen of South-West Africa when a death took place they shifted their camp and never mentioned the name of the deceased afterwards.[3]   With regard to the Tuaregs of North Africa we are told that in spite of their undaunted courage " they hate the idea of death. They do not say of any one who has died, ' he is dead ', but *Aba*, he has disappeared.   It is a sign of very bad breeding to speak of a dead relative or even to pronounce his name.   He must be alluded to as *mandam*, or such an one." [4]   Among the Lengua Indians of Paraguay the name of a dead person is never mentioned, and should it be necessary to refer to him, he is spoken of simply as " he who was ".[5]   The funeral rites of these Indians are said to aim chiefly at exorcising the dangerous spirits of the dead.[6]

The Onas, an Indian tribe of Tierra del Fuego, think it improper to mention the name of a dead

[1] J. M. Weeks, *Among the Primitive Bakongo* (London, 1914), pp. 248 *sq.*

[2] S. S. Dornan, *Pygmies and Bushmen of the Kalahari* (London, 1925), p. 279.

[3] Dornan, *op. cit.* p. 145.

[4] Lieut. Hourst, *French Enterprise in Africa*, translated by Mrs. Arthur Bell (London, 1898), p. 238.

[5] W. B. Grubb, *An Unknown People in an Unknown Land* (London, 1911), p. 170.

[6] Grubb, *op. cit.* p. 168.

man in the presence of his relations.   If it is necessary to refer to him they allude to him as " our
friend ", or " the friend of our father ", in the assur-
ance that the allusion will be understood.[1]

Thus far we have seen that by silence primitive
man has sought to elude the hearing of the dangerous
spirits of the dead ; but he has also attempted to
evade their sight.   Ancient authors tell us that
among the barbarous Sacae mourners used to descend into subterranean chambers or pits to evade
the light of the sun ; but we may conjecture that
the real motive was to avoid the ghost of the
deceased.[2]

A traveller who visited the steppes of Astrakhan
and the Caucasus in the early part of the nineteenth
century tells us that after the death of a prince his
nurses were compelled to pull out the hair of the
head, eyebrows and eyelashes.   They were then put
in a perpendicular hole in the ground.   The head
of each of them was covered with a pot, in which
there was a hole.   They received food, but being
obliged to stay in the hole for several weeks, most of
them died.[3]   The motive of this strange custom is
not mentioned by the traveller ; but we may conjecture that the intention was to avoid all contact
with the dangerous spirit of the dead prince, with
whom in his lifetime as his nurses the women had
been in a very intimate relation.

[1] C. R. Gallardo, Los Onas
(Buenos Aires, 1910), pp. 355 sq.
[2] Aelianus, Variae Historiae, ch.
xii. 38 ; Plutarch, Consolatio ad
Apollonium, c. xxii.
[3] J. Potocki, Voyage dans les
Steps d'Astrakhan et du Caucase
(Paris, 1829), ii. p. 122.

But in order to escape from the dangerous spirits of the dead, primitive man seeks not only to hide himself but also to disguise himself, so that even if the ghost sees him he will fail to recognize him. This appears to be the true explanation of mourning costume ; it is a disguise to protect the mourner against the observation of the ghost of a recently deceased person, for it is in the period immediately succeeding the death that the ghost is deemed to be particularly dangerous. In this matter the behaviour of the Nicobar Islanders, as described by the excellent observer, Mr. E. H. Man, is especially instructive. He says that in these islands after a death " a man takes a short lighted torch, made of dry coconut leaves, which he waves in all directions inside the hut with the object of driving away any evil spirits that may be lurking therein. With the further object of disguising themselves so that the departed spirits may fail to recognize them, and may do them no mischief, all the mourners shave their heads (*ikōah-kōi*), in addition to which the women shave their eyebrows (*ikōah-puyōl-okmât*), and the men eradicate with tweezers any hairs they may have on their upper lips and chins (*itōsh-enhòin*). It is also common for a mourner, for the same reason, to assume some new name for him- or herself, which, in a great measure, accounts for the fact that some individuals have borne several different names in the course of their lives. This dread of the disembodied spirits of their departed relatives and friends is induced by

the conviction that they so keenly desire to return
to the scenes and associates of their earthly existence
that they are utterly unscrupulous as to the means
and methods they adopt for the purpose of attaining their object."[1] This passage seems to me to
furnish a clue to the whole custom of mourning
costume; it is essentially a disguise to protect the
living against the spirits of the recently deceased.
A good instance of disguise assumed to elude the
observation of a recently deceased person is furnished by the Ovaherero, a tribe of South-West
Africa. As described by the Rev. G. Viehe, the
custom is as follows. " Before his death, the man
informs his relatives regarding what will happen
after his decease. This may be good (*okusera
ondaya ombua*) or bad (*okusera ondaya ombi*). The
last is done in the following manner : If the dying
man sees a person who is not agreeable to him, he
says to him : ' Whence do you come ? I do not wish
to see you here ' (or something to this effect) ; and
so saying, he presses the fingers of his left hand
together in such a way that the thumb appears between the fingers. The man spoken to now knows
that the other has decided upon taking him away
(*okutuaerera*) after his death, which means that he
must die. In many cases, however, he can avoid
this threatening danger of death. For this purpose,
he hastily leaves the place of the dying man, and
looks for an *onganga* (*i.e.* ' doctor, magician '), in

[1] E. H. Man, *The Nicobar Islands* (Royal Anthropological Institute,
N.D.), pp. 141-142.

order to have himself undressed, washed, and greased again, and dressed with other clothes. He is now quite at ease about the threatening of death caused by the deceased; for, says he, ' Now our father does not know me ' (*Nambano tate ke ndyi i*). He has no longer any reason to fear the dead." [1]

To confirm the interpretation of mourning costume as a disguise to protect mourners against the dangerous spirits of the dead it may be observed that the customs adopted in mourning are often the very reverse of those which obtain in ordinary life, for this reversal of custom may naturally be explained by the intention of baffling and deceiving the ghost, whose dull wits do not allow him to detect the subterfuge. Whatever may be its explanation, this reversal of custom in mourning was long ago noted by the shrewd and learned Plutarch, whose researches into primitive custom and belief entitle him to be called the Father of Folk-lore. Thus in his valuable treatise called *Roman Questions* he tells us that at a Roman funeral the sons of the deceased walked with their heads covered, the daughters with their heads uncovered, thus exactly reversing the ordinary usage, which was that women wore coverings on their heads while men did not. Further he proceeds to say that similarly in Greece men and women during a period of mourning exactly inverted their habits of wearing the hair—the ordinary practice of men being to cut it short, that of women to wear it long. [2]

[1] G. Viehe, "Some Customs of the Ovaherero", in *Folk-Lore Journal*, vol. i. Part III. (Cape Town) p. 51.

[2] Plutarch, *Quaestiones Romanae*, xiv.

Among the ancient Lycians it was a law that in mourning men should dress as women, thus reversing the usual apparel of the sexes.[1] A similar reversal of custom in mourning has obtained among many primitive peoples. Thus we find that savages who ordinarily paint themselves sometimes refrain from doing so after a death.[2] Again, in similar circumstances, tribes which usually go naked put on certain articles of dress. Thus in some parts of New Guinea, where the men go naked and the women wear only a short grass petticoat, women in mourning wear a net over the shoulders and breast.[3] Elsewhere in New Guinea men also wear netted vests,[4] and in another place " when in deep mourning they envelope themselves with a very tight kind of wicker-work dress, extending from the neck to the knees in such a way that they are not able to walk well."[5] On the other hand, when the Mpongwés in Western Africa are in mourning, a woman wears as few clothes as possible, and a man wears none at all,[6] though the tribe is very fond of dress, the usual garb of a man being a shirt, a square cloth falling to the ankles, and a straw hat.[7]

Whether or not these peculiar costumes (or absence of costume) were meant to disguise the

[1] Plutarch, *Consolatio ad Apollonium*, xxii; Valerius Maximus, ii. 6. 13.

[2] P. F. X. de Charlevoix, *Histoire du Paraguay* (Paris, 1756), i. p. 73.

[3] J. Chalmers and W. W. Gill, *Work and Adventures in New Guinea* (London, 1885), p. 35.

[4] Chalmers and Gill, *op. cit.* p. 130.

[5] Chalmers and Gill, *op. cit.* p. 149.

[6] J. G. Wood, *The Natural History of Man* (London, 1874–1880) i. p. 586.

[7] P. B. Du Chaillu, *Equatorial Africa* (London, 1861), p. 9. Cf. J. L. Wilson, *Western Africa* (London, 1856), c. 19.

wearers of them from the ghost of the deceased,
certain it is that disguises have been assumed as a
means of deceiving spirits. Thus the Mosquito
Indians believe that the devil (Wulasha) tries to get
possession of the corpse ; so after they have lulled
him to sleep with sweet music " four naked men
who have disguised themselves with paint, so as not
to be recognized by Wulasha, rush out from a
neighbouring hut " and drag the body to the grave.[1]
At the feast held on the anniversary of the death
these same Indians wear cloaks fantastically painted
black and white, while their faces are correspond-
ingly streaked with red and yellow, perhaps to
deceive the devil. Again in Siberia, when a Sha-
man accompanies a soul to the underworld, he
often paints his face red, expressly that he may not
be recognized by the devils.[2] In South Guinea,
when a woman is sick she is dressed in a fantastic
costume, her face, breast, arms, and legs are painted
with streaks of white and red chalk, and her head
is decorated with red feathers. Thus arrayed she
struts about before the door of the hut brandishing
a sword.[3] The intention is doubtless to deceive or
intimidate the spirit which is causing the sickness.
In Guinea, women in their pregnancy also assume a
peculiar attire ; they leave off ornaments, allow their
hair to grow, wear peculiar cuffs, and in the last eight
days their heads are thickly plastered with red clay,

[1] Bancroft, *The Native Races of
the Pacific States of North America,*
i. pp. 744 *sq.*
[2] W. Radloff, *Aus Siberien* (Leip-
sig, 1884), p. 55.
[3] J. L. Wilson, *Western Africa,*
c. 28.

which they may not leave off till the child is born.[1]
All this is probably done to disguise the women from
the demons who are commonly supposed to lie in
wait for women at such periods.

The customs of blackening the face or body and
of cutting the hair short after a death are very
widespread. But when we find these customs observed after the death, not of a friend, but of a slain
enemy, as is reported of some Indians of Central
America,[2] no one will pretend that they are intended as marks of sorrow, and the explanation that
they are meant to disguise the slayer from the angry
ghost of the slain may be allowed to stand till a
better is suggested. These disguises are meant to
serve the same purpose as the so-called purification of slayers of men and beasts. In fact "mourning" and "purification" run into each other; this
"mourning" is not mourning, and this "purification" is not purification. Both are simply pieces of
spiritual armour, defences against ghosts or demons.
In regard to "mourning" costume this appears
clearly in the Myoro custom; when the child of a
Myoro woman in Africa dies, she smears herself with
butter and ashes and runs frantically about, while
the men abuse her in foul language, for the express
purpose of frightening away the demons who have
carried off the child.[3] If the curses are meant to
frighten, are not the ashes meant to deceive the

---

[1] J. Klemm, *Allgemeine Cultur-
Geschichte der Menschheit* (Leipzig,
1844), iii. pp. 284-285.
[2] Bancroft, *The Native Races of*
the Pacific States of North America,
i. 764.
[3] J. H. Speke, *Journal of the*
Discovery of the Source of the Nile.

demon ?   Here the disguise is adopted as a protection, not against the spirit of the dead, but against
the devils which carried it off, and it is possible that
the same may be true of " mourning " costume in
other cases ;   but considering the generally vicious
and dangerous nature of ghosts, it is probable that
" mourning " costume was usually a protection
against them, rather than against devils.

The custom of cutting the hair short after a death
has been very common all over the world ;   examples
would be endless.   Here I will cite only a single
instance.   In the Babar Archipelago of the East
Indies, when a corpse is being carried to the grave
all the inmates of the houses which the funeral
procession passes cut locks of their hair and throw
them out of the house.[1]   This is probably done as
a precaution to prevent the ghost of the deceased
from entering the house and molesting the inmates,
or carrying their souls off with him to the grave.   It
may be worth while to notice that the Greeks, not
content with cutting short the hair of men in mourning, cut off the manes of their horses on the same
occasion, and a similar custom was observed in
antiquity by the ancient Persians and in modern
times by the Comanche Indians.   The Comanches
cut off the tails as well as the manes.   Possibly the
Greeks and Persians did so too, but it is only said that
they " shaved " their horses, except in Euripides,
where the shaving is distinctly confined to the

---

[1] J. H. F. Riedel, *De Sluik- en Kroesharige Rassen tusschen Selebes en
Papua*, p. 362.

manes.[1] The Turkish tribes of Central Asia, after
the death of a hero, cut off the tails of all his favourite
horses, let them go free for a year, and then sacrifice
them on his grave.[2] The opposite custom of letting
the hair grow long in mourning is much rarer ; it
has been practised by the Egyptians, Jews, Chinese,
widows on the Slave Coast, and Hindu sons in
mourning for a parent.[3] It is also observed by the
Japanese,[4] and in some districts among the Ainos.[5]
Among the Birhors, a primitive jungle tribe of Chota
Nagpur, when a death has taken place in a settlement, no man in the settlement will shave for seven
days.[6] The Nairs of Southern India do not shave
or cut the hair for a year in mourning.[7] With regard
to some of the Indians of Canada we are told by an
old Jesuit missionary that when a man had lost a
kinsman by death he used to allow his hair to grow
long in sign of mourning.[8] Among the Angoni of
British Central Africa women usually shave their
heads, but in times of sorrow and trouble, and therefore no doubt in mourning, they allow the hair to

[1] Euripides, *Alcestis*, 429 ; Plutarch, *Pelopidas*, 33 ; *Alexander*,
72 ; *Aristides*, 14 ; Herodotus, ix.
24 ; Bancroft, *op. cit.* i. 523.

[2] H. Vámbéry, *Das Türkenvolk*
(Leipzig, 1885), p. 250.

[3] For Egyptians see Herodotus, ii.
36 ; for Jews, J. Buxtorf, *Synagoga
Judaica* (Bâle, 1661), p. 706, and
Bodenschatz, *Kirchliche Verfassung
der heutigen Juden*, iv. 179 ; for
Chinese, J. H. Gray, *China* (London,
1878), i. 286 ; for Slave Coast, P.
Bouche, *La Côte des Esclaves et le
Dahomey*, p. 218 *sq.* ; for Hindus,
S. C. Bose, *The Hindus as They Are*

(London and Calcutta, 1881), p. 254.

[4] *Manners and Customs of the
Japanese in the Nineteenth Century*
(London, 1841), p. 197.

[5] B. Scheube, *Die Ainos* (Yoko-
hama), p. 22.

[6] S. C. Roy, *The Birhors* (Ranchi,
1925), p. 265. According to another
account the period of abstinence
from shaving is ten days. E. T.
Dalton, *Descriptive Ethnology of
Bengal* (Calcutta, 1872), p. 220

[7] S. Maheer, *Native Life in
Travancore*, p. 173.

[8] *Relations des Jésuites* for 1646,
p. 48.

grow. In both men and women, the dirtier they
are, the deeper the mourning.[1] The Oigób, a tribe
of Masai in East Africa, may not cut their hair for
two months after a death. In the third month, on
the sixth day after the new moon, the relations, both
men and women, cut off the hair of their head and
all the rest of their hair, go out before the village,
kill several oxen, and eat the flesh in one day.[2]
When Mutesa, king of Uganda, died, " the whole
country went into mourning, and every one allowed
his hair to grow." [3] In ordinary mourning the
Hovas of Madagascar let their hair and beards grow.
But in mourning for a sovereign the people shave
their heads.[4] Among the Chewsurs of the Caucasus
men in mourning do not shave.[5] It is reported that
in New Caledonia when a man has buried a corpse
he allows his beard and hair to grow, and covers
his hair with a sort of turban. He never uncovers
it, and if he were seen by a woman arranging his
hair he would have to perform ablutions in the
depths of the forest.[6] In Sardinia the men do not
shave for a year after the death of their wives,[7] and
in Corsica men in mourning often let their beards

[1] W. M. Kerr, " Journey from
Cape Town overland to Lake
Nyassa ", in *Proceedings of the
Royal Geographical Society*, MS.
viii (1886), p. 81.

[2] J. M. Hildebrandt, " Ethnographische Notizen über Wakamba
und ihre Nachbarn ", *Zeitschrift
für Ethnologie*, x. (1878) p. 405.

[3] R. P. Ashe, *Two Kings of
Uganda* (London, 1889), p. 79.

[4] A. Grandidier, " Des rites funéraires chez les Malagaches ", in *Revue
d'Ethnographie*, iv. (1885) p. 229.

[5] J. Radde, *Die Chews' uren und
ihr Land* (Cassel, 1878), p. 91.

[6] Ch. Lemire, *Voyage à pied en
Nouvelle - Calédonie* (Paris, 1884),
p. 117.

[7] R. Tennant, *Sardinia and its
Resources* (Rome and London, 1885),
p. 236.

grow for a long time.[1]   We have already seen that
in ancient Greece the men but not the women allowed
their hair to grow long in mourning.[2]

Among many peoples ancient and modern the
custom of cutting the hair short in mourning has
often been accompanied by the laceration of the
body of the mourner in a great variety of ways;
but there appears to be little or no evidence that this
laceration of the body is designed to deceive the
ghost of the dead by rendering the person of the
mourner unrecognizable.   On the contrary there is
some evidence to show that the laceration is intended
to please the ghost of the deceased by proving to
him the sincerity and depth of the mourners' grief.
The Australian evidence in particular points in
this direction.   For example among the Arunta of
Central Australia if a man does not cut himself
sufficiently in honour of his dead father-in-law
his wife will be given away to another man in
order to appease the angry ghost of his deceased
father-in-law.[3]   Elsewhere I have discussed the
two customs, often conjoined, of cutting the hair
and lacerating the body of the mourner, and
must refer the reader to my discussion for fuller
details.[4]

But the attempts of primitive man to deceive the

[1] F. Gregorovius, *Corsica*, translated by R. Martineau (London,
1855), p. 283.

[2] See above, p. 51.   On mourning
costumes cf. my essay " On Certain
Burial Customs as illustrative of the
Primitive Theory of the Soul ", in

Garnered Sheaves (London, 1931),
pp. 42-46.

[3] Spencer and Gillen, *Native
Tribes of Central Australia*, p. 500.

[4] *Folk-Lore in the Old Testament*,
vol. iii. pp. 270-303.

spirits of the dead are by no means limited to the assumption of mourning costume, if that indeed be, as I have suggested, the true explanation of the peculiar garb assumed by mourners. He has many other artful dodges by which he hopes to take advantage of that guilelessness and simplicity of mind which he commonly imputes to the spirits of the departed. One of these consists in the use of effigies which he attempts to palm off upon the spirits as substitutes for the living person, hoping that the threatening spirit will not notice the difference, but will accept the effigy and spare the person. Thus for example in Tahiti after a death the priest who performed the funeral rites took a number of small slips of plantain leaf-stalk, fixed two or three pieces under each arm of the corpse, placed a few on the breast, and then, addressing the dead body, said, " There are your family, there is your child, there is your wife, there is your father, and there is your mother. Be satisfied yonder (that is, in the world of the spirits). Look not towards those who are left in this world."—" The concluding parts of the ceremony were designed to impart contentment to the departed, and to prevent the spirit from repairing to the places of his former resort, and so distressing the survivors." [1] When the Galelareese of Halmahera, an island to the west of New Guinea, bury a corpse, they inter with it the stem of a banana-tree

---

[1] W. Ellis, *Polynesian Researches*, Second Edition (London, 1832), i. 402. With this and what follows compare my exposition of the same subject in *The Golden Bough: Spirits of the Corn and of the Wild*, vol. ii. pp. 97 *sqq.*, which I here closely follow.

for company, in order that the ghost of the dead person may not seek a companion among the living.[1] Just as the coffin is being lowered into the earth, one of the bystanders steps up and throws a young banana-tree into the grave, saying, " Friend, you must miss your companions of this earth ; here, take this as a comrade ". Thus in the Banks Islands, Melanesia, " the ghost of a *vasisgona*, a woman who has died in childbed, cannot go to Panoi " (the spirit land) " if her child lives, for she cannot leave her child. They therefore deceive her ghost by making up loosely a piece of a banana trunk in leaves, and laying it on her bosom when she is buried. Then, as she departs, she thinks she has the child with her ; as she goes the banana stalk slips about in the leaves and she thinks the child is moving ; and this in her bewildered new condition contents her, till she gets to Panoi and finds that she has been deceived. In the meanwhile the child has been taken to another house, because they know that the mother will come back to take its soul. She seeks everywhere for the child in grief and rage without ceasing ; and the ghost of a *vasisgona* therefore is particularly dreaded." [2] In the Pelew Islands, when a woman has died in childbed, her spirit comes and cries, " Give me the child ! " So to deceive her they bury the stem of a young banana-tree with her body, cutting it short and laying it between her

[1] M. J. van Baarda, " Fabelen, verhalen en Overleveringen der Galelareezen ", in *Bijdragen tot de Taal- Land- en Volkenkunde van* *Nederlandsch-Indië*, xlv. (1895) p. 539.
[2] R. H. Codrington, *The Mela-nesians* (Oxford, 1891), p. 275.

right arm and her breast.[1] The same device is
adopted for the same purpose in the East Indian
island of Timor.[2]   In the Niger delta when a
woman has died in childbed a piece of a plantain
stem is forced into the womb of her dead body to
make her fancy that she has her child with her in
the spirit land and so to prevent her ghost from
coming back to claim the living child.[3]   Among the
Yorubas of West Africa, when one of twins dies, the
mother carries about, along with the surviving child
a small wooden figure roughly fashioned in human
shape and of the sex of the dead twin.   This figure
is intended not merely to keep the live child from
pining for its lost comrade, but also to give the
spirit of the dead child something into which it can
enter without disturbing its little brother or sister.[4]
Among the Tschwi of West Africa a lady observed
a sickly child with an image beside it which she
took for a doll.   But it was no doll ; it was an effigy
of the child's dead twin which was being kept near
the survivor as a habitation for the little ghost, lest
it should wander homeless and, feeling lonely, call
its companion away after it to the spirit land.[5]
Among the Wajagga, a tribe of the great mountain

[1] J. Kubary, " Die Religion der
Pelauer ", in A. Bastian's *Allerlei
aus Volks- und Menschenkunde*
(Berlin, 1888), i. p. 9.

[2] W. M. Donselaar, " Aanteekeningen over het eiland Saleijer ", in
*Mededeelingen van wege het Neder-
landsche Zendlinggenootschap*, i.
(1857) p. 290.

[3] Le Comte C. N. de Cardi,
" Juju laws and customs in the Niger
Delta ", in *Journal of the Anthropo-
logical Institute*, xxix. (1899) p. 58.

[4] A. B. Ellis, *The Yoruba-
Speaking Peoples of the Slave Coast
of West Africa* (London, 1894), p. 80.

[5] Miss Mary H. Kingsley, *Travels
in West Africa* (London, 1879), p.
473.

Kilimanjaro in East Africa, it is believed that when a woman dies in childbed her affectionate ghost will return to fetch away her living child with her to the spirit land. So to prevent this from happening they place the shoot of a banana tree in the lap of her corpse when they bury it, hoping that her ghost will accept this substitute and leave her living child in peace.[1]

In San Cristoval, one of the Solomon Islands, there is a very curious custom called *ha'a ariro* or misleading the ghost. When the canoe containing the corpse is carried out of the house, all the children walk under it and back again while it is lifted high up. " Another form of puzzling the ghost, so that it will forget a child and not haunt him, is to take the young nut of a coconut and slice it in two, and then the same with another nut. Then take half of each nut and join them together and put this made-up nut under the right armpit of the dead. The ghost will be so puzzled and taken up with trying to fit together the two halves of what he supposes to be one nut that he will not haunt his child. On the south coast of Arosi half a *reremo* fruit and half a young coconut are thus joined ; in the bush half the fruit of *ahuhu* and half a canarium nut. But the idea is the same." [2]   In Ulawa, another of the Solomon Islands, the bodies of the dead are usually taken out in a canoe, and thrown into the sea, weighted with a stone, so as to sink them to the bottom. When this has been done the canoes paddle

[1] B. Gutmann, *Dichten und Denken der Dschagganeger* (Leipzig, 1909), p. 91.

[2] C. E. Fox, *The Threshold of the Pacific* (London, 1924), p. 211.

four or six times round the spot, in order to puzzle
the ghost should he seek to follow them.[1] Among
the Melanesians of the South-East Solomon Islands,
when one of a pair of twins died, a coconut was
placed beside the living twin to deceive the ghost of
his dead brother or sister, and the coconut was
spoken of as " your brother " or " your sister ".[2]
In Fiji " the spirits of women who die in childbirth,
or before the child is weaned, are greatly dreaded,
especially if the child were not born in wedlock. It
is a common custom to lay upon the breast of such
a woman a piece of a banana stem wrapped in native
cloth, and to bury it with her. This is done to cheat
her into the belief that it is her baby which she has
lying on her breast. The child in the meanwhile
is carried secretly to a distant town, that its dead
mother may be unable to find it if she discovers the
cheat. Other precautions also are taken. In some
places bits of bamboo are strung loosely on a cord
and fastened to the wrists of a corpse, so that by
their rattling they may give warning of her approach
if she takes to walking by night. Elsewhere the
poor woman is buried with her *liku* or waist-fringe
untied, that it may fall down when she rises, and
the wretched ghost may be thereby compelled to sit
down again with shame and confusion of face.

" In several parts of Fiji, when an old man dies
a curious custom is observed. Before the body is
carried forth to the burial, it is either lifted up by

---

[1] C. E. Fox, *op. cit.* pp. 256-257.   *South-East Solomon Islands* (Lon-
[2] W. G. Ivens, *Melanesians of the*   don, 1927), p. 77.

the bearers or laid upon a raised platform. A man (the brother of the child's mother) then takes the son's son of the deceased, passes him rapidly several times hither and thither, and under and over the corpse, and then runs away with him at top speed. This is done in order to bewilder the old gentleman as to the direction in which the child is taken away, it being supposed that he will be very desirous to have his grandson with him where he is, and will therefore seek to kill him. A like custom is observed when the father dies ; but it is the father's father who is especially dreaded, for it is supposed that the relationship between the paternal grandfather and his grandchild is closer than that which exists between the child and his father. This idea can be clearly traced to the former prevalence of descent through females, which indeed is still the rule among some of the Fijian tribes."[1]

Some of the aborigines in Northern Queensland, like many other Australian tribes, deposit their dead on stages at a distance from the camp. Having done so they bark the trees in the neighbourhood so as to make a false trail leading back to the stage where the corpse is lying. This is done in order to lead the wandering spirit of the dead back to his body on the stage, and to prevent him from following his friends back to their camp.[2]

---

[1] L. Fison, "Notes on Fijian Burial Customs", in *Journal of the Royal Anthropological Institute*, x. (1881) p. 145 ; *id.* L. Fison, *Tales of Old Fiji* (London, 1904), pp. 168 *sq.*

[2] J. C. Muirhead, quoted by Howitt in *Journal of the Royal Anthropological Institute*, xiii. (1884) p. 191.

The Kai tribe of Northern New Guinea often think that a death among them has been caused by the enchantments of a wicked sorcerer in a neighbouring village, and they send out a warlike expedition to take vengeance on him and his village. Sometimes, instead of sending forth a band of warriors to ravage, burn, and slaughter the whole male population of the village in which the wicked sorcerer resides, the people of one village will come to a secret understanding with the people of the sorcerer's village to have the miscreant quietly put out of the way. A hint is given to the scoundrel's next of kin, it may be his brother, son, or nephew, that if he will only wink at the slaughter of his obnoxious relative, he will receive a handsome compensation from the slayers. Should he privately accept the offer, he is most careful to conceal his connivance at the deed of blood, lest he should draw down on his head the wrath of his murdered kinsman's ghost. So, when the deed is done and the murder is out, he works himself up into a state of virtuous sorrow and indignation, covers his head with the leaves of a certain plant, and chanting a dirge in tones of heart-rending grief, marches straight to the village of the murderers. There, on the public square, surrounded by an attentive audience, he opens the floodgates of his eloquence and pours forth the torrents of an aching heart. " You have slain my kinsman," says he, " you are wicked men ! How could you kill so good a man, who conferred so many benefits on me in his lifetime ? I knew nothing of the plot. Had I had an inkling of it, I would have foiled it. How can I now avenge his death ? I have no property with which to hire men of war to go and punish his murderers. Yet in spite of everything my murdered kinsman will not believe in my innocence ! He will be angry with me ; he will pay me out ; he will do me all the harm he can. Therefore do you declare openly whether I had any share whatever in his death, and come and strew lime on my head in order that he may convince himself of my innocence." This appeal of injured innocence meets with a ready response. The people dust the leaves on his head with powdered lime ; and so, decorated with the white badge of spotless virtue, and enriched with a boar's tusk or other valuable object as the price of his compliance, he returns to his village with a conscience at peace with all the world, reflecting with satisfaction on the profitable transaction he has just concluded, and laughing in his sleeve at the poor deluded ghost of his murdered relative.

Sometimes the worthy soul who thus for a valuable consideration consents to waive all his personal feelings, will even carry his self-abnegation so far as to be present and look on at the murder of his kinsman. But true to his principles he will see to it that the thing is done decently and humanely. When the struggle is nearly over and the man is down, writhing on the grass with the murderers busy about him, his loving kinsman will not suffer them to take an unfair advantage of their superior num-

bers to cut him up alive with their knives, to chop
him with their axes, or to smash him with their clubs.
He will only allow them to stab him with their spears,
repeating of course the stabs again and again till the
victim ceases to writhe and quiver, and lies there
dead as a stone. Then begins the real time of peril
for the virtuous kinsman who has been a spectator
and director of the scene; for the ghost of the
murdered man has now deserted its mangled body,
and, still blinded with blood and smarting with pain,
might easily and even excusably misunderstand the
situation. It is essential, therefore, in order to prevent a painful misapprehension, that the kinsman
should at once and emphatically disclaim any part
or parcel in the murder. This he accordingly does
in language which leaves no room for doubt or
ambiguity. He falls into a passion; he rails at the
murderers; he proclaims his horror at their deed.
All the way home he refuses to be comforted. He
upbraids the assassins, he utters the most frightful
threats against them; he rushes at them to snatch
their weapons from them and dash them in pieces.
But they easily wrench the weapons from his un-
resisting hands. For the whole thing is only a
piece of acting. His sole intention is that the
ghost may see and hear it all, and being convinced
of the innocence of his dear kinsman may not
punish him with bad crops, wounds, sickness, and
other misfortunes. Even when he has reached
the village, he keeps up the comedy for a time,
raging, fretting, and fuming at the irreparable loss

he has sustained by the death of his lamented relative.

Similarly when a chief has among his subjects a particular sorcerer whom he fears, but with whom he is professedly on terms of friendship, he will sometimes engage a man to murder him. No sooner, however, is the murder perpetrated than the chief who bespoke it hastens in seeming indignation with a band of followers to the murderer's village. The assassin, of course, has got a hint of what is coming, and he and his friends take care not to be at home when the chief arrives on his mission of vengeance. Balked by the absence of their victim the avengers of blood breathe out fire and slaughter, but content themselves in fact with smashing an old pot or two, knocking down a deserted hut, and perhaps felling a banana-tree or a betel-palm. Having thus given the ghost of the murdered man an unequivocal proof of the sincerity of their friendship, they return quietly home.[1]

Among the Sea Dyaks of Borneo, when a death has taken place in a village, the body, wrapped in mats and covered over with a light framework of wood, is carried out of the house on the shoulders of four men. As they descend the house-ladder, ashes from the fire burnt near the corpse are thrown after them by the people who are left in the house. This is done in order that the dead man's ghost may not

---

[1] Ch. Keysser, " Aus dem Leben der Kaileute ", in R. Neuhauss, *Deutsch Neu Guinea* (Berlin, 1911), iii. pp. 148-149. Cf. J. G. Frazer, *Belief in Immortality*, i. pp. 280-282. In the text I have reproduced my English version from the latter work.

know his way back to the house, and may thus be
unable to trouble his friends afterwards.[1] This
Dyak custom has been described by a Dyak in his
native language. His account, as translated by an
English missionary, runs thus : " The burial takes
place in the early hours of the morning, at the first
sign of twilight. As soon as the corpse is carried
away from the house ashes are strewn over the footprints of the bearers. These ashes are supposed to
prevent the soul of the deceased from finding its way
back again to the house, should it desire to return and
haunt the living."[2] From this we see that a returning ghost is believed to follow the tracks of the bearers
who carried his body from the house to its last
resting-place. That is why it is necessary to conceal
the footprints of the bearers by ashes or otherwise.

Among the Tungus, a people of Siberia, on
returning from a funeral ceremony the mourners
try to efface the footprints they have made in the
snow, or else cut down trees so that they fall across
the way, in order to prevent the return of the ghost.[3]
In this case the effacing of the footprints is an alternative to blocking the path by the trunks of fallen
trees. The custom of erecting physical barriers to
prevent the return of the ghost has been illustrated
in a former part of this work.[4]

[1] E. H. Gomes, *Seventeen Years
among the Sea Dyaks of Borneo*
(London, 1911), pp. 135-136.
[2] Leo Nyuak, " Religious Rites
and Customs of the Iban or Dyaks
of Sarawak ", translated by Very
Rev. Edm. Dunn, in *Anthropos*, i.

(1906) p. 669.
[3] M. A. Czaplicka, *Aboriginal
Siberia* (Oxford, 1914), pp. 155-156,
referring to Mordvinoff, *The Natives
of the Turukhansk Country*.
[4] *The Fear of the Dead in Primitive Religion*, ii. pp. 27-52.

In ancient India, when a corpse was carried to the
pyre, a branch was tied to the body in such a way
that it brushed and effaced the footprints of the
bearers in order that death, or rather the ghost of
the dead man, might not find his way back to the
house.[1]

In South Nias, an island off the west coast
of Sumatra, the corpse is coffined outside of the
village, in order that the spirit of the dead may not
find its way back to the village to fetch somebody
there.   For this reason there is, also in North Nias,
no regular path to the cemeteries, but on each occasion
of a burial a path is cleared to the cemetery.[2]

Among the Karens, a tribe of Burma, when a
corpse has been burned on the pyre they bring back
the skull and the bones of the arms and legs to the
house. After that they adopt a sort of inverted
form of action and speech.   They winnow some rice
on a sieve turned upside down and, addressing the
spirit of the dead, they say, " See, it is necessary to
clean the rice before cooking it."   Then they set it
beside the bones of the deceased.   Next the priest
takes the skull in his hands and, showing it a vessel
of water, says, " If you are cold, bathe yourself " ;
and showing it next burning coals, says, " If you
are warm, heat yourself."   And in addressing the
ghost he adopts an inverted form of speech in which
everything is designated by a name the reverse of

[1] H. Oldenberg, *Die Religion des
Veda* (Berlin, 1894), p. 573.
[2] N. C. Rappard, " Het eiland
Nias en zijne Bewoners ", in *Bij-*
dragen tot de Taal- Land- en Volken-
kunde van Nederlandsch-Indië, lxii.
(1909) p. 573.

the real one.   Thus he calls the north the south, and
the south the north, and he calls the west the east,
and the east the west.   He speaks of the sky as the
earth, and of the earth as the sky.   In his speech
the trees have their roots in the air and their branches
in the earth.   All this the priest does, as the missionary who reports the custom rightly thought, for
the purpose of so confusing the ghost that he will
not wander and trouble the survivors.   At the conclusion of his address the priest places the skull and
the bones in a miniature house or reliquary, in which
it is apparently hoped that the spirit of the dead will
continue to reside peaceably.[1]

Among the Palaungs of Burma a very curious
mode of deceiving the ghost of a dead child has been
recorded by an excellent observer, Mrs. Leslie
Milne.   She says : " The following is a very grue-
some way of making an amulet.   When a woman
dies with her child unborn, she is rolled in a mat and
buried as soon as possible.   In the evening of the
same day the man who wished to make the amulet
goes with three or four other men to the grave where
the woman has been buried.   It would be in a
lonely place, far from the graves of others, for it is
believed that people who have died a violent death,
or on whom great misfortunes have fallen, must
have committed some terrible crime in their last
existence to come to such a terrible end.   When the
man (who wishes to have the amulet) and his

---

[1] J. B. Bringaud, " Un chapitre   Karins ", in *Missions Catholiques*,
de   l'ethnographie   des   Birmans   xxviii. (1896) p. 521.

friends reach the grave, they first make a little shrine of grass or bamboo ; then they stick a few flowers and flags of paper into it and set a bunch of bananas before it. These offerings are to appease the spirit of the dead woman. Stripping himself absolutely naked, the man then goes to the grave and digs out the earth until he reaches the mat in which the body of the dead woman is rolled. This he cuts open, then he operates on the body of the woman so as to be able to bite off the little finger of the unborn child. Having done this, he hurriedly replaces the mat, and shovels in the earth to fill up the grave. His companions, who have brought sticks with them, now give him a severe beating, to show that they are not to blame for what their companion has done, and also to make the spirit of the dead woman believe that the man who has violated her grave is being well punished for his temerity. They then withdraw, and the man dresses himself and goes home, carrying with him the little finger of the baby. He makes a large fire in the entrance-room of his house and sits as near to it as possible, as a Palaung woman would sit who had recently given birth to a child. He wraps himself in a blanket so that his clothes are hidden. He does this in order to make the child's ghost—if it has followed him to the house—believe that he is its mother. He has previously prepared cooked rice and bananas. In the middle of the night—as Palaungs believe—the ghost of the baby comes into the room to demand its finger. It is appeased at

intervals all through the night by offerings of rice
and bananas. The ghost is supposed to come for
seven nights, and each night a fresh offering of rice
and bananas is made. The seven days being over,
it is hoped that the child's spirit has gone to eat the
fruit of forgetfulness, or has become a *kar-man* in
the jungle, therefore no more offerings are made to
it. The man then gilds the finger, and Palaungs
say that any one at whom he points it—especially a
girl whom he loves—can refuse him nothing." [1]

Often in funerals the bearers of the corpse, in
carrying it to the grave or the pyre, perform certain
strange evolutions, for the purpose of so confusing
the spirit of the dead that he will not be able to find
his way back to his old home. Thus, for example,
among the Chams of Indo-China, who burn their
dead, " when at length the great day arrives the
priests construct a catafalque adorned with paper
figures, the mourners line up in procession behind,
and all proceed to the appointed place. Every
villager dons his white scarf—white being the
colour of mourning—brandishes a spear, sword, or
flag, and joins in the cortège. The bearers perform
the most remarkable evolutions with the body,
carrying it now feet first, now head first, or turning
it round and round in order to confuse the spirit
and prevent it from finding its way back. This
essential object is also secured by a priest, known on

[1] Mrs. Leslie Milne, *The Home of an Eastern Clan* (Oxford, 1924), p. 266. In the Palaung language *kar-man* denotes a spirit of the dead inhabiting a tree, water, air, earth or stone : see Mrs. Leslie Milne, *op. cit.* p. 342.

these occasions as *Po Damôeun* or ' Lord of Sorrow ', who remains in the house of the deceased shuts himself in, and calls on every object, animate and inanimate, to prevent the soul from entering and molesting the living ".[1] At a funeral in Burma, when a corpse is being carried to the pyre to be burnt, the bearers of the bier engage in grotesque dances, sometimes allowing it to advance, and sometimes to recede, as if its possession were being contested ; and at the pyre, before they lay the coffin on the wood, they sway it backwards and forwards seven times before the sacred *Bo* tree.[2] The writers who describe this ceremony do not explain the reasons for the grotesque dances and other movements of the bearers ; but probably their motive was the usual one of confusing the ghost, and so preventing his return. Among the Bataks of Sumatra, before carrying a corpse out of a house, the bearers first walk backwards and forwards several times, as if to confuse the dead and prevent him from finding his way back again.[3] In the Adelaide tribe of the Australian aborigines, when a man dies " a rude bier is prepared by fastening together ten or twelve branches, so as to form the radii of a circle ; and, when the body is lifted upon this bier, the ground upon which the man died is dug up by his wives or women related to him, with their long

[1] Commandant Baudesson, *Au pays des superstitions et des rites* (Paris), p. 249 ; Captain H. Baudesson, *Indo-China and its Primitive People*, p. 313. I quote from the English translation.

[2] M. and B. Ferrars, *Burma* (London, 1900), p. 195.

[3] J. Freiherr von Brenner, *Besuch bei den Kannibalen Sumatras* (Würzburg, 1894), p. 235.

sticks, occasionally assisted by the men. A little
heap of earth is thus formed, supposed to contain
the ' wingko ', or breath that has left the body, and
which this digging is intended to set free. While
this is being done, the bier is raised upon the shoulders of several men, each one taking a branch, and
some facing one way, others another. They move
slowly off from the spot, stopping at intervals, and
performing a quick rotatory motion in one direction,
and, when they can do so no longer, in the opposite
one. All this while a man stands under the centre
of the bier, assisting to support it with his head ;
and, after each rotation, he addresses the deceased,
asking him how and why he died, who killed him,
etc. The group of men surrounding the bier and
its supporters are all armed with their spears and
other weapons, and the women carry their long
sticks and bags. Sometimes the bearers move forward as if by a consentaneous impulse, and, at
others, one of the bystanders beckons to a spot to
which the body is immediately borne, and the rotations are repeated. Even the presence of the
feather of some rare bird upon the ground will
attract their attention to that particular place, and
the circumvolutions will there be renewed with
increased energy. If there happens to be large
trees in the neighbourhood, they walk quickly up to
one and then another, resting the bier against them ;
and, on every such occasion, the deceased is interro-
gated as before. Between every act of rotation,
their march is more extended ; so that they thus

by degrees proceed farther from the place where the death occurred, until at last they walk off altogether to a distant locality, in which it is resolved to bury the body ; the ceremony occasionally continuing more than one day. The place of burial being fixed upon, the earth or sand is loosened by the digging-sticks, and thrown out by the hands ; the body is laid in the grave on one side, and the hole being filled up again, is usually covered with branches and bark of trees ".[1] The writer who describes these burial rites does not explain the motive for the rotations and other odd behaviour of the bearers ; but probably we shall not err in supposing that their aim is to lure the spirit of the dead far away from his old home, and so to bewilder him on his last journey that he will never find his way back to trouble his family and friends.

The peasants of Ho-nan, in China, fear the ghosts of young children even more than the ghosts of grown men, for when they die children receive no ancestral honours in the domestic shrine, and accordingly their ghosts are angry and seek to avenge themselves on their family by killing the cattle or the fish on which the people live. However, their relations have a mode of guarding themselves against these dangerous spirits. When a child is sick, and at the point of death, they expose or drown or bury the little sufferer, and the man who carries the dying child to its last home is careful not to walk

[1] W. Wyatt, " Some Account of the Manners and Customs of the Adelaide and Encounter Bay Tribes ", in *The Native Tribes of South Australia* (Adelaide, 1879), pp. 164-165.

in a straight line. He moves in a zigzag, going and returning, pacing now to the east and now to the west, describing a confusion of triangles, in order that in this labyrinth of broken lines the ghost of the child may never be able to trace its way home. So the family in the house are quite at their ease, thinking that they will never be troubled by the depredation of their child's ghost on the domestic cattle and fish.[1]

The Koryaks, a primitive tribe in the extreme north-east of Siberia, burn their dead, and when they have placed a body on the pyre they take measures to prevent the dangerous spirit of the deceased from following them back to the house. Mr. Jochelson, who witnessed the cremation of a girl's body, has described their precautions as follows : " When the clothes were burned, and the child's head appeared, her grandfather took a pole, and, thrusting it into the body, said, 'Of yonder magpie pricked ' (*A'nalan vaki'tha ti'npinen*) ; or, in a free translation, ' This is the magpie of the underworld which pricked '. He imitated the actions of the magpie of the world of the dead, in order to inform the deceased that she was passing to another world, and must not return to the house. The further actions of the dead girl's grandfather had the same end in view. When the flames of the pyre were dying away, he broke some twigs from the alder and willow bushes that were growing near by,

---

[1] A letter of the missionary Delaplace, dated Moncy-te-Fou, 25 September 1851, in *Annales de la* *Propagation de la Foi*, xxiv. (1852) pp. 250 *sqq.*

and strewed them around the pyre. These twigs represented a dense forest which was supposed to surround the burning-place. We left the place while the pyre was still burning. Before leaving, the grandfather went around the pyre, first from right to left, them from left to right, in order so to obscure his tracks that the deceased would not be able to follow him. Then, stepping away from the pyre towards the houses, he drew with his stick a line in the snow, jumped across it, and shook himself. The others followed his example. The line was supposed to represent a river which separated the village from the burning-place. All these actions are identical with episodes in the tales of the 'magic flight'. After being taken out of the house, the deceased is apparently regarded as a spirit hostile to the living."[1]

Often the bearers of a corpse, before they convey the body to the grave or pyre, walk or run with it at full speed round the house, in order to confuse the spirit of the dead, and thus to prevent him from returning to his old dwelling. Thus, for example, in Siam the bearers carry the coffin thrice round the house, running at full speed, for they believe that if they did not take this precaution, the spirit of the dead would recall the road by which he had passed, and would return during the night to play some mischievous prank upon his family.[2] In

[1] Waldemar Jochelson, *The Koryaks* (Memoir of the American Museum of Natural History: The Jesup North Pacific Expedition) (Leiden and New York, 1905), i. p. 112.

[2] "Lettre de Mgr. Bruguière, évêque de Capse, à M. Bousquet,

Minahassa, a district in the north of the island of Celebes, before a corpse is carried to the grave, it is borne thrice round the house where the death took place. The bearers who carry it walk or run at a quick pace, with comic gestures which excite the amusement rather than the sorrow of the spectators. The corpse is seated on a chair placed on the bier, and if the deceased was a mother one of her daughters will sit on the bier with bells fastened to her body which jingle with the movements of the bier. The jingle of the bells may be intended to hasten the departure of the mother's ghost to the spirit land.[1]

Among some of the Indians of Bolivia, when a death has taken place in a house, it is customary to shift the door to the other side of the house in order that the returning ghost may not be able to find it, and to effect an entrance into the dwelling.[2] A similar precaution to baffle a returning ghost is reported from various parts of Africa. After a death has taken place, and the body has been buried, the Barundi of Tanganyika adopt various precautions to prevent the return of the dreaded ghost. In the hut where the death occurred they shift the entrance to the other side of the hut, renew

vicaire-général d'Aire ", in *Annales de la Propagation de la Foi*,v. (1831) p. 174. Cf. Mgr. Pallegoix, *Description du royaume Thai ou Siam* (Paris, 1854), p. 245, and E. Young, *The Kingdom of the Yellow Robe*, p. 246.

[1] " Een blik op de Minahassa ", in *Tijdschrift voor Nederlandsch-Indië*, 1845, Part IV, p. 330; N.

Graafland, *De Minahassa* (Rotterdam, 1867), i. p. 331.

[2] *Exploraciones y noticias hidrograficas de los Rios del Norte de Bolivia* : Segunda Parte (La Paz, 1890), p. 20. Cf. Chr. Nusser-Asport, " Padre Armentias Reise in den Bolivianischen Provinz Caupolican ", in *Globus*, lx. (1891) p. 120.

the hearthstone, and move the place of the bed and
all the other furniture in the hut, all no doubt to
deceive the ghost so that even if he returned to the
hut he could not recognize his old dwelling.[1] A
similar precaution taken by some of the Kafirs of
South Africa is reported by Mr. Dudley Kidd.   He
says : " Another strange case was told me.   At the
funeral of a small child the people buried the blankets
and ornaments used by the child, and then went and
fetched the door of the hut in which the baby had
lived.   This also they buried, substituting a new
door for the old one ; they said they did so to bam-
boozle the spirit of the baby.   When it came wandering round at night it would find a new door on the
hut, and would think it had made a mistake ; whereupon it would wander about until it found the old
familiar door in the earth, and it would then settle
down contentedly, and not trouble the people in the
kraal."[2]

A common, almost a world-wide way of deceiving
a ghost, is to carry his body out of the house, not by
the door, but through a special opening in a wall of
the house, which is immediately afterwards closed
up.   The belief seems to be that the returning ghost
can enter his old home only through the opening by
which his body was carried out, so that when he
arrives at the opening and finds it blocked up he is
puzzled, and being unable to find the door he cannot
enter the house.   A custom of this kind has been

[1] H. Meyer, *Die Barundi*, p.
114.

[2] Dudley Kidd, *The Essential
Kafir* (London, 1904), p 251.

reported from many parts of the world, both in ancient and modern times, and the explanation of it which has just been given is assigned for it by many of the peoples who practise it.   But sometimes the true original reason is forgotten and a mistaken reason substituted for it.   In the east, where the houses are often raised above the ground on piles, the corpse is often passed through a hole in the floor instead of through a hole in the wall, but the intention is the same.   Sometimes it is not all the dead who are thus carried out, but only the remains of those whose ghosts are specially dreaded, particularly the corpses of women who have died in childbed. We will now take examples of this curious custom, arranging them so as to illustrate the geographical. diffusion of the practice.   We have already seen that the custom obtains in Siam, for the purpose of excluding the ghost of the dead from the house.[1]

In Laos, a province of Siam, it is especially the bodies of women dying in childbed which are thus taken out of the house by a special opening; in their case the corpse is taken out through a hole in the floor, and not in the wall of the house.[2]   The people of

[1] See above, *Fear of the Dead in Primitive Religion*, vol. ii. p. 102, and for the authorities see Bruguière in *Annales de l'Association de la Propagation de la Foi*, v. (Lyons and Paris, 1831) p. 180; Mgr. Pallegoix, *Description du royaume Thai ou Siam* (Paris, 1854), p. 245; Sir John Bowring, *The Kingdom and People of Siam* (London, 1857), i. 122; E. Young, *The Kingdom of the Yellow Robe*, p. 246.   Mr. P. A. Thomson thinks that the custom is observed from a fear that if the corpse were not carried through a special opening the spirit of the dead would refuse to go out through the door and so would remain in the house. See P. A. Thomson, *Lotus Land* (London, 1906), p. 136. This explanation appears to be erroneous. Why should a dead man refuse to go out by the door which he has gone out so often in his lifetime?

[2] Carl Bock, *Temples and Elephants* (London, 1884), p. 262.

Annam, which borders on Siam, sometimes observe a similar custom. The writer who reports it says that the Annamites resort to every kind of device to prevent the spirits of the dead from returning to the house. For this purpose the funeral procession follows a roundabout way to the tomb, thinking so to deceive the spirit, and to complete his confusion the bearers of the bier turn it about several times. Or they take the corpse out of the house, not by the door, but by a special opening, sometimes breaking a hole in a wall of the house for the purpose.[1] The Moï, a primitive race who inhabit the mountainous region of Indo-China, from China on the north to Cambodia on the south, observe a similar custom for a similar reason. The writer who reports it says that among them, when a death has taken place, " the bearers take up the body, convey it rapidly through every room in the house, and after wrapping it in large palm leaves secure it to a stout bamboo pole. The next matter is to get it out of the house in such a way that it will never know the point of exit. Otherwise the spirit will surely find its way back and continue to haunt the living. Accordingly, an opening is very carefully made in the thatched walls or roof, so that the breach will close of itself when the corpse has passed through." [2] The Kachins of Burma carry out the corpses of women dying in childbed not through the door of the house but through an opening made for the purpose in a wall

[1] P. Giran, *Magie et religion Annamites* (Paris, 1912), p. 393.
[2] Captain Baudesson, *Indo-China* and its Primitive People, p. 170; id. Commandant Baudesson, *Au pays des superstitions et des rites*, 127.

or in the floor of the house. This they do to prevent
the return of her dangerous ghost, and for the same
purpose they resort to other devices, which we shall
have occasion to notice later on.[1] We have already
seen that for a similar purpose the Shans of Burma
take out the corpse of a woman dying in childbed
through a hole in the wall of the house, and that the
Palaungs of Burma lower the corpses of such women
through a hole in the floor, always for the sake of
preventing the return of the much-dreaded ghost.[2]

In China it seems to have been an ancient practice
to knock down part of the wall of a house for the
purpose of carrying out a corpse, for the custom is
alluded to in the Lî-Kî, one of the sacred books of
the Chinese.[3] The custom is said to have been particularly observed for members of the royal family ;
when one of them died ancient usage required that
the corpse should be carried out of the palace, not
through the door, but through a breach made for the
purpose in the wall.[4] At Mukden in Mongolia, the
body of a dead child " must not be carried out of a
door or window, but through a new or disused opening, in order that the evil spirit which causes the
disease may not enter. The belief is that the
Heavenly Dog, which eats the sun at the time of an

---

[1] Ch. Gilhodes, " Naissance et
enfance chez les Katchins (Birmanie) ", in *Anthropos*, vi. (1911)
pp. 872 *sq.*

[2] *The Fear of the Dead*, vol. ii.
pp. 112 *sq.*, referring to Mrs. Leslie
Milne, *The Shans at Home*, p. 96,
and *The Home of an Eastern Clan*,
pp. 304 *sq.*

[3] *The Sacred Books of China*,
translated by James Legge, Part III.,
The Lî-Kî, i.-x. (Oxford, 1885) pp.
144 *sq.* (Book II. Sect. I. Part II. 33)
(*Sacred Books of the East*, vol. xxvii.).

[4] J. F. Lafitau, *Mœurs des
sauvages amériquains* (Paris, 1724),
ii. 401 *sq.*, citing Le Comte, *Nouv.
mémoires de la Chine*, vol. ii. p. 187.

eclipse, demands the bodies of children, and that if they are denied to him he will bring certain calamity on the household." [1]   This explanation of the custom is apparently an afterthought which has displaced the original motive, the fear of the ghost of the dead child and a desire to prevent it from returning to the house.   In the extreme east of Siberia the primitive Reindeer Koryaks do not carry out their dead by the usual door, but under the edge of the tent-cover, which is lifted up for the purpose. [2]   Among the primitive Chukchee, neighbours of the Koryaks on the north, a corpse is usually drawn up through a hole in the roof or in the back of the tent, and then all traces of the passage are removed, to prevent the possible return of the dead. [3]   The Samoyeds of Siberia carry out the dead, not through the door of the hut, but through an opening made by lifting up the roof or covering of the hut, for they think that, were the corpse carried out by the door, the ghost of the deceased would soon return to fetch away another of the family. [4]

The custom with which we are here concerned has been observed by various peoples of the Indian Archipelago, for example, by the Gajos of Sumatra. [5]

[1] Mrs. Bishop, *Korea and Her Neighbours* (London, 1898), pp. 239 *sq.*

[2] W. Jochelson, *The Koryak* (New York and Leiden, 1908), pp. 110 *sq.* (The Jesup North Pacific Expedition: Memoir of the American Museum of Natural History).

[3] W. Bogaras, *The Chukchee* (publication of the Jesup North Pacific Expedition, vol. vii.   Memoir of the American Museum of Natural History) (New York, 1904-1910), p. 525. Cf. M. A. Czaplicka, *Aboriginal Siberia* (Oxford, 1914), pp. 146 *sq.*

[4] P. S. Pallas, *Reise durch verschiedene Provinzen des russischen Reichs* (St. Petersburg 1771-1776), iii. 75 ; Middendorff, *Reise in den aussersten Norden und Osten Siberiens,* iv. 1464.

[5] C. Snouck Hurgronje, *Het Gajo-*

Among the Kayans in the interior of Borneo, whose houses are raised above the ground on piles, the coffin containing the corpse is lowered to the ground with rattans, either through the floor, planks being taken up for the purpose, or under the eaves at the side of the gallery. " In this way they avoid carrying it down the house-ladder ; and it seems to be felt that this precaution renders it more difficult for the ghost to find its way back to the house." [1] Among these Kayans it is especially the bodies of women dying in childbed which are carried out by removing boards in the back wall of the dwelling, for the ghosts of these women are here, as usual, much dreaded, and special precautions have to be taken to prevent their return. [2] The Toradyas of Central Celebes usually pass a corpse out of the house by the window, but if the window is too small to permit of the passage of the body they break an opening through a wall of the house, and so pass the corpse through it. The dead body of a child is passed out of a house through a hole in the floor. [3] The Buginese of South Celebes never carry a corpse out of the house by the ordinary door, but always break a hole in one of the walls of the house for the purpose. [4] Among the Buginese and Macassars of South

---

land en zijne Bewoners (Batavia, 1903), p. 313.

[1] C. Hose and W. McDougall, The Pagan Tribes of Borneo (London, 1912), i. 35. Cf. W. H. Furness, The Home-life of Borneo Headhunters (Philadelphia, 1902), p. 52.

[2] Dr. A. W. Nieuwenhuis, Quer durch Borneo (Leiden, 1904), p. 91.

[3] N. Adriani and A. C. Kruijt, De Bare'e-sprekende Toradja's van Midden-Celebes (s'Gravenhage, 1912), i. p. 236 ; ii. pp. 97, 99.

[4] Adriani and Kruijt, op. cit. vol. i. p. 356.

Celebes there is in the king's palace a window reaching to the floor through which on his decease the king's body is carried out.[1] That such a custom is only a limitation to kings of a rule which once applied to everybody becomes all the more probable, when we learn that in the island of Saleijer, which lies to the south of Celebes, each house has, besides its ordinary windows, a large window in the form of a door, through which, and not through the ordinary entrance, every corpse is regularly removed at death.[2] In Bali, a small island to the north of Java, when a queen of the island died, " the body was drawn out of a large aperture made in the wall to the right-hand side of the door, in the absurd opinion of *cheating the devil*, whom these islanders believe to lie in wait in the ordinary passage."[3] Probably the true original motive of the custom was to prevent the dead queen's ghost from coming back to disturb her successor on the throne. In Fiji, when a certain king died, the side of the house was broken down to allow the body to be carried out, though there were doorways wide enough for the purpose close at hand.[4] The missionary who records the fact could not learn the reason of it, but here

[1] B. F. Matthes, *Bijdragen tot de Ethnologie van Zuid-Celebes* (The Hague, 1875), p. 139 ; *id.*, " Over de *ádá's* of gewoonten der Makassaren en Boegineezen ", *Verslagen en Mededeelingen der Koninklijke Akademie van Wetenschappen*, Afdeeling Letterkunde, Derde Reeks, ii. (Amsterdam, 1885) p. 142.

[2] W. M. Donselaar, " Aantekeningen over het eiland Saleijer ",

Mededeelingen van wege het Nederlandsche Zendelinggenootschap, i. (1857) p. 291.

[3] Prevost, quoted by John Crawford, *History of the Indian Archipelago* (Edinburgh, 1820), ii. 245. Cf. Adolf Bastian, *Die Volker des östlichen Asien*, v. (Jena, 1869), p. 83.

[4] Thomas Williams, *Fiji and the Fijians*, Second Edition (London, 1860), i. 197.

again we may suppose that the carrying out of the
royal body through a breach in the wall of the house
was a precaution to prevent the deceased monarch's
ghost from coming back to haunt and trouble his
successor on the throne.

In India, among the Birhors, a primitive tribe of
Chota Nagpur, " a woman dying within twenty-one
days of childbirth or a child dying within twenty-one
days of birth may never be admitted into the community of ancestor-spirits, as their spirits are always
dangerous.   In their case, therefore, a new doorway
to the hut is opened to take their corpses to the grave.
These corpses are buried in a place apart from where
other corpses are buried." [1]   Speaking of the Hindoos, a French traveller in India of the eighteenth
century says that instead of carrying the corpse out
by the door they make an opening in the wall by
which they pass it out in a seated posture, and the
hole is closed up after the ceremony. [2]   Among
various Hindoo castes it is customary, if a death
occurs on an inauspicious day, to remove the corpse
from the house not through the door, but through a
temporary hole made in the wall. [3]   Another high
authority on India gives us more precise information
as to those unlucky days which necessitate this
change in the ordinary mode of burial.   He tells us
that the Hindoos attribute to the moon a kind of
zodiac composed of twenty-seven constellations

[1] S. C. Roy, *The Birhors* (Ranchi, 1925), p. 266.
[2] Sonnerat, *Voyage aux Indes orientales et à Chine* (Paris, 1782), i.
p. 86.
[3] E. Thurston, *Ethnographic Notes in Southern India* (Madras, 1906), p. 226.

which preside each over one of the twenty-seven days of its periodic course. The five last days of the moon are all deemed more or less disastrous. Woe to the relatives of a person who dies on one of these ill-omened days. The corpse of the unfortunate must not be carried out through the door or the window : it is absolutely necessary for the purpose to make a hole in the wall of the house, through which the corpse is passed out.[1] In Travancore the body of a dead rajah " is taken out of the palace through a breach in the wall, made for the purpose, to avoid pollution of the gate, and afterwards built up again so that the departed spirit may not return through the gate to trouble the survivors".[2] Another writer describes as follows this mode of carrying out the corpse of a dead rajah of Travancore. " Before the body is taken from the palace, a hole is made in the wall of the compartment where it rested, and through this the corpse is conveyed outside. This is a custom even with the Sûdras, the reigning family of Travancore being Kshatrias. What the exact superstition, or idea, is, I am not in a position to say, but I fancy that there is a belief that if the corpse is conveyed through the door, other deaths will immediately follow."[3] We may suppose that such a death would be ascribed to the maleficent influence of the deceased rajah's ghost, who might have effected an entrance into the palace

[1] Abbé J. A. Dubois, *Mœurs, institutions et cérémonies des peuples de l'Inde* (Paris, 1825), ii. 225.
[2] S. Mateer, *Native Life in* Travancore (London, 1883), p. 137.
[3] A. Butterworth, " Royal Families in Travancore ", in the *Indian Antiquary*, xxxi. (1902) p. 251.

by the ordinary door. Among the Brahuis, a
Dravidian-speaking people of Baluchistan, if the
door of a house faces south they think that it will be
very unlucky to carry out a corpse for burial through
the door on the third or fourth day of the new moon.
Hence on any such day it is necessary to make a
breach in the wall of the house facing the door, for
the sake of carrying out through it the corpse of the
deceased.[1] The Lepchas of Sikkim take a corpse
out of the house by a hole made in the floor. Their
houses are generally built on pillars or wooden posts.[2]
Among the Persians the custom of carrying out a
corpse through a breach in the wall of a house would
seem to be very ancient, for in their sacred book, the
Zend-Avesta, it is prescribed that, when a death has
occurred, a breach shall be made in the wall and the
corpse carried out through it by two men, who have
first stripped off their clothes.[3]

Among the Sakalava and Antimerina of Madagascar, when a sovereign or a prince of the royal
family dies within the enclosure of the king's palace,
the corpse must be carried out of the palace, not by
the door, but by a breach made for the purpose in the
wall ; the new sovereign could not pass through the
door that had been polluted by the passage of a dead
body.[4] Here again we may suppose that as in
Celebes and Travancore the rule for the burial of

[1] Denys Bray, Life-History of a
Brahui (London, 1913), p. 123.
[2] J. A. H. Louis, The Gates of
Thibet (Calcutta, 1894), p. 114.
[3] The Zend-Avesta, Part I., The
Vendidâd, translated by James

Darmesteter (Oxford, 1880), p. 95
(Fargard, viii. 2, 10), Sacred Books
of the East, vol. iv.
[4] Arnold van Gennep, Tabou et
totémisme à Madagascar (Paris,
1904), p. 65, quoting Dr. Catat.

sovereigns is or has been formerly the rule for the burial of their subjects likewise ; kings are commonly conservative of ancient usages.

In Africa the custom of carrying the dead out of a house by an opening made specially for the purpose is practised by many tribes in many parts of the continent. Thus, for example, " the Ashantis, and some others of the northern tribes, bury their dead outside, and the body is taken out of the house through a hole which is made in the wall, for a corpse may not pass through any door. This superstition appears to have been borrowed from the Mohammedan peoples inland, for it is held by the Fulas, Houssas, Dagombas, and others, and also by the Mandingos and Jolloffs far to the north ; while it is unknown to the southern Tshi-speaking tribes."[1] Among the Ewe-speaking peoples of Togo the body of a priest may not be carried out through the door of a house ; a hole is made in the roof of the house, and the priest's corpse is pushed through it. The German missionary who reports the custom thinks that this is done to prevent the priest's ghost from finding the door of the house and so entering and troubling the survivors.[2] Among the Ibibios of Southern Nigeria " a woman who dies in giving birth to twins, or before the end of her year of purification after such an event, may not be carried to her last resting-place through the house-door, any more than she may go out by it on leaving home to

[1] A. B. Ellis, *The Tschi-speaking Peoples of the Gold Coast of West Africa* (London, 1887), pp. 239 *sq.*

[2] J. Spieth, *Die Ewe-Stämme* (Berlin, 1906), p. 756.

spend the prescribed twelve moons in the twin
women's town. Such sad exiles must pass through
a hole purposely broken in the wall, by which exit
the unfortunate babes are also carried forth. Further, the body of a twin mother may on no account
be borne along a road by which ordinary people pass
to and fro, but only by a little path specially cut
through the bush to the place where it is to be flung.
The reason given for this prohibition is much the
same as that given in Cambodia for carrying a dead
body feet foremost, *i.e.* 'that it may not see the
house, in which event other sickness and other
deaths would result'. Ibibios say, too, that should
the ghost return and try to enter her former home
she would be unable to do so since the place by
which the body was carried forth has been blocked
up, and wraiths can only enter by the same way
through which their bodies were borne forth." [1] The
general Nigerian custom at a burial is described briefly
as follows, by another authority : " Superstition
does not permit of the corpse being carried through
a door, and a hole for its egress has to be made in
the wall ".[2] Among the Bambara, a tribe in the
upper valley of the Niger, this mode of carrying a
corpse out of a house to burial appears to be reserved
for the bodies of social outcasts.[3] Among the Mossi,
a tribe of the Western Sudan, a corpse is regularly

[1] D. Amaury Talbot, *Woman's
Mysteries of a Primitive People*
(London, 1918), p. 215.
[2] Lieut.-Col. A. F. Mockler-
Ferryman, *British Nigeria* (London,

1912), p. 234.

[3] Abbé Jos. Henry, *L'Âme d'un
peuple africain: les Bambara*
(Münster, 1910), p. 231.

carried out of the hut, not by the door, but through an opening made for the purpose in the wall of the hut.[1] Among the Bubis of Fernando Po, when an eminent person dies the corpse is carried out of the house, not by the door, but by a hole broken through that wall of the house near which the dying man lay.[2] Among the Wajagga of Mount Kilimanjaro in East Africa, the dead body of a childless woman is never carried out of the hut by the door, but always through a breach made in the opposite wall of the house. She is buried in the depth of the forest ; but never in a place which the natives expect to cultivate. Apparently they think that the corpse of a childless woman would render the ground barren. It is safe therefore to infer that the carrying out of her body through a special opening in the hut is intended to prevent her dangerous ghost from returning to blight her friends and the land.[3] Similarly among the Kavirondo, near neighbours of the Wajagga, " when a woman dies without having borne a child, she is carried out of the back of the house. A hole is made in the wall and the corpse is ignominiously pushed through the hole and carried some distance to be buried, as it is considered a curse to die without a child. If the woman has given birth to a child, then her corpse is carried out through

[1] P. E. Mangin, " Les Mossi ", in *Anthropos*, ix. (1909) p. 729.

[2] L. Janikowski, " L'Ile de Fernando-Poo, son état actuel et ses habitants ", in *Bulletin de la Société*

de Geographie, vii. (1886) p. 563.

[3] B. Gutmann, " Trauer und Begräbnis-Sitten der Wadschagga ", in *Globus*, lxxxix. (1906) p. 200.

the front door and buried in the veranda of the house." [1]

In describing a burial among the Ngoni (Angoni) of Nyassaland a missionary tells how the bearers carried out the corpse, not through the door of the hut, but by a hole broken through the wall of the hut, and then laid it in the grave. " All the dishes, pots, clothes, and articles of personal use belonging to the deceased were buried with him. But no metal goods were buried, whether hoes, or arrows, or brass ornaments. It was feared that these would give the ghost opportunity to return with anger to hurt the friends." [2] Among the Atonga of Nyassaland the dead are carried out of a hut, not by the door, but by a special opening opposite the door, which has been broken through the wall of the hut.[3] Among the Thonga, a Bantu tribe of South-East Africa, a corpse may not be carried out of a hut by the door : it must be passed out through a hole made in the wall of the hut on the right-hand side if the deceased is a man, or presumably on the left-hand side if the deceased be a woman. It is buried in a grave either behind the hut or in the neighbouring forest.[4] A missionary who has described the customs and religion of the Bantu tribes of South-East Africa between Cape Colony and Natal tells us that the dead body of a chief is never carried out

[1] Rev. N. Stam, " The Religious Conceptions of the Kavirondo ", in *Anthropos*, v. (1910) p. 361.

[2] D. Fraser, *Winning a Primitive People* (London, 1914), p. 158.

[3] Rev. A. C. MacAlpine, in A. Werner, *The Natives of British Central Africa* (London, 1906), p. 161.

[4] H. A. Junod, *The Life of a South African Tribe*, Second Edition (London, 1927), i. 138.

of the hut by the door, but always by a special opening made for the purpose in the wall of the hut.[1]
Among the Basutos, another Bantu tribe of South
Africa, a corpse is carried out of the hut, not through
the door, but through an opening made in the wall
of the hut opposite to the door.[2] So among the
Bechuanas, another Bantu tribe of South Africa, a
corpse is not carried out of the hut by the door, for
that is reserved for the use of the living. It is
carried out through an opening made in the fence,
and buried in the cattle kraal.[3] Describing the
burial customs of the South African tribes among
which he laboured, the missionary Dr. Moffat says
that " the body is not conveyed through the door
of the fore-yard or court connected with each
house, but an opening is made in the fence for that
purpose ".[4] The Hottentots of South Africa, who
are not a Bantu tribe, practise a similar custom.
They carry a corpse out of a hut, not by the door,
but by an opening specially made for the purpose
in the wall of the hut.[5] According to the French
missionaries, Arbousset and Daumas, some of the
Bushmen observe a similar custom ; when a person
dies they wrap up his body in his ordinary attire,

[1] Rev. Jas. Macdonald, *Light in Africa* (London, 1890), p. 166. Cf. Dudley Kidd, *The Essential Kafir* (London, 1904), p. 247.

[2] Rev. E. Casalis, *The Basutos* (London, 1861), p. 202.

[3] " Extrait du Journal des Missions evangeliques ", in *Bulletin de la Société de Géographie*, xx. (1833) p. 196. Cf. C. G. Andersson, *Lake Ngami, or Explorations and Dis-* coveries, Second Edition (London, 1856), p. 446.

[4] R. Moffat, *Missionary Labours and Scenes in Southern Africa* (London, 1842), p. 307.

[5] P. Kolben, *The Present State of the Cape of Good Hope* (London, 1731–1738), i. 316 ; Adolph Bastian, *Der Mensch in der Geschichte* (Leipzig, 1860), vol. ii. pp. 322 *sq.*

and carry it out of the hut, not by the door, but by a large opening made in the wall.[1]

A like burial custom has been observed for like reasons by many of the aboriginal inhabitants of America, both Eskimo and Indian. Thus, for example, among the Greenlanders " if a person dies in the house, his body must not be carried through the ordinary entry of it, but conveyed out at the window ; and if he dies in a tent, he is brought out at the back part of it. At the funeral, a woman lights a stick in the fire, brandishing the same and saying, *piklerrukpok*, that is, Here is no more to be got."[2] Among the Eskimos of Hudson Bay, when a death has taken place in a snow house (*igloo*) or a tent the relatives try to bury it before the sun has risen. But if the sun has risen while the corpse is still in the house or tent the body must be kept there for three or five days. At the end of that time the corpse must be carried out, not by the door, but by a special opening made in the wall of the house or by raising a corner of the tent.[3] With regard to the Eskimos of the Ungava District in the Hudson Bay Territory we are told that " the nearest relatives on approach of death remove the invalid to the outside of the house, for if he should die within he must not be carried out of the door but through a hole cut in the side wall, and it must then be carefully closed

[1] T. Arbousset and F. Daumas, *Relation d'un voyage d'exploration* (Paris, 1842), pp. 502 *sq.*

[2] Hans Egede, *Description of Greenland*, Second Edition (London, 1818), pp. 152 *sq.* Cf. David

Crantz, *History of Greenland* (London, 1767) i. 237.

[3] Mgr. A. Turquetil, " Notes sur les Esquimaux de Baie Hudson ", in *Anthropos*, xxi. (1926) p. 432.

to prevent the spirit of the person from returning ".[1]
To the same effect Rink, who seems to have spent
much of his time in Greenland, in speaking of the
Eskimos in general, says, " the bodies of those who
died in a house were carried out through a window, or
if in a tent, underneath the back part."[2] When
C. F. Hall was living with the Eskimos of Cumber-
land Inlet, a young child died in a snow house
(*igloo*).   In order to bury the body a passage was
cut through the wall of the snow house, and through
this opening the little body was carried by its mother,
accompanied or followed by Hall and the other
mourners.[3]   Among the Eskimos of Hudson Strait,
with whom Captain G. F. Lyon wintered, " the
dead are in most cases carried through the window,
in preference to the door of a snow hut, which, after
the three days of mourning have expired, is for-
saken, at least by the family of which the deceased
had formed a part ".[4]

Among the Unalit Eskimos of Bering Strait a
corpse is usually removed from the house by being
raised with cords through the smoke-hole in the
roof ; but is never passed through the doorway.
Should the smoke-hole be too small to allow of the
passage of the corpse, an opening is made in the rear

[1] Lucien M. Turner, " Ethnology
of the Ungava District, Hudson Bay
Territory ", in *Eleventh Annual
Report of the Bureau of Ethnology*
(Washington, 1894) p. 191.
[2] H. J. Rink, *Tales of the Eskimo*
(London, 1875), p. 55.
[3] C. F. Hall, *Narrative of the*
*Second Arctic Expedition made by
Charles F. Hall* (Washington, 1879),
p. 265.
[4] Capt. G. F. Lyon, *The Private
Journal of Captain G. F. Lyon, of
H.M.S. Hecla, during the recent
voyages of discovery under Captain
Parry* (London, 1824), p. 369.

of the house, and the body is carried through it.[1]
Among the Tuski, an aboriginal but not Indian tribe
of Alaska, "those who die a natural death are carried
out through a hole cut in the back of the hut or
yaráng. This is immediately closed up, that the
spirit of the dead man may not find his way back."[2]
Among the Tlingit Indians of Alaska, when a chief
dies his body is taken out of the house by an opening
made in the back wall of the dwelling.[3]   Among
the Haida Indians of Queen Charlotte Island, British
Columbia, when a chief died his body was carried
out to the grave through an opening made for the
purpose in a wall of the house.   His near relatives
and friends cut their hair short and put pitch on their
faces in sign of mourning.   If he was a great chief
all the people of the town sometimes followed their
example.[4]   Among the Kwakiutl Indians of British
Columbia a corpse " must not be taken out of the
door, else other inmates of the house would be sure
to die soon.   Either a hole is made in one of the
walls, through which the body is carried out, or it
is lifted through the roof.   It is placed behind the
house to be put into the box that is to serve as a
coffin.   If it were placed in the coffin inside the
house, the souls of the other inmates would enter

[1] E. W. Nelson, " The Eskimo
about Bering Strait ", in the
*Eighteenth Annual Report of the
Bureau of American Ethnology*
(1896–1897), Part I. (Washington,
1899) p. 310.
[2] W. H. Dall, *Alaska and its
Resources* (London, 1871), p. 382.

[3] Aurel Krause, *Die Tlinkit-
Indianer* (Jena, 1885), p. 225.
[4] J. R. Swanton, *Contributions to
the Ethnology of the Haida* (The
Jesup North Pacific Expedition:
Memoir of the American Museum of
National History) (Leiden and New
York, 1905), pp. 52, 54.

the coffin too, and then all would die soon."[1] Among the Lkuñgen Indians, in the south-east part of Vancouver Island, after a death the corpse is at once carried out of the house through an opening which has been made by removing some boards of the back wall of the house. They think that the ghost would kill every one in the house if the corpse were allowed to remain in it.[2]

Concerning some of the Indians of Canada near the St. Lawrence River, we are told by a Jesuit missionary of the seventeenth century that among them a corpse was never carried out of a hut by the door, but always through a hole made in a wall of the hut by removing some of the bark.[3] The Ojebway Indians greatly fear the spirits of the lately deceased. Hence they bury their dead as soon as possible. They do not carry them out of the doorway, but cut a hole in the bark of the lodge and thrust the body out, for they fear that if the dead person remained in the house his spirit would carry off the souls of the survivors, and they would die. Hence they not only pull down the whole house and put out the fire, but are very careful not even to light the new fire in the new house with a spark or sticks from the old one. A new fire and new wood must be taken. Nor do they build the new lodge

[1] Franz Boas, "Notes on the Kwakiutl", in *Eleventh Report on the North-Western Tribes of Canada* (Report of the British Association for 1890), Sixth Report on the Indians of British Columbia, p. 574.
[2] Franz Boas, *Sixth Report of the Committee on the North-Western Tribes of Canada* (Report of the British Association for 1890), p. 23.

[3] *Relation des Jésuites*, 1633, p. 11; *id.*, 1634, p. 23 (Canadian reprint, Quebec, 1858).

on the old spot, but choose another place as far from it as possible.[1]

Among the Catios Indians of Columbia in South America a corpse may not be carried out of the house by the usual house-ladder, lest the spirit of the deceased should find his way back to the house ; but the missionaries who report the custom and the reason for it do not inform us through what part of the hut a corpse is passed out.[2]   The custom of blocking up the entrance to a hut for the purpose of excluding the returning ghost of a recently deceased person has been well described by the missionary, Mr. Grubb, in a particular case among the Lengua Indians of Paraguay.   After speaking of the death of an old man among these Indians he says, " The people had built their shelters on the forest side of my hut, but, although they had promised not to destroy the village nor vacate it, they had taken the precaution to pull down their booths and re-erect them on the farther side of my hut, so that, whatever happened, I, at any rate, should be between them and the ghost, and therefore be the first to suffer. The witch-doctor, the most intelligent man of the party, had, a week or two previously, under strong persuasion from me, erected for himself quite a superior kind of hut, with a small opening for a door.   His wife and family, however, although they did not remove the hut, made very considerable

---

[1] J. G. Kohl, *Kitchi-Gami : Wanderings round Lake Superior* (London, 1860), p. 106 n.

[2] Joseph and Maria Schilling, " Religion und soziale Verhältnisse der Catios-Indianer in Kolumbien ", in *Archiv für Religionswissenschaft* (Leipzig), xxiii. (1925) p. 296.

alterations to it, the chief of which was that they securely blocked up the doorway, making it appear like a part of the wall, and opened a small gap on the opposite side instead. As the old wizard afterwards explained to me, this was done on purpose to puzzle the ghost. He, while in the body, knew the house well, but the alterations were so considerable that it was supposed his ghost would not recognize it, and would be especially nonplussed when it made for the entrance to find a solid wall."[1]

In Europe the custom of carrying the dead out of the house by a special opening which is then closed to prevent their ghosts from re-entering the dwelling has been observed by several peoples at various times, both ancient and modern. Thus among the Cheremiss of Russia, "old custom required that the corpse should not be carried out by the door but through a breach in the north wall, where there is usually a sash window. But the custom has long been obsolete, even among the heathen, and only very old people speak of it. They explain it as follows : to carry it out by the door would be to show the *Asyrèn* (the dead man) the right way into the house, whereas a breach in the wooden wall is immediately closed by replacing the beams in position, and thus the *Asyrèn* would in vain seek for an entrance."[2] With regard to the

[1] W. B. Grubb, *An Unknown People in an Unknown Land*, pp. 165 *sq.*

[2] S. K. Kusnezow, " Über den Glauben vom Jenseits und den Todtencultus der Tscheremissen ", *Internationales Archiv für Ethnographie*, ix. (1896) p. 157.

Russian custom we are told that " the corpse was often carried out of a house through a window, or through a hole made for the purpose, and the custom is still kept up in many parts ".[1]   In Denmark corpses used to be carried out of the house, not through the door, but through an opening made in the wall for the purpose, especially in the wall of the principal room.   After the corpse had been carried through, the opening was immediately bricked up before the mourners returned from the grave.   Such customs used to be common among the Danish peasantry : each peasant house commonly had its corpse-door of this sort, which could be distinguished from the outside at the gable end of the house.   The practice is now nearly, if not totally, extinct.[2]   " In Sweden it is said that all the gates along the road through which a corpse has been carried to the churchyard are hung upside down, so that they open the opposite way.   And if a ghost has begun to haunt a house, it is generally sufficient to alter the position of the door, then he has to remain outside.   It is impossible for him to find his way in again."[3]   It was an old Norse rule that a corpse might not be carried out of the house by the door which was used by the living ; hence a hole was made in the wall at the back of the dead man's head and he was taken out through it backwards, or a hole was dug in the ground under the south wall and the body was drawn out through

---

[1] W. R. S. Ralston, *The Songs of the Russian People* (London, 1872), p. 318.

[2] Dr. H. F. Feilberg, " The Corpse-Door : a Danish Survival ", in *Folk-Lore*, xviii. (1907) pp. 364-375.

[3] Dr. Feilberg, *op. cit.* p. 369.

it.[1] The practice is repeatedly alluded to in the old Norse sagas.[2] Old German law required that the corpses of criminals and suicides should be taken out of a house through a hole under the threshold.[3] In the Highlands of Scotland the corpses of suicides used to be carried out of the house not through the door but through an opening made between the thatched roof and the top of the wall. They were buried, along with the bodies of unbaptized children, outside the common churchyard.[4] In Mecklenburg " it is a law regulating the return of the dead that they are compelled to return by the same way by which the corpse was removed from the house. In the villages of Picher, Bresegard, and others the people used to have moveable thresholds at the house-doors, which, being fitted into the door-posts, could be shoved up. The corpse was then carried out of the house under the threshold, and therefore could not return over it." [5] In Perche, a province of France, the bodies of still-born children are not taken out by the door, but are passed through a window for burial. The reason for the custom is not explained, but probably the original motive was to prevent the return of their unhappy spirits to the house.[6]

[1] W. Weinhold, *Altnordisches Leben* (Berlin, 1856), p. 476.

[2] Dr. Feilberg, *loc. cit.*

[3] J. Grimm, *Deutsche Rechtsalterthümer*[3] (Gottingen, 1881), pp. 726 sq.

[4] J. G. Campbell, *Superstitions of the Highlands and Islands of Scotland* (Glasgow, 1900), p. 242.

[5] Karl Bartsch, *Sagen, Märchen, und Gebräuche aus Meklenburg* (Vienna, 1879–1880), ii. § 358.

[6] F. Chapiseau, *Le Folk-lore de la Beauce et du Perche* (Paris, 1902), i. 164.

CHAPTER III

I. *Ghosts of the Slain*

HITHERTO I have spoken for the most part of the spirits of the dead in general, as if all these spirits were equally feared by primitive man. That is by no means the case. He distinguishes sharply between ghosts and ghosts, particularly according to the death they died, and some of them he deems much more dangerous than others and takes special precautions against them. In general the spirits of all who have died a violent death are classed among the dangerous ghosts. Their span of life has been cut prematurely short : they feel that they have been wronged, and seek to avenge themselves on the authors of their death if they can discover them. And since, in their wrath, they do not always discriminate nicely between the innocent and the guilty, they may become a danger, not only to individuals, but to a whole community. Among these the spirits of the slain are the most commonly feared,

and with these we shall begin our survey of dangerous ghosts.[1]

The Arunta of Central Australia, like many
other savage tribes, think that a death among them
is often caused by the nefarious arts of a sorcerer in
a neighbouring tribe, and they send out a party of
men to take vengeance by killing the supposed culprit. When they have accomplished their mission
of blood by taking the life of the reputed sorcerer,
the avengers return to their own camp, which may
be a long way distant. On the whole of the return journey they think they are followed by the
spirit of the man whom they have murdered. It
takes the form of a little bird called the *chichurkna*,
and may be heard crying like a child in the distance
as it flies. If any of the slayers should fail to hear
its cry, he would become paralysed in his right arm
and shoulder. At night-time especially, when the
bird is flying over the camp, the slayers have to lie
awake and keep the right arm and shoulder carefully hidden, lest the bird should look down upon
and harm them. When once they have heard its
cry their minds are at ease, because the spirit of the
dead then recognizes that he has been detected, and
can therefore do no mischief. On their return to
their friends, as soon as they come in sight of the
main camp, they begin to perform an excited war-
dance, approaching in the form of a square and

[1] With what follows compare *The
Golden Bough : Taboo and the Perils
of the Soul*, pp. 177 *sqq.* ; *Psyche's
Task* (*The Devil's Advocate*), pp.
113 *sqq.* Much of the evidence cited
in these passages is here repeated,
with the addition of some fresh
examples.

moving their shields as if to ward off something which was being thrown at them. This action is intended to repel the angry spirit of the dead man, who is striving to attack them. Next, the men who did the deed of blood separate themselves from the others, and forming a line, with spears at rest and shields held out in front, stand silent and motionless like statues. A number of old women now approach with a sort of exulting skip and strike the shields of the man-slayers with fighting-clubs till they ring again. They are followed by men who smite the shields with boomerangs. This striking of the shields is supposed to be a very effective way of frightening away the spirit of the dead man. The natives listen anxiously to the sounds emitted by the shields when they are struck; for if any man's shield gives forth a hollow sound under the blow, that man will not live long, but if it rings sharp and clear, he is safe. For some days after their return the slayers will not speak of what they have done, and continue to paint themselves all over with powdered charcoal, and to decorate their foreheads and noses with green twigs. Finally, they paint their bodies and faces with bright colours, and become free to talk about the affair; but still of nights they must lie awake listening for the plaintive cry of the bird in which they fancy they hear the voice of their victim.[1]

The Fijians used to bury the sick and aged alive,

[1] Spencer and Gillen, *Native Tribes of Central Australia*, pp. 493-495; *id.*, *Northern Tribes of Central Australia*, pp. 563-568.

and having done so they always made a great up-roar with bamboos, shell-trumpets and so forth in order to scare away the spirits of the buried people and prevent them from returning to their homes ; and by way of removing any temptation to hover about their former abodes they dismantled the houses of the dead and hung them with everything that in their eyes seemed most repulsive.[1] When the cannibal Melanesians of the Bismarck Archi-pelago have eaten a human body, they shout, blow horns, shake spears and beat the bushes for the purpose of driving away the ghost of the man or woman whose flesh has just furnished the banquet. Before doing so they considerately offer to their victim's ghost a portion of his or her own flesh.[2] When a Maori warrior had slain his foe in combat, he tasted his blood, believing that this preserved him from the avenging spirit (*atua*) of his victim ; for they imagined that " the moment a slayer had tasted the blood of the slain, the dead man became a part of his being and placed him under the pro-tection of the *atua* or guardian spirit of the de-ceased ".[3] In the Pelew Islands the relations of a man whose head has been taken by enemies are secluded and purified for fear of the ghost, which is angry with them ; after the purification the ghost

[1] John Jackson, in J. E. Erskine's *Journal of a Cruise among the Islands of the Western Pacific* (London, 1853), p. 477.

[2] George Brown, D.D., *Mela-nesians and Polynesians* (London,

1910), pp. 142, 145.

[3] J. Dumont D'Urville, *Voyage autour du monde et à la recherche de la Pérouse* (Paris, 1832–1833), iii. 305.

goes away to the land of the enemy and pursues his murderer.[1]

Among the Kiwai of British New Guinea, " the warrior who has killed is, as only might be expected, in continual danger from the ghosts of those he has slain. Consequently he must for a month refrain from intercourse with women and eat no crabs, crocodile, sago, or pig. If he did, the ghost would enter into his blood and he would certainly die. As a further precaution against the power of ghosts, food and a bowl of *gamada* are set aside and flung away with a warning to the dead to return to their own place." [2] Among the tribes at the mouth of the Wanigela River, in New Guinea, " a man who has taken life is considered to be impure until he has undergone certain ceremonies : as soon as possible after the deed he cleanses himself and his weapon. This satisfactorily accomplished, he repairs to his village and seats himself on logs of sacrificial staging. No one approaches him or takes any notice whatever of him. A house is prepared for him which is put in charge of two or three small boys as servants. He may eat only toasted bananas, and only the centre portion of them —the ends being thrown away. On the third day of his seclusion a small feast is prepared by his friends, who also fashion some new perineal beads for him. This is called *ivi poro*. The next day the man dons all his best ornaments and badges for

[1] J. Kubary, *Die socialen Ein-*
richtungen der Pelauer (Berlin,
1885), pp. 126 *sq.*

[2] W. N. Beaver, *Unexplored New
Guinea* (London, 1920), p. 174.

taking life, and sallies forth fully armed and parades
the village.　The next day a hunt is organized, and
a kangaroo selected from the game captured.　It is
cut open and the spleen and liver rubbed over the
back of the man.　He then walks solemnly down to
the nearest water, and standing straddle-legs in it
washes himself.　All the young untried warriors
swim between his legs.　This is supposed to impart
courage and strength to them.　The following day,
at early dawn, he dashes out of his house, fully
armed, and calls aloud the name of his victim.
Having satisfied himself that he has thoroughly
scared the ghost of the dead man, he returns to his
house.　The beating of flooring-boards and the
lighting of fires is also a certain method of scaring
the ghost.　A day later his purification is finished.
He can then enter his wife's house." [1]

In the Namau district of British New Guinea, on
returning to their village after a raid, warriors who
had slain their enemies took great precautions to
drive away the vengeful ghosts of their enemies,
which had followed them to the village.　These precautions were often witnessed by a missionary who
has graphically described them as follows : " In
Namau the spirits of enemy warriors were regarded
very seriously, and dealt with very systematically
on the night immediately after a fight.　They were
supposed to follow their dead bodies back to the
village of the victors, and there conceal themselves

[1] R. E. Guise, "On the Tribes
inhabiting the Mouth of the Wani-
gela River, New Guinea", in the　　*Journal of the Royal Anthropological Institute*, xxviii. (1899) pp.
213 *sq.*

in every possible nook and cranny to await a favour-
able opportunity to torture the men who had over-
thrown them in the fight.   As soon as night had set
in the old men provided themselves with coconut-
palm flares and torches, paraded the village from
end to end, pushed their flares into every possible
hiding-place of a spirit until they were satisfied that
they had rid their village of their presence.   I have
a dim recollection that this practice was observed
by the Ibi tribes in the long ago, but I have no data
by me to confirm it.   Whereas I saw the driving-
out of the spirits in the Namau villages, as described
above, so frequently that, alas, I cannot forget it." [1]
One such ceremony witnessed by him in a village
of the Purari delta is described by the same observer
as follows : " Darkness I have said ; but there was
no darkness in the village that night other than the
darkness of heathenism, and it was terrible indeed.
Fires were kindled on every open space ; torches of
coconut palms were lit and carried into every dark
recess of the village ; drums were beaten ; conch
shells were blown ; everybody yelled who had a
yell left ; all this was done to drive away the spirits
of the victims from the village." [2]

Among the Orokaiva, in the east of British New
Guinea, a native who has slain an enemy has to
perform a number of curious rites.   Among other
things he has to climb into a tree and submit to be
severely bitten by a vicious species of green ant

[1] J. H. Holmes, *In Primitive New Guinea* (London, 1924), p. 184.
[2] J. H. Holmes, *op. cit.* p. 174.

which haunts its branches. Also a coconut was broken over his head, and he was soused with its milk. Mr. Williams, who reports these and the other observances and restrictions imposed upon a man-slayer among the Orokaiva, was informed directly that they are meant to drive away the *asisi*, or spirit, of the slain man.[1]

Among the Kai of Northern New Guinea, when a party of warriors has stormed a village, and killed many of the inmates, they beat a hasty retreat, in order to reach their own, or a friendly village, before nightfall. Their reason for haste is the fear of being overtaken in the darkness by the ghosts of their slaughtered foes, who, powerless by day, are very dangerous and terrible by night. Restlessly through the hours of darkness these unquiet spirits follow like sleuth-hounds in the tracks of their retreating enemies, eager to come up with them and by contact with the bloodstained weapons of their slayers to recover the spiritual substance which they have lost. Not till they have done so can they find rest and peace. That is why the victors are careful not at first to bring back their weapons into the village, but to hide them somewhere in the bushes at a safe distance. There they leave them for some days until the baffled ghosts may be supposed to have given up the chase and returned, sad and angry, to their mangled bodies in the charred ruins of their old home. The first night after the return of the warriors is always the most anxious time; all the

[1] F. E. Williams, *Orokaiva Society* (London, 1930), p. 175.

villagers are then on the alert for fear of the ghosts ;
but if the night passes quietly, their terror gradually subsides and gives place to the dread of their
surviving enemies. As the victors in a raid are
supposed to have more or less of the soul-stuff
or spiritual essence of their slain foes adhering to
their persons, none of their friends will venture to
touch them for some time after their return to the
village. Everybody avoids them and goes carefully
out of their way, and any ache or ailment which he
or she may experience during this time is set down
to indirect contact with one of the slayers.[1] Similarly the Yabim of Northern New Guinea dread the
spirit of a murdered man because he is believed to
haunt his murderer and to do him a mischief. Hence
they drive away such a dangerous ghost with shouts
and the beating of drums ; and by way of facilitat-
ing his departure they launch a model of a canoe,
laden with taro and tobacco, in order to transport
him with all comfort to the land of souls.[2] When
the Bukaua of Northern New Guinea have won a
victory over their foes, and have returned home,
they kindle a fire in the middle of the village and
hurl blazing brands in the direction of the battlefield, while at the same time they make an ear-
splitting din, to keep at bay the angry spirits of the
slain.[3] Similarly in the Doreh district of Dutch New

[1] Ch. Keysser, " Aus dem Leben
der Kaileute ", in R. Neuhauss,
Deutsch Neu Guinea, iii. (Berlin,
1911) pp. 64 *sq.*, 147 *sq.*, 132.
[2] K. Vetter, in *Nachrichten über*

*Kaiser Wilhelms-Land und den
Bismarck-Archipel*, 1897, p. 94.
[3] S. Lehner, " Bakaua ", in R.
Neuhauss, *Deutsch Neu Guinea*, iii.
p. 444.

Guinea, if a murder has taken place in the village, the inhabitants assemble for several evenings in succession and utter frightful yells to drive away the ghost of the victim in case he should be minded to hang about the village.[1]   In Windessi, Dutch New Guinea, when a party of head-hunters has been successful, and they are nearing home, they announce their approach and success by blowing on triton shells.   Their canoes are also decked with branches. The faces of the men who have taken a head are blackened with charcoal.   If several have taken part in killing the same victim, his head is divided among them.   They always time their arrival so as to reach home in the early morning.   They come rowing to the village with a great noise, and the women stand ready to dance in the verandahs of the houses.   The canoes row past the *room sram* or house where the young men live, and as they pass the murderers throw as many pointed sticks or bamboos at the wall or roof as there were enemies killed.   The day is spent very quietly.   Now and then they drum or blow on the conch ; at other times they beat the walls of the houses with loud shouts to drive away the ghosts of the slain.[2]

In Timor, an island of the Indian Archipelago, when a warlike expedition has returned in triumph bringing the heads of the vanquished foe, the leader of the expedition is forbidden by religion and custom

<hr>

[1] H. von Rosenberg, *Der malay-ische Archipel* (Leipsic, 1878), p. 461.

[2] J. L. D. van der Roest, " Uit het leven der Bevolkung van Windessi ", in *Tijdschrift voor Indische Taal- Land- en Volkenkunde*, xl. (1890) pp. 157 *sq.*

to return at once to his own house. A special hut is prepared for him, in which he has to reside for two months, undergoing bodily and spiritual purification. During this time he may not go to his wife nor feed himself; the food must be put in his mouth by another person.[1] That these observances are dictated by fear of the ghosts of the slain seems certain; for from another account of the ceremonies performed on the return of a successful head-hunter in the same island we learn that sacrifices are offered on this occasion to appease the soul of the man whose head has been taken. The people think that some misfortune would befall the victor were such offering omitted. Moreover, a part of the ceremony consists of a dance accompanied by a song in which the death of the slain man is lamented and his forgiveness is entreated. " Be not angry ", they say, " because your head is here with us; had we been less lucky, our heads might now have been exposed in your village. We have offered the sacrifice to appease you. Your spirit may now rest and leave us at peace. Why were you our enemy? Would it not have been better that we should remain friends? Then your blood would not have been spilt and your head would not have been cut off." [2]

The Bare'e-speaking Toradyas of Central Celebes

---

[1] S. Muller, *Reizen en Onderzoekingen in den Indischen Archipel* (Amsterdam, 1857), ii. 252.

[2] J. S. G. Graamberg, " Eene maand in de binnenlanden van Timor ", in *Verhandelingen van het Bataavisch genootschap van Kunsten en Wetenschappen*, xxxvi. (1872) pp. 208, 216 *sq.*

are greatly concerned about the souls of men who have been slain in battle. They appear to think that men who have been killed in war instead of dying by disease have not exhausted their vital energy and that therefore their departed spirits are more powerful than the common ruck of ghosts ; and as on account of the unnatural manner of their death they cannot be admitted into the land of souls they continue to prowl about the earth, furious with the foes who have cut them off untimely in the prime of manhood, and demanding of their friends that they shall wage war on the enemy and send forth an expedition every year to kill some of them. If the survivors pay no heed to this demand of the bloodthirsty ghosts, they themselves are exposed to the vengeance of these angry spirits, who pay out their undutiful friends and relatives by visiting them with sickness and death. Hence with the Toradyas war is a sacred duty in which every member of the community is bound to bear a part ; even women and children, who cannot wage real war, must wage mimic warfare at home by hacking with bamboo swords at an old skull of the enemy, while with their shrill voices they utter the war-whoop.[1]

In the Andaman Islands, if a man has killed another in a fight between two villages or in a private quarrel, he leaves his village and goes to live in the jungle, where he must stay for some weeks, or even months. His wife may attend him in his seclusion.

---

[1] N. Adriani and Alb. C. Kruijt, *De Bare'e-sprekende Toradjas van Midden-Celebes*, i. 285, 290 *sq.*

For several weeks the homicide must observe several taboos. He may not handle a bow or arrow. He may not feed himself or touch food with his hands, but must be fed by his wife or a friend. He must keep his neck and upper lip covered with red paint, and must wear plumes of shredded *Tetrathera* wood in his belt before and behind, and in his necklace at the back of his neck. If he breaks any of these taboos it is believed that the spirit of the man whom he killed will make him ill. After this he undergoes a kind of purification. His hands are first rubbed with white clay, and then with red paint. He is then rid of the taboos; he may handle bows and arrows, and feed himself with his own hands; but he retains the plumes of shredded wood for a year of so.[1]

Among the Kachins of Burma, when a man has committed a murder it is necessary for him to take immediate precautions against the spirit of his victim, which will become a malignant *nat*, and will assuredly follow the murderer and wreak its vengeance on him. Because of this danger he may not enter his or any other village until a certain ceremony has been performed. Near the sacred grove (*num-shang*) of the village the sacred *kumbang* grass is planted in the ground. Next to it, in the direction of the village, a wooden rice-pounder is laid; next to the pounder, one of the smooth stones used for sharpening *dahs* (large knives); and finally a small fire. A sacrifice must be offered to the spirit of the

---

[1] A. R. Brown, *The Andaman Islanders*, pp. 133, 164.

murdered man, and the most effective is that of a dog ; but if a dog is not available and the matter is urgent, a fowl or a pig will answer the purpose. The sacrificial animal is killed over the pounder, and the murderer steps over the *kumbang* grass, the pounder, the sacrificed animal, the stone and the fire. Having done so, he bends back the grass in the direction away from the pounder, and he may then enter the village and his home, both of them now being considered secure from the unpleasant attentions of the murdered man's ghost. Under no circumstances will anybody use or even touch the pounder, stone, or, if a pig or fowl has been sacrificed, the flesh of the sacrificed animal. These remain lying in the sacred grove.[1]

The Lushai of North-Eastern India believe that if a man kills an enemy the ghost of his victim will haunt him and he will go mad, unless he performs a certain ceremony which will make him master of the dead man's soul in the other world. The ceremony includes the sacrifice of an animal, whether a goat, a pig, or a mithran.[2]

Among the Lakhers, a tribe of head-hunters in the same region, as soon as the warriors have returned from a successful raid, all those who have been lucky enough to take an enemy's head must perform a certain ceremony called the *Ia*, the object

[1] W. J. S. Carrapiett, *The Kachin Tribes of Burma* (Rangoon, 1929), pp. 29, 69.

[2] Lieut.-Col. J. Shakespear, " The Kuki-Lushai clans ", in the *Journal of the Royal Anthropological Institute*, xxxix. (1909) p. 380; *id.*, *The Lushei Kuki Clans* (London, 1912), pp. 78 *sq.*

of which is twofold : first to render the spirit of the
slain, which is called *saw*, harmless to his slayer,
and secondly to ensure that the spirit of the slain
shall be the slave of the slayer in the next world.
It is believed that unless the *Ia* ceremony is performed over the heads of men killed in war, their
ghosts (*saw*) will render their slayers blind, lame, or
paralysed, and that if by any lucky chance a man
who has omitted to perform the *Ia* ceremony escapes
these evils, they will surely fall upon his children or
his grandchildren. Again, if the *Ia* ceremony is
not performed the spirit of the slain man will not
accompany his slayer to the spirit land as his slave,
but will go to a special abode of the dead where
dwell the spirits of all those who have died violent
deaths. The *Ia* ceremony varies somewhat from
village to village ; but it always includes a dance
round either the captured head or an artificial head
carved out of a gourd. On the night of the ceremony and all the next day dancing and singing continue. The following day is a holiday (*aoh*). No
work is done in the village, and no one leaves it.
The next day each man who has taken a head kills
a pig, and then goes and bathes and thoroughly
cleanses himself of all bloodstains, so that the spirits
of the dead shall not be able to recognize their
slayers. While the *Ia* ceremony is in progress the
man performing it may not sleep with his wife.
Not till he has cleansed himself may he resume
conjugal relations. The belief is that during the *Ia*
ceremony the spirit of the deceased is hovering

round, and if it saw the man who had slain him sleeping with his wife, it would say, "Ah, you prefer women to me ", and would inform all the spirits, and the man who had done what is forbidden would not be allowed to take any more heads. In the village of Chapi some special precautions are taken to guard the slayer against the vengeful ghost of the man whom he has slain. On the return of the warriors from a raid, a dog is sacrificed by each warrior who has taken a head, and its skull is hung up above the head of the man slain. This is a preliminary precaution to guard the slayer against the angry ghost of the man whom he has slain. They think that the dog's ghost will bark at the dead man's ghost, and so hinder him from harming his slayer. After that the warriors enter the village and perform the rest of the *Ia* ceremony, by sacrificing a pig and dancing round an artificial head. Then in the evening each man who has taken a head goes into his house with the cook, the rice-beer maker, the drummers and the person who played the gongs at the *Ia* feast, and they must all remain inside the house for five days. On the morning of the sixth day the man who has taken a head rises at cockcrow and goes and bathes in the nearest stream. He then returns to his house and in front of it plants two chestnut poles. The persons who have kept him company inside the house during these five days hold on to the chestnut poles, and the head-taker says, " The spirit of the man I have killed has now departed ". Then they sacrifice a

pig and eat it, so finishing the ceremony. The
reason why the cook, the rice-beer maker, the
drummer and the gong-player are shut up for five
days with the head-taker is that it is believed that
if they go home before the whole ceremony is
finished they will take the deceased's ghost with
them and will become ill. During these days it is
taboo for the head-taker to sleep with his wife. If
he did so he would take no more heads, for the
reason already given.

Among these Lakhers, a man who has taken a
head in war, although by doing so he has acquired
great renown, is none the less regarded as unclean.
On his return to the village a head-taker is taboo
(*pana*) until the *Ia* ceremony has been performed to
lay the dangerous ghost of the man killed ; and it
is not until a formal purification—at which the hands
and feet are washed in the blood of the pig sacrificed
and the whole body is washed in water—has been
accomplished, that a head-taker resumes his ordinary family and social relations. The temporary
separation of a head-taker from the rest of the community is especially marked among the Sabeu, the
tribe inhabiting the Chapi group of villages.
Among this tribe the ghost (*saw*) of the deceased is
regarded as so powerful that it is believed that it
will do harm to all who helped the head-taker to
perform the *Ia* ceremony and to their family unless
they remain with him apart until the ghost (*saw*) has
finally been laid and the head-taker cleansed. All
Lakhers share this view, but their ceremonies are

less elaborate than those of the Sabeu. It is not only men who have taken heads in war who are bound to cleanse and purify themselves, murderers are also under the same obligation. Although head-taking on a raid is deemed meritorious, while murder is regarded as a social sin, it makes no difference to the fact that after taking human life a man must purify himself; but even after purification a murderer labours under certain social disadvantages, while a head-taker does not.[1]

Among the Oraons of Chota Nagpur in India the angry spirit of a murdered man is propitiated by sacrifice, and is sometimes reckoned among the ancestral spirits of his murderer. For example, " in village Siligain two Oraons, related to each other as cousins, had a quarrel over a piece of land ; and one of them, in a sudden fit of anger, thrust his axe into the bowels of the other man. The man, thus struck, at once ran to his assailant's house and, pressing his wounded stomach with his hands, sat down at one corner of the hut and exclaimed, ' Here I establish myself,' and then ran out again to the field in dispute and dropped down dead. To this day, the descendants of the murderer propitiate the murdered man's spirit. After the harvest, the first sheaf of paddy from the field on to which he dropped down dead is offered to the spirit of the murdered man at the same corner of the house where he sat down before his death. The descendants of the murdered man too are allowed access to the same

[1] N. E. Parry, *The Lakhers* (London, 1932), pp. 213-218.

spot for making similar offerings."[1] In Travancore the ghosts of murderers who have been hanged are thought to be especially dangerous and are believed to haunt the place of execution and its neighbourhood. To prevent this it used to be customary to cut off the criminal's heels with a sword or to hamstring him as he was turned off.[2]

In Africa also the belief is very widespread that the ghosts of the slain are dangerous to their slayers, or to the community in general, and special precautions are taken to guard against them. For this purpose among the Kabyles of North Africa a murderer tries to leap seven times over the grave of his victim within three or seven days, believing that if he can do so he will be safe from the pursuit of the ghost. Hence the fresh grave of a murdered man is carefully guarded.[3] Among the Ibibio of Southern Nigeria, when a murderer thinks that he is haunted to his hurt by his victim's angry ghost, he offers a dog in sacrifice to the offended spirit. Should the sacrifice prove unavailing he catches a male lizard, and, with this carefully caged, goes to a place where cross-roads meet. There, by the wayside, he makes a tiny gallows, and taking out the lizard from its prison, passes it three times round his head, crying, " Here I give you a man instead of me. Take him and leave me free." After this he places a noose round the neck of the lizard and hangs it upon the miniature gallows, hoping that the ghost will accept

[1] S. C. Roy, *Oraon Religion and Custom* (Ranchi, 1928), pp. 69 *sq.*

[2] Rev. S. Mateer, *The Land of* *Charity* (London, 1871), pp. 203 *sq.*

[3] J. Liorel, *Kabyle du Jurjura* (Paris, N.D.), p. 441.

the lizard instead of himself or another human victim.[1]

The Yendang, a tribe of Northern Nigeria, were formerly head-hunters like all their neighbours. Among them men who had taken heads were obliged to have their bodies washed in beer by an old man in order to safeguard themselves from pursuit by the ghosts of their victims.[2] Again, among the Katab, another tribe of Northern Nigeria, who were also of old head-hunters, when a warrior had taken a head he used to make off with it at full speed, and when he was free from pursuit one of his friends made him drink immediately a concoction of the bark of the locust and male shea-trees, at the same time striking him on the chest and back with locust-bean leaves. These rites were designed to protect the warrior from assault from the dead man's ghost.[3] The Chiwai, another tribe of Northern Nigeria, used also to be head-hunters, like all their neighbours. Among them all heads taken had to be brought immediately to the priestly chief of the village. The heads were boiled, and pieces of the flesh eaten by the priest, after which the skulls were deposited in the sacred hut of the village. During the performance of these rites each man who had taken a head remained in concealment, and he was anointed with a filthy mixture, which included the intestines of a porcupine, in order to ward off pursuit by the dead

[1] P. A. Talbot, *Life in Southern Nigeria*, p. 245; *id.*, *The Peoples of Southern Nigeria* (London, 1926), iii. 866.

[2] C. K. Meek, *Tribal Studies in Northern Nigeria* (London, 1931), i. 487.

[3] C. K. Meek, *op. cit.* ii. 69.

man's ghost.[1]   Among the Yungur, another tribe
of head-hunters in Northern Nigeria, it was customary for a warrior on taking a head to lick off the
blood from his weapon in order to prevent his victim's
ghost from pursuing him.[2]   Among the Igara, yet
another tribe of head-hunters in Northern Nigeria,
a warrior who had taken a head used to propitiate
the spirit of his dead foe annually by pouring the
blood of a sacrificed pullet over his enemy's skull
before he might eat of the new yams.[3]   And in this
tribe when a man had taken a head it was deemed
necessary for him to perform a purificatory rite for
the purpose of warding off the angry ghost of his
victim.   With this object the slayer partook of a
magical medicine, which was made up by grinding
into powder a portion of the lips, nose, eyes, eyebrows, genital organs, liver and heart of his enemy,
together with various herbs.   The eating of this
concoction was considered to destroy the power of
the ghost of his dead foe to harm the eater.[4]

The Dinka, a pastoral people of the Upper Nile,
believe that a homicide is likely to be haunted by his
victim's ghost, and in consequence to grow thinner
and weaker until he dies.[5]   Among the Shilluk,
another tribe of the Upper Nile, warriors used to
engage the services of a medicine man to invoke their
ancestors that the spirits of their slain enemies might

---

[1] C. K. Meek, *op. cit.* ii. 156.
[2] C. K. Meek, *op. cit.* ii. 458.
[3] Capt. J. R. Wilson-Haffenden,
The Red Men of Nigeria (London,
1930), p. 215.

[4] Capt. J. R. Wilson-Haffenden,
op. cit. pp. 216 *sq.*
[5] C. G. and B. L. Seligman, *Pagan
Tribes of the Nilotic Sudan* (London,
1932), p. 177.

do them no harm.   For this purpose a sheep was sacrificed, and part of its entrails buried in a pot as an offering to the spirits of the underworld.[1]   Among the Lango, a Nilotic tribe of Uganda, on the morning after a battle every man who has slain an enemy brings a goat or a sheep for a sacrifice, because the killing of an enemy entails great dangers from his ghost.   The ghost is supposed to have a deadly influence on his slayer, afflicting him with attacks of giddiness and frenzy, during which he may do himself or the bystanders mortal mischief.   It makes his brain reel, and dances in his head until he is not responsible for his actions.   For this reason, and also lest in the heat of the conflict a leprous or cancerous man has been speared, the slayers sacrifice goats and sheep, which may be of any colour, unless the slayer feels the influence of a ghost already beginning to affect him, in which case he must kill a black goat.   The whole community joins in eating the meat of the sacrificial victims.   The undigested matter from the intestines of the slaughtered goats is smeared over the bodies of the warriors to protect them from the ghosts of their dead enemies, and all the bones are burned to ashes, which the warriors throw broadcast to the winds.   The ghost of the slain man has also to be appeased by making cicatrices on the bodies of his slayers.   This has to be done by the slayer himself : he cuts rows of these scars on his shoulder and upper arm, the number of

[1] W. Hofmayr, *Die Shilluk* (Vienna, 1925), p. 230; *id.*, C. G. Seligman, *op. cit.* p. 97.

the scars varying according to his ability to stand the pain up to three and a half rows. Finally each slayer has to shave his head in a particular fashion called *atira*.[1]

Among the Nilotic people of Kavirondo, to the east of Lake Victoria Nyanza, when a warrior has killed another in battle he is isolated from his village, lives in a separate hut for about four days, and is fed by an old woman because he may not touch food with his hands. On the fifth day he is escorted to the river by another man, who washes him. A white goat is killed and cooked by the attendant, who feeds the man with the meat. The goat-skin is cut into strips and put upon the slayer's wrists and round his head, and he returns to his temporary home for the night. The next day he is again taken to the river and washed, and a white fowl is presented him. He kills it and it is cooked for him, and he is again fed with the meat. He is then pronounced to be clean, and may return to his home. It sometimes happens that a warrior spears another man in battle and the latter dies from the wound some time after. When he dies the relatives go to the warrior and inform him of the death, and he is separated at once from the community until the ceremonies above described have been performed. The people say that the ceremonies are necessary in order to release the ghost of the dead man, which is bound to the warrior who slew him and is only

---

[1] J. H. Driberg, *The Lango, a Nilotic Tribe of Uganda* (London, 1923), pp. 110 *sq.*

released on the fulfilment of the ceremonies. Should a warrior refuse to fulfil the ceremonies, the ghost will ask, " Why don't you fulfil the ceremonies and let me go ? " Should the man still refuse to comply, the ghost will take him by the throat and strangle him.[1]

Among these Nilotic people of Kavirondo the ceremonial treatment of a murderer closely resembles the treatment of a warrior who has killed a foe in battle, and the reason is that both treatments are dictated by a fear of the ghost of the slain. When a murder has been committed the murderer seldom seeks safety in flight, and often confesses his guilt without any trial. But he must undergo a cere- mony of purification. He is first separated from the members of his village and lives in a hut with an old woman who attends to his wants, cooks for him and also feeds him, for he may not touch food with his own hands. The seclusion lasts three days, after which a man who is himself a murderer, or has at some time killed a man in battle, leads the murderer to a stream and washes him all over. He then kills a goat and cooks the meat, takes four sticks and places a piece of meat on each stick and gives the man the meat to eat from each stick in turn. When the meat has been eaten, he gives him four pieces of porridge made into balls and put on the sticks. After this the goat-skin is cut into strips, which are put round the neck and round each wrist of the murderer. This ceremony is performed by the two

---

[1] J. Roscoe, *The Northern Bantu* (Cambridge, 1915), p. 289.

men who are alone at the river, and after it the murderer is free to return home. It is said that until this ceremony is performed the ghost cannot take its departure for the place of the dead, but hovers about the murderer.[1]

Among the Basoga, a Bantu people of Uganda, on the northern shore of Lake Victoria Nyanza, when a murder has been committed by a member of another clan, the clan whose member has been killed seeks to capture a member of the offending clan and kill him. Sometimes they succeed in capturing one of its members, most often a youth in the road. They drag him away to the grave of the murdered man and there cut his throat and leave the body lying at the grave as an atonement to the ghost of the murdered.[2] Among the Bagesu, a cannibal tribe of Mount Elgon in Kenya, when a murderer belongs to the same clan as his victim he must leave his village and find a new home, even though the case may be settled amicably. But before quitting the village the murderer has to take a goat, kill it, smear his chest with the contents of the stomach, and take the remainder and throw it upon the roof of the house of the murdered man to appease the ghost of his victim.[3]

Among the Banyankole, a pastoral people of Southern Uganda, "a warrior who had killed a man was treated like a murderer or a hunter who had killed a lion, leopard, antelope, or hyaena (because

[1] J. Roscoe, *op. cit.* p. 281.   [2] J. Roscoe, *op. cit.* p. 243.
[3] J. Roscoe, *op. cit.* p. 98.

these animals belonged to the gods) ; he was not allowed to sleep or eat with others until he had been purified, for the ghost of the man was upon him ".[1] Among the Bakitara, a powerful tribe of Uganda, when a rebellious prince had been killed it was necessary that he should be speared, even after his death, by a man of royal blood, for no ordinary man might shed royal blood, and the prince's ghost might be a dangerous enemy to the man who had done such a deed.[2] Similarly among the Bakunta, a small tribe on the shores of Lake Edward in Uganda, the princes of the royal family often rose in rebellion against the king. If the king was killed in the fight, the man who did the deed was raised to a position of authority and importance at the time, but when later any misfortune or illness attacked members of the royal house, the priests would declare that the ghost of the last monarch desired vengeance on his murderer, and the dead king's successor would be persuaded to arrest and kill the man whose act had put him on the throne. If it was the rebellious prince who had been killed, the same treatment would be meted out to his slayer, for none might shed royal blood with impunity.[3]

Among the Kikuyu, a Bantu tribe of Kenya, when a man has killed a person of his own clan, it is deemed necessary to perform certain ceremonies for the purpose of guarding him against the dangerous

[1] J. Roscoe, *The Banyankole* (Cambridge, 1923), p. 161.
[2] J. Roscoe, *The Bakitara or Banyoro* (Cambridge, 1923), p. 314.
[3] J. Roscoe, *The Bagesu and other Tribes of the Uganda Protectorate* (Cambridge, 1924), p. 159.

ghost of his victim.   Among other things, the elders go to the local sacred fig-tree and kill a sheep there. They deposit some of the fat, the chest bone, the intestines, and the more important bones at the foot of the tree.   The rest of the carcase is eaten by the elders.   They say that the ghost of the murdered man will visit the tree that night in the shape of a wild cat and eat the meat, and that this offering will prevent the ghost of the deceased from coming back to his village and troubling the occupants.[1] Among the Bantu tribes of Kavirondo, when a man has killed an enemy in warfare he shaves his head on his return home, and his friends rub a medicine, which generally consists of goat's dung, over his body to prevent the spirit of the slain man from troubling him.[2]   Exactly the same custom is observed for the same reason by the Wageia of Tanganyika.[3]   With the Ja-Luo of Kavirondo the custom is somewhat different.   Three days after his return from the fight the warrior shaves his head. But before he may enter the village he has to hang a live fowl, head uppermost, round his neck ; then the bird is decapitated and its head is left hanging round his neck.   Soon after his return a feast is made for the slain man, in order that his ghost may not haunt his slayer.[4]   When a Ketosh warrior of

---

[1] C. W. Hobley, " Kikuyu Customs and Beliefs ", in *Journal of the Royal Anthropological Institute*, xl. (1910) pp. 438 *sq.*

[2] Sir H. Johnston, *The Uganda Protectorate*, ii. 723 ; C. W. Hobley, *Eastern Uganda*, p. 20.

[3] M. Weiss, *Die Völkerstämme im Norden Deutsch-Ostafrikas* (Berlin, 1910), p. 198.

[4] Sir H. Johnston, *The Uganda Protectorate*, ii. 794 *sq.* ;   C. W. Hobley, *Eastern Uganda*, p. 31.

Kenya who has killed a foe in battle returns home, " it is considered essential that he should have connection with his wife as soon as convenient ; this is believed to prevent the spirit of his dead enemy from haunting and bewitching him ".[1]

Among the Ba-Yaka, a Bantu people of the Congo Free State, a man who has been killed in battle is supposed to send his soul to avenge his death on the man who killed him ; but the slayer can escape the vengeance of the dead by wearing the red tail-feathers of the parrot in his hair, and painting his forehead red.[2]

Among the Boloki, a people of the Upper Congo, " a homicide is not afraid of the spirit of the man he has killed when the slain man belongs to any of the neighbouring towns, as disembodied spirits travel in a very limited area only ; but when he kills a man belonging to his own town he is filled with fear lest the spirit shall do him some harm. There are no special rites that he can observe to free himself from these fears, but he mourns for the slain man as though he were a member of his own family. He neglects his personal appearance, shaves his head, fasts for a certain period, and laments with much weeping." [3] By this display of sorrow he doubtless hopes to soften the heart of his victim's ghost, and so to induce him to spare his slayer.

[1] C. W. Hobley, " British East Africa ", in *Journal of the Anthropological Institute*, xxxiii. (1903) p. 353.
[2] E. Torday and T. A. Joyce, " Notes on the Ethnography of the Ba-Yaka ", in the *Journal of the Royal Anthropological Institute*, xxxvi. (1906) pp. 50 *sq.*
[3] J. H. Weeks, *Among Congo Cannibals* (London, 1913), p. 268.

Among the Angoni, a Zulu tribe settled to the north of the Zambesi, warriors who have slain foes on an expedition smear their bodies and faces with ashes, and hang garments of their victims on their persons. This costume they wear for three days after their return, and rising at break of day they run through the village uttering frightful yells to banish the ghosts of the slain, which otherwise might bring sickness and misfortune on the people.[1] Among the Ila-speaking peoples of Northern Rhodesia, who were head-hunters, the warrior who had taken a head in battle had afterwards to undergo purification. The doctor or medicine-man put a little medicine on the tongue of the slayer that the ghost of the man he had slain might not trouble him. This he did to each of the warriors who had taken a head in battle. Further, each warrior was bathed in the fumes of certain medicines burnt in a sherd. The ashes were afterwards placed in a koodoo horn and planted at the threshold of his hut to drive off the ghost of the person he had killed.[2]

In these tribes a man who has committed a murder is believed to be possessed by the ghost of his victim, which renders him very uneasy in his mind ; but the ghost can be expelled by the taking of an emetic or by cupping, and so the slayer's peace of mind can be restored ; he has either vomited up the ghost or ejected him in the blood of

[1] C. Wiese, " Beiträge zur Geschichte der Zulu im Norden des Zambesi ", in *Zeitschrift für Ethnologie*, xxxii. (1900) pp. 197 *sq.*

[2] Rev. E. W. Smith and Capt. A. M. Dale, *The Ila-speaking Peoples of Northern Rhodesia* (London, 1920), i. 179.

his body.[1] Among the Awemba, a tribe of Northern Rhodesia, "according to a superstition common among Central African tribes, unless the slayers were purified from blood-guiltiness they would become mad. On the night of return no warrior might sleep in his own hut, but lay in the open *nsaka* in the village. The next day, after bathing in the stream and being anointed with lustral medicine by the doctor, he could return to his own hearth, and resume inter-course with his wife."[2] In all such cases the mad-ness of the slayer is probably attributed by the natives to the ghost of the man he has slain, which has taken possession of him.

Among the Thonga, a Bantu tribe of South Africa, about Delagoa Bay, " to have killed an enemy on the battlefield entails an immense glory for the slayer ; but that glory is fraught with great danger. They have killed. . . . So they are ex-posed to the mysterious and deadly influence of the *nuru* and must consequently undergo a medical treatment. What is the *nuru* ? *Nuru*, the spirit of the slain which tries to take its revenge on the slayer. It haunts him and may drive him to insanity : his eyes swell, protrude, and become inflamed. He will lose his head, be attacked by giddiness, and the thirst for blood may lead him to fall upon members of his own family and to stab them with his assegay. To prevent such misfortunes, a special medication is required, the slayers must *lurulula tiyimpa ta bu*,

[1] Smith and Dale, *op. cit.* ii. pp. 136 *sq.*
[2] J. H. West Sheane, "Wemba Warpaths ", in *Journal of the African Society*, No. 41 (October, 1911), pp. 31 *sq.*

take away the *nuru* of their sanguinary expedition.
. . . In what consists this treatment ? The slayers
must remain some days at the capital. They are
taboo. They put on old clothes, eat with special
spoons, because their hands are ' hot ', and off special
plates (*mireko*) and broken pots. They are forbidden
to drink water. Their food must be cold. The chief
kills oxen for them ; but if the meat were hot it
would make them swell internally ' because they are
hot themselves, they are defiled (*ba na nsila*) '. If
they eat hot food, the defilement would enter into
them. ' They are black (*ntima*). This black must
be removed.' During all this time sexual relations
are absolutely forbidden to them. They must not
go home to their wives. In former times the Ba-
Ronga used to tattoo them with special marks from
one eyebrow to the other. Dreadful medicines were
inoculated in the incisions, and there remained
pimples ' which gave them the appearance of a
buffalo when it frowns '. After some days a medicine-
man comes to purify them, ' to remove their black '.
There seems to be various ways of doing it, according to Mankhelu. Seeds of all kinds are put into a
broken pot and roasted, together with drugs and
psanyi[1] of a goat. The slayers inhale the smoke
which emanates from the pot. They put their hands
into the mixture and rub their limbs with it, especially the joints. . . . Insanity threatening those who
shed blood might begin early. So, already on the

[1] *Psanyi* is half-digested grass
found in the stomachs of sacrificed
goats. See Henri A. Junod, *The*
Life of a South African Tribe,
Second Edition (London, 1927), i.
477 *sqq.*

battlefield, just after their deed, warriors are given a preventive dose of the medicine by those who have killed on previous occasions. . . . The period of seclusion having been concluded by the final purification, all the implements used by the slayers during these days, and their old garments, are tied together and hung by a string to a tree, at some distance from the capital, where they are left to rot." [1]

Among the Basutos of South Africa ablution is especially performed on return from battle. It is absolutely necessary that the warriors should rid themselves, as soon as possible, of the blood they have shed, or the ghosts of their victims would pursue them incessantly, and disturb their slumbers. They go in procession, and in full armour, to the nearest stream. At the moment they enter the water a diviner, placed higher up, throws some purifying substance into the current. The spears and battle-axes also undergo the process of washing. [2]

Among the Thompson Indians of British Columbia, when a man had killed his enemy he used to blacken his own face, believing that if he failed to do so the ghost of his victim would blind him. [3] On the evening of the day on which they had tortured a prisoner to death, the American Indians used to run through the village with hideous yells, beating with sticks on the furniture, the walls, and the roofs of the huts to prevent the angry ghost of

[1] H. A. Junod, *op. cit.* i. 477 *sqq.*
[2] Rev. E. Casalis, *The Basutos* (London, 1861), p. 258.
[3] J. Teit, *The Thompson Indians*, p. 357.

their victim from settling there and taking vengeance for the torments that his body had endured
at their hands.[1] " Once," says a traveller, " on
approaching in the night a village of Ottawas, I
found all the inhabitants in confusion : they were
all busily engaged in raising noises of the loudest
and most inharmonious kind. Upon inquiry, I
found that a battle had been lately fought between
the Ottawas and the Kickapoos, and that the object
of all this noise was to prevent the ghosts of the
departed combatants from entering the village." [2]
Amongst the Omaha Indians of the United States
a murderer whose life had been spared by the kinsmen of his victim had to observe certain stringent
rules for a period which varied from two to four
years. He must walk barefoot, and he might eat
no warm food, nor raise his voice, nor look around.
He had to pull his robe around him and to keep it
tied at the neck, even in warm weather ; he might
not let it hang loose or fly open. He might not
move his hands about, but had to keep them close
to his body. He might not comb his hair, nor
might it be blown about by the wind. No one would
eat with him, and only one of his kindred was allowed
to remain with him in his tent. When the tribe
went hunting, he was obliged to pitch his tent about
a quarter of a mile from the rest of the people,
" lest the ghost of his victim should raise a high

---

[1] P. F. X. de Charlevoix, *Histoire
de la Nouvelle-France* (Paris, 1744),
vi. 77, 122 *sq.* ; J. F. Lafitau, *Mœurs
des sauvages ameriquains*, ii. 279.

[2] W. H. Keating, *Narrative of an
Expedition to the Source of the St.
Peter's River* (London, 1825), i. 109.

wind which might cause damage."[1] The reason
here alleged for banishing the murderer from the
camp of the hunters gives the clue to all the other
restrictions laid on him : he was haunted by the
ghost and therefore dangerous. Speaking specially
of the Creek Indians in the south-east of the United
States, James Adair, who knew them well, tells us
that after a successful expedition the Indians cut the
scalps into several pieces and place them on the
tops of the winter houses of their deceased relations,
whose deaths, if by the hand of the enemy, they
esteem not revenged until then ; and thus their
ghosts are enabled to go to their intermediate place of
rest, till after a certain time they return to live for
ever in that tract of land which pleased them best
when in their former state. They dance for three
days and nights for their victory, and for the happiness of sending the spirits of their killed relations
from the eaves of their houses which they haunted,
mourning with plaintive notes, like owls in winter.[2]
From observing the great respect paid by the
Indians to the scalps they had taken, and listening
to the mournful songs which they howled to the
shades of their victims, the painter Catlin was convinced that " they have a superstitious dread of the
spirits of their slain enemies, and many conciliatory
offices to perform, to ensure their own peace."[3]

[1] Rev. J. Owen Dorsey, " Omaha
Sociology ", in *Third Annual Report
of the Bureau of Ethnology* (Washington, 1884), p. 369.
[2] James Adair, *History of the*

American Indians (London, 1775),
p. 397.
[3] G. Catlin, *North American
Indians*, Fourth Edition (London,
1844), i. 246.

Among the Natchez, an Indian tribe of the lower Mississippi, young braves who had taken their first scalps were obliged to observe certain rules of abstinence for six months. They might not sleep with their wives, nor eat flesh ; their only food was fish and hasty-pudding. If they broke these rules, they believed that the soul of the man they had killed would work their death by magic, that they would gain no more successes over the enemy, and that the least wound inflicted on them would prove mortal.[1]

The Indians of British Guiana in South America believe that an avenger of blood who has slain his man must go mad unless he tastes the blood of his victim ; in order to avert this consequence the Indian man-slayer resorts on the third night to the grave of his victim, pierces the corpse with a sharp-pointed stick, and withdrawing it sucks the blood of the murdered man. After that he goes home with an easy mind, satisfied that he has done his duty and that he has nothing more to fear from the ghost.[2] Among the Lengua Indians of Paraguay a murderer is not only put to death, but his body is burned, and his ashes scattered to the four winds. These Indians believe that after this treatment his spirit cannot take human form, and remains in the after-world shapeless and unrecognizable, and

[1] " Relation des Natchez ", *Voyages aux Nord* (Amsterdam, 1737), ix. 24 ; *Lettres édifiantes et curieuses* (Paris, 1780–1783), vii. 26 ; Charlevoix, *Histoire de la Nouvelle-France.*

[2] Rev. J. H. Bernau, *Missionary Labours in British Guiana* (London, 1847), pp. 57 sq. ; R. Schomburgk, *Reisen in British Guiana* (Leipsic, 1847–1848), ii. 497 ; W. H. Brett, *Indian Tribes of Guiana* (London, 1868), pp. 358 *sq*

therefore unable to mingle with its kindred spirits, or to enjoy such social intercourse as exists.[1]   In that disabled and melancholy state the spirit of the murderer must clearly be incapable of harming the survivors.

Like so many savages, the ancient Greeks believed that the soul of any man who had just been killed was angry with his slayer and troubled him ; hence even an involuntary homicide had to depart from his country for a year until the wrath of the dead man had cooled down ; nor might the slayer return until sacrifice had been offered and ceremonies of purification performed.   If his victim chanced to be a foreigner, the homicide had to shun the country of the dead man as well as his own.[2]   The legend of the matricide Orestes, how he roamed from place to place pursued and maddened by the ghost of his murdered mother, reflects faithfully the ancient Greek conception of the fate which overtakes the murderer at the hands of the ghost.[3]

But it is important to observe that to Greek thinking not only does the hag-ridden homicide go in terror of his victim's ghost ; he is himself an object of fear and aversion to the whole community on account of the angry and dangerous spirit which dogs his steps.   It was probably more in self-defence than out of consideration for the man-

---

[1] W. B. Grubb, *An Unknown People in an Unknown Land*, p. 120.
[2] Plato, *Laws*, ix. 8, pp. 865D-866A ; Demosthenes, xxiii. pp. 683 *sq.* ; Hesychius, *s.v.* ἀπενιαυτισμός.

[3] Aeschylus, *Choephor*, 1021 *sq.* ; *Eumenides*, 85 *sqq.* ; Euripides, *Iphig. in Tauri*, 940 *sqq.* ; Pausanias, ii. 31. 8, viii. 34. 1-4.

slayer that Attic law compelled him to quit the
country. This comes out clearly from the provisions of the law. For in the first place, on going
into banishment the homicide had to follow a prescribed road:[1] obviously it would have been
hazardous to let him stray about the country with a
wrathful ghost at his heels. In the second place,
if another charge was brought against a banished
homicide, he was allowed to return to Attica to
plead in his defence, but he might not set foot on
land ; he had to speak from a ship, and even the
ship might not cast anchor or put out a gangway.
The judges avoided all contact with the culprit,
for they judged the case sitting or standing on the
shore.[2] Plainly the intention of this rule was
literally to insulate the slayer, lest by touching
Attic earth even indirectly through the anchor or
gangway he should blast it by a sort of electric shock,
as we might say ; though doubtless the Greeks
would have said that the blight was wrought by
contact with the ghost, through a sort of effluence
of death. For the same reason if such a man, sailing the sea, happened to be wrecked on the coast of
the country where his crime had been committed,
he was allowed to camp on the shore till a ship
came to take him off, but he was expected to keep
his feet in sea-water all the time,[3] evidently to
neutralize the ghostly infection, and prevent it from

[1] Demosthenes, xxiii. pp. 643 *sq.*
[2] Demosthenes, xxiii. pp. 645 *sq.* ;
Aristotle, *Constitution of Athens*,
57 ; Pausanias, i. 28. 11 ; Pollux,
viii. 120 ; Helladius, quoted by
Photius ; *Bibliotheca*, p. 535A, lines
28 *sqq.*, ed. I. Bekker (Berlin, 1824).
[3] Plato, *Laws*, ix. 8, p. 866C, D.

spreading to the soil. For the same reason, when
the turbulent people of Cynaetha in Arcadia had perpetrated a particularly atrocious massacre and had
sent envoys to Sparta, all the Arcadian states
through which the envoys took their way ordered
them out of the country ; and after their departure
the Mantineans purified themselves and their belongings by sacrificing victims and carrying them
round the city and the whole of their land.[1]   So
when the Athenians had heard of a massacre at
Argos, they caused purificatory offerings to be
carried round the public assembly.[2]   No doubt
the root of all such observances was a fear of the
dangerous ghost which haunts the murderer and
against which the whole community as well as the
homicide himself must be on its guard. The
Greek practice in these respects is clearly mir-
rored in the legend of Orestes ; for it is said
that the people of Troezen would not receive him
in their houses until he had been purified of his
guilt,[3] that is, until he had been rid of his mother's
ghost.

At a sanctuary of the goddesses of madness—the
Maniae—in Arcadia, on the road from Megalopolis
to Messene, a curious legend ran that on his wanderings Orestes came thither and there, maddened by
the murder of his mother, bit off one of his fingers,
whereupon the black Furies of his murdered mother,
who had driven him crazy, appeared to him white,

[1] Polybius, iv. 17-21.   xvii. 9.
[2] Plutarch, *Praecept. ger. reipub.*   [3] Pausanias, ii. 31. 8.

and he was at once healed of his madness.[1] The
legend perhaps contains a reminiscence of a drastic
mode of appeasing the angry ghost of a murdered
person, to which Greek murderers may sometimes
have resorted. In savage society, as we have seen,
man-slayers are often supposed to be driven mad by
the ghosts of their victims, and have resort to many
ceremonies for the purpose of ridding themselves
of these dangerous spirits. With this object Greek
murderers may sometimes have sacrificed a finger.
The sacrifice of a finger, or rather the joint or joints
of a finger, in mourning and on other occasions, has
been a common custom in many parts of the world,
including Australia, Polynesia, India, Africa, and
America.[2]

[1] Pausanias, viii. 34. 2, with my
commentary upon the passage in
Pausanias's Description of Greece,
iv. pp. 355-357.
[2] See my note on Pausanias, *loc.
cit.* For further references to the
custom see J. C. van Eerde:
" Fingermutilatie in Centraal Nieuw-
Guinea ", in *Tijdschrift van het
Koninklijk Nederlandsch Aardrijk-
skundig Genootschap*, 2de Serie, Deel
xxviii. (1911) pp. 49-65 ; P. J. de
Smet, *Western Missions and Missionaries* (New York, 1863), p. 135.
(at the first peal of thunder in
spring) ; G. B. Grinnell, *Blackfoot
Lodge Indians* (London, 1893), pp.
194, 258 ; J. Mathew, *Eaglehawk
and Crow* (London and Melbourne,
1899), p. 120 ; Chevron, in *Annales
de l'Association de la Propagation de
la Foi*, xiv. (1842) p. 192 (sacrifice
for a sick parent in Fiji) ; *op. cit.*
xvii. (1845) pp. 74 *sqq.* (in Australia,
sacrifice to serpents, fish, or kanga-
roos in infancy) ; *op. cit.* xviii. (1846)
p. 6 (Wallis Island, Pacific : a
general custom) ; *op. cit.* xxiii.
(1851) p. 314 (Mandan and Big-
Belly Indians, North America : in
mourning for children or grandchildren) ; *op. cit.* xxxii. (1860) p. 95
(Futuna Island, Pacific : Sacrifice at
illness or death of parent) ; Max
Bartels, " Isländischer Brauch und
Volksglaube in Bezug auf die Nach-
kommenschaft ", in *Zeitschrift für
Ethnologie*, xxxii. (1900) p. 74 (Ice-
and : mother bites off child's finger
to prolong child's life) ; Mgr. Le
Roy, " Les Pygmées ", in *Les
Missions Catholiques*, xxix. (1897)
p. 90 (Ba-Bongo of Upper Ogowe
River, Africa : mutilation of children's fingers after death of first-born
child) ; Buchanan Hamilton, cited
in *The Indian Antiquary*, xxiv.
(Bombay, 1895) p. 303 (Mysore,
India : amputation of mother's
finger joints at betrothal of her

II. *Ghosts of Suicides*

The spirits of persons who have taken their own life are commonly regarded with dread and fear,

daughter); A. W. Howitt, *Native Tribes of South-East Australia* (London, 1904) pp. 746 *sq.* (Australia, tribes of eastern coast: amputation of joints of little finger or whole little finger of all women in childhood); Dudley Kidd, *The Essential Kafir* (London, 1904) pp. 203, 262 *sq.* (Africa, Kafirs: amputation of finger in mourning or childhood or to give strength. Amputated joint placed in roof to counteract evil magic of enemies); A. Karasek, " Beiträge zur Kenntnis des Waschambaa ", in *Baessler-Archiv* (Berlin and Leipzig), i. (1911) p. 171 (Africa, the Wachamba: mother amputates joint of her little finger and drops the blood into the eye of her child to heal malady of eyes. If hut falls on man and he escapes unhurt he amputates a joint of his little finger, buries it, and sacrifices a goat); E. Thurston, *Ethnographic Notes in Southern India* (Madras, 1906), pp. 390-396 (India, Mysore: amputation of first joints of third and fourth fingers of mother's right hand before her daughter's ears are pierced as a preparation for marriage); *id.*, Thurston, *Castes and Tribes of Southern India* (Madras, 1909), v. pp. 75 *sqq.*; *Ethnographic Survey of Mysore* (Preliminary Issue), No. xv. pp. 8 *sq.*, 10 *sq.*; Rev. A. G. Morice, " The Great Déné Race ", in *Anthropos*, i. (1906) p. 724 (N. America, Déné Indians: in mourning for child or husband); *Voyage de la Pérouse autour du monde* (Paris, 1797), iii. 254 (Tonga and other Polynesian islands: in mourning for dead relative or friend);

Labillardière, *Relation du voyage à la recherche de la Pérouse* (Paris, 1800), p. 151 (Tonga: to heal sickness); Rev. G. Brown, " Notes on a Recent Journey to New Guinea and New Britain ", in *Seventh Report of the Australasian Association for the Advancement of Science*, 1898; *id.*, G. Brown, *Melanesians and Polynesians* (London, 1910), pp. 241, 394 (New Guinea, New Britain, and Eastern Polynesia: amputation of finger-joints in mourning, and for benefit of sick friends); John Williams, *Narrative of Missionary Enterprises in the South Sea Islands* (London, 1838), pp. 470 *sq.*; L. Degrandpré, *Voyage à la côte occidentale d'Afrique* (Paris, 1801), ii. pp. 93 *sq.* (Africa: amputation of finger-joints among Bushmen as cure for sickness); Father Betaillon, in *Annales de la Propagation de la Foi*, xiii. (1841) p. 20 (Wallis Island, Pacific: little fingers amputated in mourning and thrown on bier); J. B. Stair, *Old Samoa* (London, 1897), p. 117 (Samoa: amputation of finger or finger-joints in mourning); J. E. Erskine, *Journal of a Cruise among the Islands of the Western Pacific* (London, 1863), p. 123 (Tonga Island: in mourning and depreciation of sickness); R. W. Williamson, *The Mafulu* (London, 1912), p. 247 and note (New Guinea: in woman's mourning for children and other relatives); Baldwin Spencer, *Native Tribes of Northern Australia* (London, 1914), p. 10 (North Australia, Larakia Tribe: amputation of joint of index finger of woman by her mother in

and special precautions are taken by the living to guard against these dangerous ghosts. Among the Ewe tribes of Togo in West Africa, when a man is in great anger or trouble, he will sometimes go into the forest and hang himself on a tree. When this becomes known, if it is night, no one but the relations of the suicide will go to look for the body ; but next morning other people will go in search of it. They do it, however, in great fear, and hang magic strings about them, while others smear their faces with a magical powder, in order that the ghost of the suicide may not molest them. If a man hangs himself at midday, after previously making an unsuccessful attempt at suicide, the neighbours will not go to look for him, or if they go it is a mere pretence, and they leave to his relatives the trouble of finding his body. For they believe that the man who should first set eyes on the suicide would be unlucky and troubled by the dead man's ghost. Hence the people will not approach the body. When one of the searchers catches sight of the body he throws grass upon it, saying, " I pity you, I pity you ". Then the others come up, and

childhood, or at a later time) ; John Turnbull, *A Voyage Round the World in 1800–1804*, Second Edition, (London, 1813), p. 100 (Australia, New South Wales : amputation of first two joints of little finger of right hand of female child in infancy. Severed part thrown into sea, that the woman may thereafter be fortunate in fishing) ; David Collins, *Account of the English Colony in New South Wales*, Second Edition (London, 1804), pp. 358 *sq.* ; J. Irle, *Die Herero* (Gutersloh, 1906), p. 155 (South-West Africa, in tribe Bergdamra : first joint of little finger of left hand of every child amputated at birth as tribal mark) ; G. W. Stow, *Native Races of South Africa* (London, 1905), pp. 129, 152. See further my discussion of the subject in *Folk-Lore in the Old Testament*, iii. 198-241.

cut down the tree on which the man has hanged himself. After that they cut off the branch on which he hanged himself. On this branch they lay the corpse, and drag it ruthlessly over stones and through thorns to the place set apart for the burial of persons who have died a violent death (*Blutmenschen*). There they dig a small hole, shove the body in, and huddle it up in all haste. Should one of them have pity on the dead man he may fire a few shots from his musket. If a man has hanged himself in the neighbourhood of a village, they thrust a stake through his breast, carry him like a pig into the forest, and there give him a hasty burial. But if the man was unpopular, then they drag his body along the ground to the place of burial.

The branches of the tree on which he hung himself are then cut off and laid on his grave, in order that his remains may not be dragged out by wild beasts. After the burial the relations of the suicide must pay a fine of cowries and a goat to the villagers, because their kinsman has defiled the village by the manner of his death. A portion of the cowrie fine is used to defray the expenses of purifying the village from the defilement it has incurred through the death of the suicide. What remains of the fine is distributed among the villagers. Nine days later the people assemble to hold the final ceremony. They have bought palm-wine and collected provisions for the purpose. The brothers of the deceased on his father's side spread a new mat upside down on the

road, and heap provisions of all kinds upon it, of
which some of the people freely partake. Then
they fill a small pot with palm wine, smear it with
white earth, and bind its neck with the bark of the
raffia palm. Next they cut three pieces of firewood,
and put them together as if to form a hearth, and
they place the pot upon the wood, but kindle no fire.
In the evening they take the pot, together with all
the provisions that lie upon the mat, carry them
away, and set them down at the edge of the path
near the suicide's grave. After that they go home
and fire two musket shots, which ends the death
ceremony. Afterwards the priests, for a fee, call
the spirit of the suicide into the house of the earth-
gods (*Trōhaus*). Arrived there, the spirit of the
suicide makes his excuses to the deities for his crime.
He may say, for example, that spirits have driven
him mad, and so goaded him into crime. Or he may
say that his dead brothers, who have also died unhappy deaths, have lured him to his doom, in order
to have his company in the spirit land.

Among these people, when a man has taken his
life, smarting under an insult which has been offered
to him by a kinsman, his body is not buried until
his relatives have paid a fine to the villagers, because
his spirit is believed to render the ground barren,
and to hinder the rain from falling, so that the whole
tribe suffers from the effects of his crime. The
member of his family who insulted the deceased is
also called to account and must pay a fine before
the body of his kinsman may be laid in the earth.

If the motive to suicide has been shame at the failure to keep a solemn promise which the man made in his life, his body is denied honourable burial, and the place where he did the deed must be purified by a sacrifice to the earth god (*trõ*).[1]

The Baganda of Central Africa were very superstitious about suicides. They took innumerable precautions to remove the body and destroy the ghost, lest he should cause trouble to the living. Shame for crime committed sometimes led to suicide, but this occurred rarely in any section of the community, and most rarely among women. When a man committed suicide, he hanged himself on a tree in his garden or in his house. In the former case the body was cut down, and the tree felled also, then both the tree and the corpse, the latter tied to a pole like the carcase of an animal, were taken to a distant place where cross-roads met, and the body was burned, the tree being used for firewood. When the suicide had taken place in the house the dwelling was pulled down, and the materials were taken with the body and burned in the road. People feared to live in a house in which a suicide had taken place, lest they too should be tempted to commit the same crime. Those who had burned the corpse afterwards washed their hands carefully at the place of burning with sponges made from plantains, and threw them on the pyre. When women passed the place where a suicide had been burned, they threw grass or sticks upon the heap, to prevent the ghost from

[1] J. Spieth, *Die Ewe-Stämme* (Berlin, 1906), pp. 272-277.

entering into them and being reborn. The intention
in burning the body was, if possible, to destroy the
ghost. If the suicide had been a man of no social
importance his body was regularly burnt to ashes
on a piece of waste land beside the road, or at
cross-roads, in order to destroy the ghost.[1] If,
however, he had been a person of some position,
and his relatives claimed the body, it was first
charred by fire before it was handed over to them.
Everyone passing the spot where the corpse of a
suicide had been burned took the precaution to
throw some grass, or a few sticks, on the place, so
as to prevent the ghost from catching him, in case it
had not been destroyed.[2]

Among the Wachagga of Mount Kilimanjaro in
East Africa the bodies of suicides are buried like
those of other people, but the place where the crime
was committed must be purified or, to use the expression of our authority, " pacified " by being
sprinkled with water drained from the blossom of a
certain sacred yellow flower. Further, they take the
noose of the rope with which the man had hanged
himself, and bringing a goat, hang it in the noose,
and then offer it in sacrifice. In this way they
attempt to appease the ghost of the suicide, and to
prevent him from tempting other people to imitate
his crime.[3] Among the Wachamba of Usambara

[1] J. Roscoe, The Baganda (London, 1911), pp. 20 sq.

[2] J. Roscoe, op. cit. p. 289.

[3] B. Gutmann, Dichten und
Denken der Dschagganeger (Leip-
zig, 1909), p. 141. Cf. Gutmann,
" Trauer und Begräbnis-sitten der
Wadschagga ", in Globus, lxxxix.
(1906) p. 200.

in Central Africa, the bodies of suicides do not receive a regular burial, but are huddled away in holes
in the rocks or in the forest.   There a tree is felled,
and laid over his body. With the exception of his axe,
knife, spear and sword the property of the deceased,
and especially his clothing, is thrown away in the
wood.   If he had hanged himself on a tree, the tree
is torn up by the roots.   They take a goat and kill it,
and having extracted the entrails they throw them
together with the animal's bones into the hole from
which the tree has been torn up.   If the tree were
not thus torn up, it is believed that the children and
relatives of the suicide would immediately die.   If
the suicide was committed in a hut in the field, the
hut is at once burned.[1]   The Sakalava of Madagascar have so firm a belief in a life after death that
they will sometimes threaten that after their decease
their ghosts will haunt and persecute such as had
offended them in life.   When the persons so threat-
ened hear it they seek to effect a reconcilement,
fearing apparently that the persons who threaten
them might make good their threats by taking their
own lives, and then attacking such as had given
umbrage in life.   A traveller in the south of Madagascar has reported that when the Mahafali desire
to avenge themselves speedily on their enemies they
will sometimes take their own lives in order that
their ghosts may at once take vengeance on their foes.
Among the young men of the Mahafali tribe this

---

[1] A. Karasek, " Beiträge zur   *Baessler-Archiv*, i. (1911) pp. 190
Kenntnis der Waschambaa ", in   *sq.*

belief has been known to create a regular epidemic
of suicides.[1]

Suicide as a method of wreaking a ghostly vengeance after death for a wrong done in life has been
practised as a regular part of their profession by
the Chārans, a sub-division of the Bhāts, a caste of
bards and genealogists in India, who are found all
over the Central Provinces and Birār. By profession they were bards and heralds, and they
travelled from court to court without fear of molestation from robbers or enemies. But the mere
reverence for their calling would not have sufficed to
protect them from the attacks of robbers and others.
They derived a greater security from their readiness
to mutilate, starve or kill themselves, rather than
yield up any property committed to their care ;
and it was a general belief that their ghosts would
then haunt the persons whose ill-deeds had forced
them to take their own lives. It was on this fear
of their ghosts that the Chārans relied, nor did they
hesitate a moment to sacrifice their lives in defence
of any obligation they had undertaken or of property
committed to their safe-keeping. When plunderers
carried off any cattle belonging to the Chārans, the
whole community would proceed to the spot where
the robbers resided ; and if restoration of the property were not made they would cut off the heads
of several of their old men and women. In such
cases many instances occurred of a man dressing

---

[1] H. Russillon, *Un culte dyn-
astique avec évocation des morts*   *chez les Sakalavas de Madagascar*
(Paris, 1912), pp. 47 *sq.*

himself in cotton-quilted cloths, steeped in oil, which he set on fire at the bottom, and thus danced against the criminal until he himself dropped down dead and was burned to ashes. To do this was to perform the ceremony of *trāga* against the male-factor.

The following account of a suicide and actual haunting of his ghost is reported by Mr. R. V. Russell from the *Rāsmālā*. A Chāran asserted a claim against the chief of Siela in Kathiawar, which the latter refused to pay. The bard then went to Siela, taking forty of his caste with him, with the intention of sitting *Dharna*, as the ceremony is called, at the chief's door, and preventing any one from coming out or going in until the claim was settled. However, the chief, having got wind of it, ordered the gates of the town to be closed against them. The Chāran to whom the debt was due thus remained outside the walls, and for three days he abstained from food. Finally, after sacrificing the life of several of his company he dressed himself in clothes wadded with cotton steeped in oil, and having set fire to them burned himself to death. But as he died he cried out : " I am now dying ; but I will become a headless ghost in the palace, and will take the chief's life and cut off his prosperity". After this sacrifice the rest of the bards returned home.

On the third day after the creditor's suicide his ghost (*Bhūt*) threw the chief's wife downstairs, so that she was much injured. Many people too beheld the headless phantom in the palace. At last the ghost entered the chief's own head and set him trembling. At night he would throw stones at the palace, and he killed a female servant outright. At length, in consequence of the many acts of violence committed by the ghost of the suicide, none dared to approach the chief's palace even by broad daylight. In order to exorcize the ghost Fakirs and Brahmans were summoned from many different places ; but whoever attempted the cure was immediately assailed by the ghost in the chief's body, and that so furiously that the courage of the exorcizer failed him. Moreover the ghost would cause the chief to tear the flesh off his own arms with his teeth. Besides this, several persons died of injuries received at the hands of the ghost ; but nobody had the power to expel him. At last a foreign astronomer came, who had a great reputation for charms and magic, and the chief sent for him and paid him honour. The sage tied all round the house threads which he had charged with a charm ; then he sprinkled charmed milk and water all round ; then he drove a charmed iron nail into the ground at each corner of the mansion, and two at the door. He purified the house and continued his charms and incantations for forty-one days, each day making sacrifices at the cemetery to the ghost of the suicide. He himself lived in a room in the chief's house which was securely fastened up ; but people say that while he was muttering his charms stones would fall and strike the windows. Finally the astrologer brought the chief, who had been living in a separate room, and tried to exorcize the ghost that was possessing him. The patient began by being very violent, but a sound thrashing which the astrologer and his assistants administered unsparingly at last reduced the sufferer to a better frame of mind. A sacrificial fire-pit was made and a lemon placed between it and the chief. The astrologer commanded the ghost to enter the lemon. But the ghost, speaking from the chief's body, said, "Who are you? If one of your gods were to come, I would not quit this man for him." Thus they went on from morning till noon. At last they came outside, and, by burning various kinds of incense and sprinkling many charms, they induced the ghost to enter into the lemon. When, thus inspired, the lemon began to bounce about, the whole of the spectators praised the astronomer, crying out, "The ghost has gone into the lemon! The ghost has gone into the lemon!" The chief himself who had been possessed was now perfectly satisfied that the ghost had gone out of him and into the lemon. The astronomer then drove the lemon out of the city, followed by drummers and trumpeters, and if the lemon diverged from the right path, the astrologer with a tap of his wand would guide it back into the way it should go. On the track they sprinkled mustard and salt and finally buried the lemon in a pit seven cubits deep, throwing into the hole above it mustard and salt, and above these dust and stones, and filling in the space between the stones with lead. At each corner too, the astrologer drove in an iron nail, two feet long, which he had previously charmed.   The lemon thus buried and nailed down, the people returned home, and we are told, and without being unduly credulous we may readily believe, that nobody ever saw that ghost again.[1]

Akin to the process of *trāga* is the process of *Dharna*, which was commonly practised by a creditor to extort payment from a recalcitrant debtor.   The ordinary method of *Dharna* was for the creditor to sit starving himself at the door of the person from whom redress was sought until the debtor consented to pay his debt, from fear of being haunted by his creditor's ghost if he starved himself to death.   Or instead of threatening to starve himself to death the creditor might stand at his debtor's door with an enormous weight on his head, and to declare that if payment were refused he would stand there till he died.   This seldom failed to produce the desired effect, but if he actually died under the weight, the debtor's house was razed to the ground and he and his family were sold for the benefit of the creditor's heirs.[2]

In China a similar dread of the ghosts of suicides has prevailed, and has led to similar practices. We are told that among the Chinese " the firm belief in ghosts and their retributive justice has still other effects. It deters from grievous and provoking injustice, because the wronged party, thoroughly sure of the avenging power of his own spirit when

[1] R. V. Russell, *The Tribes and Castes of the Central Provinces of India* (London, 1916), ii. pp. 259-262.

[2] R. V. Russell, *op. cit.* ii. pp. 265 *sq.*

disembodied, will not always shrink from converting himself into a wrathful ghost by committing suicide. It is still fresh in our memory how such a course was followed in 1886 by a shopkeeper in Amoy, pressed hard by a usurer, who had brought him to the verge of ruin. To extort payment, this man ran off with the shutters of his shop, thus giving its contents a prey to burglars ; but in that same night the wretch hanged himself against his persecutor's door-post, the sight of his corpse setting the whole ward in commotion at daybreak, and bringing all the family he had storming to the spot. The usurer, frightened out of his wits, had no alternative but to pay them a considerable indemnification, with an additional sum for the burial expenses, on which they pledged their promise to abstain from bringing him up before the magistrate. Pending those noisy negotiations, the corpse remained untouched where it hung. Thus the usurer had a hairbreadth escape from jail, flagellation and other judicial woes, but whether he slipped also through the hands of his etherized victim, we were never told. It impressed us on that occasion to hear from the Chinese that occurrences of this kind were very far from rare, and they told us a good many, then fresh in everybody's memory."[1]

Again we read that " the prevalence of suicide is a feature of Mukden as of most Chinese cities. Certain peculiarities of Chinese justice render it a

[1] J. J. M. De Groot, *The Religious System of China* (Leiden, 1901), vol. v. Book II. pp. 450 *sq*.

favourite way of wreaking spite upon an employer or neighbour, who is haunted besides by the spirit of the self-murderer. Hence servants angry with their masters, shopmen with their employers, wives with their husbands, and above all daughters-in-law with their mothers-in-law, show their spite by dying on their premises, usually by opium, or eating the tops of lucifer matches ! It is quite a common thing for a person who has a grudge against another to go and poison himself in his courtyard, securing revenge first by the mandarin's inquiry and next by the haunting terrors of his malevolent spirit. Young girls were daily poisoning themselves with lucifer matches to escape from the tyranny of mothers-in-law and leave unpleasantness behind them." [1] With regard to the Chinese fear of the ghosts of suicides we are informed that they are taught in their almanacs that if on any given day and hour of any month they feel headache or pain in their bones " it is because they have unwittingly come in contact, at some corner of their house within or without, with the ghosts of men or women who have committed suicide by drowning or hanging or poison. In consequence of this impolite approach to the spirits, the god of the furnace is ill at ease, or the ancestors of the man are disturbed. The remedy is to make an apology to the ghost so rudely offended, and to present a propitiatory offering consisting of two or five hundred paper cash, a paper horse on which the ghost is requested to ride away, and a

---

[1] Mrs. Bishop, *Korea and Her Neighbours* (London, 1898), i. 241.

bowl of water and rice as an inducement to commence the journey requested."[1]

The Wotyaks, a people of Asiatic affinities settled
in Russia, stand in great fear of the spirits of the
dead, and in particular of the ghosts of suicides.
Hence when a man has a grudge at somebody he
will sometimes hang himself in his enemies' courtyard, or stab himself to death, in order that after
his death his ghost may haunt and persecute his foe.
The writer who reports this custom suggests that the
peaceable disposition of the Wotyaks is partly to be
explained by this fear of the spirits of the dead, fear
being apparently among them a more potent motive
than love in their attitude towards the departed.[2]

With regard to the Bannavs, a people of Indo-
China inhabiting the mountains between Tonkin
and Siam, we are told that suicide has a stigma in
their penal code. The suicide is buried in a corner
of the forest far from the graves of his brethren, and
all who have assisted at the burial are required to
purify themselves afterwards in a special manner.[3]
Though we are not informed of it by our authority
we may assume that this purification is intended to
free the mourners from the dangerous influence of
the suicide's ghost.

In ancient Greece it was customary at Athens
to cut off the right hand of a suicide and bury it

[1] J. Preston, " Charms and Spells
in use amongst the Chinese ", in
China Review, vol. ii. (1873-1874)
p. 169.
[2] Max Buch, *Die Wotjaken* (Hel-
singfors, 1882), 147 *sq.*
[3] Le Compte in M. H. Mouhot,
*Travels in the Central Parts of
Indo-China* (London, 1864), ii. pp.
27 *sq.*

apart from his body, no doubt in order to disarm
his ghost, by depriving him of the use of his right
hand.[1] Similar precautions have been taken in
modern Europe to prevent the ghosts of suicides
from doing a mischief to the living. In England a
person against whom a coroner's jury had found a
verdict of suicide used to be buried at cross-roads
with a stake driven through the body, no doubt to
prevent the ghost from walking, and attacking the
survivors.[2] In Pomerania and West Prussia the
ghosts of suicides are much feared. Such persons
are buried, not in the churchyard, but at the place
where they took their lives, and every passer-by
must cast a stone or a stick on the spot, or the ghost
of the suicide will haunt him by night and give him
no rest. Hence the piles of sticks or stones accumu-
lated on the graves of these poor wretches sometimes attain a considerable size.[3] With regard to
the customs and beliefs concerning suicides in Denmark, Dr. Feilberg, an excellent authority on the
folk - lore of his native land, writes as follows:
"Whilst on the subject I will mention a custom of
earlier times when burying suicides ; the dead
person was not carried through the churchyard gate,
but lifted over the outer mound, dragged down on
the opposite side, and placed to the north of the
church. In times still further back a rope was

[1] Aeschines, *In Ctesiphontem*, 244.
Cf. E. Westermarck, *The Origin and
Development of the Moral Ideas*
(London, 1908), ii. 248.
[2] Westermarck, *op. cit.* ii. 256.
[3] A. Treichel, " Reisig- und Stein-
häufung bei Ermordeten oder Selbst-
mördern ", in *Verhandlungen der
Berliner Gesellschaft für Anthropologie, Ethnologie und Urgeschichte*
(1888), p. 569, bound up with *Zeitschrift für Ethnologie*, xx. (1888).

attached to the body, it was then dragged by wild horses and buried wherever the rope happened to break, or else the corpse was thrown among carrion in the gallows ditch, whereby one also interfered with the suicide after death. For no poor human soul can find rest unless the funeral rites have been properly observed, and to these belong more especially according to the popular belief, the having prayers read over him, and being buried in consecrated ground. When manners became milder, the suicide was allowed to rest in the churchyard, but was to be buried either before sunrise or after sunset. I myself have been present on such occasions. The grave, to distinguish it from those of the honest dead, might be dug from north to south instead of from east to west. That is an insult, and has been done towards other dead (besides suicides) to tease them. The intended insult has always been felt by the person in question, and been revenged by malicious haunting. When one compares all the many other examples which point in the same direction, I have no doubt that when the suicide's coffin is carried in over the mound, it is to prevent its ghost finding its way out of the churchyard, as it will be stopped by the hedge." [1] In Bulgaria the bodies of suicides may not be buried at all in the churchyard.[2] A similar prohibition to bury the bodies of suicides within a churchyard used to be strictly observed in the north-east of Scotland. On this

[1] Dr. H. F. Feilberg, " The Corpse Door ", in *Folk-Lore*, xviii. (1907) pp 369 *sq*.

[2] A. Strauss, *Die Bulgaren* (Leipzig, 1898), p. 455.

subject the Rev. Walter Gregor, a high authority
on the folk-lore of that district, writes as follows.
" Peculiar horror was manifested towards suicides.
Such were not buried in the churchyard. It is not
much over half a century since a fierce fight took
place in a churchyard in the middle of Banffshire,
to prevent the burial of a suicide in it. By an early
hour all the strong men of the parish who were
opposed to an act so sacrilegious were astir and
hastening to the churchyard with their weapons of
defence—strong sticks. The churchyard was taken
possession of, and the walls were manned. The
gate and more accessible parts of the wall were
assigned to picked men. In due time the suicide's
coffin appeared, surrounded by an excited crowd,
for the most part armed with sticks. Some, however, carried spades sharpened on the edge. Fierce
and long was the fight at the gate, and not a few
rolled in the dust. The assailing party was beaten
off. A grave was dug outside the churchyard, close
beneath the wall, and the coffin laid in it. The lid
was lifted, and a bottle of vitriol poured over the
body. Before the lid could be again closed, the
fumes of the dissolving body were rising thickly
over the heads of actors and spectators. This was
done to prevent the body from being lifted during
the coming night from its resting-place, conveyed
back to its abode when in life, and placed against the
door, to fall at the feet of the member of the family
that was the first to open the door in the morning.
The self-murderer's grave was on the boundary of

two lairds' lands, and was marked by a single stone or a small cairn, to which the passing traveller was bound to cast a stone. It was the prevailing idea that nothing would grow over the grave of a suicide, or on the spot on which a murder had been committed. After the suicide's body was allowed to be buried in the churchyard, it was laid below the wall in such a position that one could not step over the grave. This was done under the belief that, if a woman *enceinte* stepped over such a grave, her child would quit this earth by her own act." [1] In Scotland the bodies of suicides are now buried on the north side of the churchyard with the head to the east whereas all other dead are buried with their feet to the east. The fisher folk think that after such a burial the herring will forsake the coast for seven years. Hence sometimes they dig up the corpse by night and bury it on the shore at low water mark, or on the top of a mountain out of sight of the sea, that the herring may not be scared. Such burials have occurred on the top of Aird Dubh, and also on a mountain bounding Inverness and Ross-shire.[2] At Lochbroom, in Scotland, the people believe that if the body of a suicide be interred within any burial ground which is within sight of the sea or of cultivated land this would prove disastrous both to fishing and agriculture, or, in the words of the people, would cause " famine (or dearth) on sea and land " ; hence the custom has been to bury suicides in out-

[1] W. Gregor, *Notes on the Folk-lore of the North-east of Scotland* (London, 1881), pp. 213 *sq.*

[2] C. F. Gordon Cumming, *In the Hebrides* (London, 1883), p. 185.

of-the-way places among the lonely solitudes of the mountains.[1]

III. *Ghosts of Persons who have died a violent death other than murder or suicide*

The souls of persons who have been killed either by others or by themselves are by no means the only spirits of the dead whom primitive man regards with a more than ordinary degree of apprehension. In his list of peculiarly dangerous ghosts he includes the spirits of all who have died a violent death other than murder or suicide; for, their natural term of life having been prematurely cut short, he believes that they are indignant and ready to visit their displeasure on all and sundry, without discriminating nicely between the innocent and the guilty. In countries like India, where wild beasts abound, and are the causes of many deaths, the real terror of such a death is augmented or even redoubled in the minds of the natives by the purely imaginary terror of the victim's ghost. Thus, for example, among the Baigas, a primitive Dravidian people of the Central Provinces in India, when a man has been killed by a tiger, a Baiga priest goes to the spot and there makes a small cone out of the blood-stained

---

[1] E. Westermarck, *op. cit.* ii. 255, citing Ross in *Celtic Magazine*, xii. p. 350 *sq.* On the customs and superstitions as to suicide, see further A. Wuttke, *Der deutsche Volksaberglaube der Gegenwart* (Berlin, 1869), § 756; Dr. R. Lasch, " Die Behandlung der Leiche des Selbstmörders ", in *Globus*, lxxvi. (1899) pp. 63 *sqq.*; E. Westermarck, *op. cit.* ii. pp. 229-264.

earth. This must represent a man, either the dead man or one of his living kinsmen. His companions having retired a few paces, the priest goes on his hands and knees and performs a series of antics which are supposed to represent the tiger in the act of destroying the man, at the same time seizing the lump of blood-stained earth in his jaws. One of the party then runs up and taps him on the back with a small stick. This perhaps means that the tiger is killed or otherwise rendered harmless; and the Baiga immediately lets the mud cone fall into the hands of one of the party. It is then placed in an ant-hill and a pig is sacrificed over it. The next day a small chicken is brought to the place, and when a mark supposed to be the dead man's name has been made on its head with red ochre, it is thrown back again into the forest, the priest crying out, "Take this and go home". The ceremony is supposed to lay the dead man's ghost, and at the same time to prevent the tiger from doing any further damage. The Baigas believe that the ghost of the victim, if it is not charmed to rest, will reside on the head of the tiger and incite him to further deeds of blood, rendering him also secure from harm by his preternatural watchfulness.[1] Among the Bhatra, another primitive tribe in the Central Provinces in India, when a man has been killed by a tiger his spirit must be propitiated. The priest ties strips of tiger-skin to his arms, and the feathers

[1] R. V. Russell, *The Tribes and Castes of the Central Provinces of India*, ii. 84 ; and Capt. J. Forsyth, *The Highlands of Central India* (London, 1871), pp. 362 *sq.*

of the blue jay to his waist, and thus disguised
jumps about pretending to be a tiger. A package
of two hundred pounds of rice is made up, and the
priest sits on it and finally takes it away with him.
If the dead man had any ornaments they must all
be given, however valuable, lest his ghost should
hanker after them and return to look for them in
the shape of a tiger. The large quantity of rice
given to the priest is also probably intended as a
provision of the best food for the dead man's spirit,
lest it be hungry and come in the shape of a tiger
to satisfy its appetite upon the surviving kinsfolk.
The laying of ghosts of persons killed by tigers is
thus a very profitable affair for the priests.[1] The
Dumāl are an agricultural caste of the Central
Provinces in India who have recently been transferred to Orissa and Bihār. Among them if two
or more persons in a family have been killed by
tigers, a magician is called in, and he pretends to
be the tiger, and to bite someone in the family,
who is carried as a corpse to the burial-ground,
there buried for a short time, and then taken out
again. All the ceremonies of mourning are observed for him for one day. This proceeding is
believed to secure immunity for the family from
further attacks ; doubtless also it is thought to
appease the ghosts of the men whose bodies have
been devoured by tigers. In return for his services
the magician gets a share of everything in the house
corresponding to what he would receive, supposing

<hr/>

[1] Russell, *op. cit.* ii. 274 *sq.*

he were a member of the family, on a partition.[1]
Among the Gonds of Bastar, a great Dravidian
tribe of India, when a man has been killed by a
tiger and his widow marries again, she goes through
the ceremony not with her new husband but with
a lance, axe, or sword, or with a dog.   It is believed
that the tiger into which her first husband's spirit
has entered will try to kill her second husband, but
owing to the precaution taken he will either simply
carry off the dog or will himself get killed by an
axe, sword or lance.[2]   Among these Gonds also
the soul of a man who has been devoured by a
tiger must be specially propitiated, and ten or twelve
days are occupied in bringing it back.   To ascer-
tain when the soul has come back a thread is tied
to a beam and a copper ring is suspended from it,
being secured by twisting the thread round it and
not by a knot.   A pot full of water is placed below
the ring.   Songs are then sung in propitiation of
the spirit, and a watch is kept day and night.   When
the ring falls from the thread and drops into the
water it is believed that the soul has come back.
If the ring delays to fall they implore the dead man
to come back and ask where he has gone to and why
he is tarrying.   Animals are sacrificed to the ring
and their blood poured over it, and when it finally
falls they rejoice greatly and say that the dead man
has come back.   A man who has been killed by a
tiger or a cobra may receive general veneration,
for the purpose of propitiating his spirit, and so may

---

[1] Russell, *op. cit*. ii. 536.   [2] Russell, *op. cit*. iii. 81.

become a village god.[1] Among the Halbas, a
caste of cultivators and farm-servants in the Central
Provinces of India, if a person has been killed by a
tiger, the people go out, and if they find any remains of the body these are burned on the spot.
The priest is then invoked to call back the spirit of
the deceased, which is deemed a most essential precaution.   In order to do this he suspends a copper
ring on a long thread above a vessel of water and
then burns butter and sugar on the fire, muttering
incantations, while the people sing songs and call
on the spirits of the dead man to return.   The
thread swings to and fro, and at length the ring falls
into the pot, and this is accepted as a sign that the
spirit has come and entered the vessel.   The mouth
of the vessel is immediately covered and it is buried
or kept in some secure place.   The people believe
that unless the dead man's spirit is thus secured it
will accompany the tiger and lure solitary travellers
to destruction.   This is done by calling out and
offering them tobacco to smoke, and when they go
in the direction of the voice the tiger springs out
and kills them.   " The malevolence thus attributed
to persons killed by tigers is explained by their
bitter wrath at having encountered such an untimely death and consequent desire to entice others
to the same." [2]   The Kalanga, a caste of cultivators in the Central Provinces of India, make offerings to the spirits of their dead in a certain month of
the year ; but they make no such offerings to the

[1] Russell, *op. cit.* iii. 95.   [2] Russell, *op. cit.* iii. 195 *sq.*

spirits of persons who have died a violent death. The spirits of these latter must be laid lest they should trouble the living, and this is done in the following manner : a handful of rice is placed at the threshold of the house, and a ring is hung by a thread so as to touch the rice. A goat is then brought up, and when it eats the rice the spirit of the dead person is believed to have entered into the goat, which is thereupon killed and eaten by the family so as to dispose of him once for all. If the goat will not eat the rice it is forced to do so. The spirit of a man who has been killed by a tiger must, however, be laid by the sorcerer of the caste, who goes through the ceremony of pretending to be a tiger and of mauling another sorcerer.[1] Among the Kawars, a primitive tribe in the Central Provinces in India, when a man has been killed by a tiger they perform a ceremony called " Breaking the string " or the connexion which they believe the animal establishes with a family on having tasted its blood. Otherwise they think that the tiger would gradually kill off all the remaining members of the family of his victim. In this ceremony the village medicine-man (*Baiga*) is painted with red ochre and soot to represent the tiger, and proceeds to the place where the victim was carried off. Having picked up some of the blood-stained earth in his mouth, he tries to run away to the jungle, but the spectators hold him back until he spits out the earth. This represents the tiger being forced

[1] Russell, *op. cit.* iii. 308.

to give up his prey. The medicine-man then ties
a string round all the members of the dead man's
family standing together. He places some grain
before a fowl saying, " If my charm has worked,
eat of this " ; and as soon as the fowl has eaten
some grain the medicine-man states that his efforts
have been successful and the attraction of the man-
eater has been broken. He then breaks the string
and all the party return to the village. A similar
ceremony is performed when a man has died of
snake-bite.[1] In both cases the ceremony is probably supposed to appease the angry ghosts of the
persons killed by a tiger or a cobra.

Among the Kir, a caste of cultivators in the
Central Provinces of India, great respect is paid to
the spirit of a relative who has died a violent death,
or died as a bachelor or without progeny, the spirits
of such persons being always prone to trouble their
living kinsfolk. In order to appease them songs are
sung in their praise on important festivals, the members of the family staying awake the whole night,
and wearing their images on a silver piece round
the neck. When they eat and drink they first touch
the food with the image by way of offering to the
dead, so that their spirits may be appeased and
refrain from harassing the living.[2] The Kurmis,
a great cultivating class of Hindustan, believe that
the spirits of their dead return to their old homes
in the dark fortnight of the month Kunwār (Sep-
tember-October). On the thirteenth day of that

---

[1] Russell, *op. cit.* iii, 398–399.   [2] Russell, *op. cit.* iii. 483.

fortnight come the spirits of all those who have died
a violent death, as by a fall, or have been killed
by wild animals or snakes.   The spirits of such persons are supposed, on account of their untimely end,
to entertain a special grudge against the living.[1]
Among the Panwar, a famous Rajput clan found
in the Central Provinces of India, when a man has
been killed by a tiger (*bagh*) he is deified and worshipped as the tiger god (*Bagh Deo*).   A hut is made
in the yard of the house, and an image of a tiger
placed inside and worshipped on the anniversary
of the man's death.   The members of the household will not afterwards kill a tiger, because they
think that the animal has become a member of the
family.   A man who dies from the bite of a cobra
(*nag*) is similarly worshipped as the cobra god (*Nag
Deo*).   The image of a snake made of silver or iron
is venerated by the family, and the members of it
will not kill a snake.   If a man is killed by some
other animal, or by drowning or a fall from a tree,
his spirit is worshipped as the forest god (*Ban Deo*)
with similar rites, being represented by a little lump
of rice and red lead.[2]   Before sacrificing to their beneficent ancestral spirits, the Sansia or Uria—a caste
of masons and navvies in the Central Provinces of
India—are wont to offer two sacrifices to the spirits
of ancestors who have died a violent death or have
committed suicide, and to the spirits of relatives
who died unmarried, for fear lest these unclean and
malignant spirits should seize and defile the offer-

---

[1] Russell, *op. cit.* iv. 79 *sq.*   [2] Russell, *op. cit.* iv. 346 *sq.*

ings made to the kindly ancestral spirits.[1]   Among
the Savars, a primitive tribe of the Central Provinces in India, if a man has died a violent death, a
small platform is raised in his honour under a teak
tree, in which the ghost of the dead man is supposed
to take up its residence, and nobody thereafter may
cut down that tree.   In such a case the Uriya Savars
take no special measures unless the ghost of such a
man appears to somebody in a dream and asks to
be worshipped as Baghiapat (tiger-eaten) or Masan
(serpent-bitten).   When this happens they consult a
sorcerer, and take such measures as he may prescribe
to appease the dead man's ghost.[2]

The Oraons, a primitive aboriginal tribe, inhabiting the secluded plateau of Chota Nagpur in Northern India, believe that the spirits of persons who
have been killed by tigers assume the form of tigers
and prowl about at night near their old homes
which they seek to enter.   To drive away these
unquiet spirits the help of a spirit-doctor is called
in.   A man not belonging to the family is made to
personate the tiger.   His body is painted in colours
like those of the tiger, coloured earth being used
for the purpose.   A tail is also provided.   Thus arrayed, the man stands in the manner of a tiger on
his hands and legs, to which four ropes are tied.
Four men hold him by the ropes, and he is led on,
all the while fretting and fuming and snarling and
gnashing his teeth and otherwise imitating the
manner of a tiger.   The spirit-doctor follows the

---

[1] Russell, *op. cit.* iv. 498.   [2] Russell, *op. cit.* iv. 507.

mock tiger, and makes a show of driving it away.
As this sham tiger is driven away from the village
the ghost of the tiger's victim is supposed to be
simultaneously banished from the neighbourhood.
A fowl or some other sacrifice as dictated by the
spirit-doctor is offered to the tiger-ghost by the
spirit-doctor, as a further inducement for him to go
away.   Then the sham tiger is bathed and brought
back home.   At the house a feast is provided for
the family and fellow-villagers.[1]

Among the Kachins of Burma the souls of persons who have died a violent or unnatural death do
not receive the usual funeral honours, because it is
believed that they have become malignant spirits
ready and willing to cause harm and misfortune to
the living.   In these cases the body is invariably
cremated, never buried, and no time is lost in disposing of the corpse. All the usual marks of respect
are omitted, and the priest does not even go through
the ceremony of sending off the spirit to the spirit
land.   The place for the cremation is chosen as far
from the village as possible.   All the property of
the deceased goes with him, and food and some fire
from the house are placed beside the open hollow
in which his body has been cremated.   A white
cord is drawn round four saplings stuck in the
ground near the property.   The spirits of all such
persons go west, in the direction of the setting sun,
so the priest gives no directions as to the route to

[1] S. C. Roy, *Oraon Religion and
Custom* (Ranchi, 1928), p. 98. Cf.
S. C. Roy, " Magic and Witchcraft
on the Chota Nagpur Plateau ", in
the *Journal of the Royal Anthropological Institute*, xliv. (1914) p. 346.

be followed.   Nevertheless every Kachin house contains an image of the Gumgun nat ; that is, the spirit
of an ancestor who has met with a violent or unnatural death and whose spirit has returned to its
former home or the home where kinsfolk are living,
and requires propitiation, and can in turn help the
living.   The altar to the spirit is usually placed
against the left-hand walling of each house nearest
the back entrance.   The altar may not be touched :
any stranger interfering with it would give great
offence and might meet with violence.[1]   Among
the Palaungs of Burma, when anyone dies a mys-
teriously sudden death, or is killed, his body is
buried as quickly as possible in a lonely part of
the jungle at some distance from the village.   The
grave is generally dug beside a large tree, because
the spirits of all people dying suddenly are believed
to remain near their bodies, haunting the place where
they are buried.   Their time to die had not yet
come, and the spirit could not yet go to eat of the
fruit of forgetfulness.   Such a spirit is wicked, hurt-
ful, and jealous, and the only hope for its happiness is to give it the chance of a pleasant and shady
tree for its home.   The funeral customs, such as
tying coins to the wrist, are the same as usual ;
but if the person has been found dead in the jungle,
his corpse would not be brought back to the village,
but would be buried near where he died.[2]   There is
a general belief among the Burmese and Shans that

[1] W. J. S. Carrapiett, *The Kachin*
Tribes of Burma (Rangoon, 1929),
pp. 46, 78.

[2] Mrs. Leslie Milne, *The Home*
of an Eastern Clan, p. 304.

the spirits of human beings who have been killed by an elephant ride on the animal's head, warning him of his approach to pitfalls and hunters, and guiding him to where he may kill people, so as to add to their own ghostly company.[1]   In Cambodia all persons who die a natural death are buried according to the course of the sun with their heads to the west ; but all who die a violent death or by accident—such as by a fall—or drowning, or murder, or suicide, or the sting or bite of wild animals, are buried across the course of the sun, with their heads to the north, in order to prevent their spirits from returning to afflict their families.[2]   In Korea the spirits of all those who die sudden or violent deaths are believed to become evil demons who haunt and torment the living in endless ways.[3]

Like so many other peoples, the Kiwai Papuans of British New Guinea greatly fear the ghosts of persons who have met with a violent death, or have otherwise died in some unusual way.   The spirits of people who have been drowned or killed by a crocodile or a snake, and also those of suicides, are greatly feared because they will try to entice friends into a like death.   The spirit of a man killed by a crocodile is called *sibara-adíri*.   It is thought to carry on its back a " ghost-crocodile ", which it may throw upon another man, who is then doomed

[1] H. S. Hallett, *A Thousand Miles on an Elephant in the Shan States* (Edinburgh and London, 1890), pp. 377 *sq.*
[2] M. S. Aymonier, " Notes sur les coutumes et croyances super- stitieuses des Cambodgiens ", in *Excursions et reconnaisances*, No. 16 (Saigon, 1883), p. 202.

[3] Mrs. Bishop, *Korea and its Neighbours*, ii. 242.

to be killed in the same way. The "ghost-crocodile" is believed to be carried by the man's ghost all the way to the land of the dead ; and this may reveal the cause of death to people who have the faculty of seeing spirits. Such an apparition forbodes a similar death to anyone to whom it appears, but this fate can be averted if some friend of the man involved contrives to separate the crocodile from its bearer ; otherwise it is inevitable. In order to lay the ghost of a man killed by a crocodile the people build a small hut, like that erected on graves, at the place where the man met his death, and put food inside. They wish the spirit to remain there, and say to him, " Do not come back to where people are living. You are now a ghost : stay here, this is your house." If this is not done, the ghost, who does not wish to be alone, will come and fetch one of his friends to suffer the like fate. Another means of protection against such a fate is this : a man will burn part of a crocodile's tail to ashes and mix them with clay, and out of this form a ball, which he throws far away into the river. Or he fastens the piece of crocodile's tail to a stick, wades into the water with it, and fixes the stick to the bottom. In both cases he utters the following spell : " You are a crocodile spirit. Go far away, and stay there for ever." This adjuration prevents the crocodile ghost from attacking people.[1]

Among the Wandamba of Tanganyika in East Africa, if the hunter of an elephant has the mis-

---

[1] G. Landtman, *The Kiwai Papuans of British New Guinea*, pp. 283 *sq.*

fortune to be killed by an animal, his companions
bury him on the spot, and the chief medicine-man
puts some powder and medicine into the dead man's
hands, and also pours a little on the ground at the
foot of an adjacent tree, and sweeps round the grave
vowing vengeance on the animal, for the death of
their friend.   Then the party go off, and when they
have killed the elephant the head medicine-man
puts a little powder into the palm of his hand and
blows it away to let the dead man know that he had
been avenged.   Afterwards he returns to the hunter's
grave with some of the elephant's blood, which he
pours on the powder to appease the spirit of the
deceased.[1]   The curious rites which the Ewe people
of Togo perform after the death of a person who
has been killed by snake-bite have already been
described.[2]

   Among the Huron Indians of Canada, when anyone died by drowning or cold it was believed that
Heaven was angry with the people, and must be
appeased by sacrifice.   They summoned the inhabitants of the neighbouring villages and held
a feast and distributed presents freely, thinking
that the matter concerned the whole country.   The
corpse was carried to the cemetery and laid on a mat.
On one side of it a grave was dug in the ground
and on the other side a fire was made for the sacrifice.
At the same time several young men chosen by their

[1] A. G. O. Hodgson, "Some Notes
on the Hunting Customs of the
Wandamba of the Wanga Valley,
Tanganyika", in the *Journal of the*
Royal Anthropological Institute, lvi.
(1926), p. 64.

[2] See above, p. 11.

relations took their stand round about the corpse with their knives in their hands. The priest, who was described as the protector of the deceased, marked with charcoal the parts of the corpse which were to be cut. The young men set to work with their knives hacking off the fleshy parts. Finally they cut open the body and drew out the entrails and threw them on the fire together with the fleshy parts which they had severed. Then they laid the mangled remains in the grave. While the young men were hacking at the corpse women went round them, encouraging them to ply their work well for the good of the whole country, at the same time putting beads as a further encouragement into the mouths of the operators. Sometimes the mother of the deceased, bathed in tears, joined the party, lamenting the death of her son in a doleful chant. By these rites the Hurons believed that they appeased the wrath of Heaven; but if they were to omit them they thought that any accidents or misfortunes that might befall them were the effects of Heaven's displeasure at the sacrilege.[1]

IV. Ghosts of Women dying in Childbed

The ghosts of women dying in childbed are commonly believed to be dangerous in a peculiarly high degree, and very special precautions are taken

---

[1] *Relations des Jésuites*, 1636 (Canadian reprint, Quebec, 1858) p. 108. P. F. X. de Charlevoix, *Histoire de la Nouvelle - France* (Paris, 1744), v. 110.

to guard against them.[1]   The belief and the practice consequent upon it are particularly prevalent in some parts of India, and all over the Malay region to the east.   Thus the Hindus of the Punjab believe that if a mother dies within thirteen days of her delivery, she will return in the guise of a malignant spirit to torment her husband and family.   To prevent this some people drive nails through her head and eyes, while others also knock nails on either side of the door of the house.[2]   A gentler way of attaining the same end is to put a nail or a piece of iron into the clothes of the poor dead mother.[3]   The ghost of such a woman is called a Churel.   She is particularly malignant towards members of her own family. She appears in various forms, sometimes she is fair in front and black behind, but she invariably has her feet turned round, heels in front and toes behind. However she generally assumes the form of a beauti-ful woman and seduces youths at night, especially the handsome.   She carries them off to some king-dom of her own, and if they venture to eat the food offered to them there she keeps them till they lose their manly beauty.   Then she sends them back to the world grey-haired old men, where, like Rip Van Winkle, they find all their friends dead long ago.[4] Among the Gurao, a caste of village priests in the

[1] Cf. *Psyche's Task* (*The Devil's Advocate*), pp. 133 *sqq.*, where some of the evidence here cited has been previously adduced.

[2] H. A. Rose, "Hindu Birth Observances in the Punjab", in *Journal of the Royal Anthropological Institute*, xxxvii. (1907) pp. 225 *sq.*

[3] G. F. D'Penha, "Superstitions and Customs in Salsette", in *The Indian Antiquary*, xxviii. (1899) p. 115.

[4] W. Crooke, *Popular Religion and Folk-lore of Northern India* (Westminster, 1896), i. pp. 269 *sq.*

Central Provinces of India, when the corpse of a woman who has died in childbed is being carried to the burning ground various rites are observed to prevent her spirit from becoming a malignant ghost (*Churel*) and troubling the living. A lemon charmed by a magician is buried under her corpse and a man follows the body strewing the seeds *rala*, while nails are driven into the threshold of the house.[1] Among the Kurmis, the representative cultivating caste of Hindustan, if a woman has died in childbirth, or after the birth of a child and before the performance of the sixth-day ceremony of purification, her hands are tied with a cotton thread when she is buried, in order that her spirit may be unable to rise and trouble the living. It is believed that the souls of such women become evil spirits (*Churels*). Thorns are also placed over her grave for the same purpose.[2] In Bombay it is believed that the souls of women dying in childbed enter the order of ghosts variously known as *Chudels*, *Vantris*, or *Takshamis*. In order that the spirit of such a woman may not return from the cremation ground, mustard seeds are strewn along the road behind her bier, for a belief prevails that her ghost can only succeed in returning if she can gather all the mustard seeds thus strewn on the way. In some places loose cotton-wool is thrown over the bier so as to be scattered all along the road to the cemetery. It is thought that the ghost can only return to the house if she can collect

---

[1] R. V. Russell, *Tribes and Castes of the Central Provinces*, ii. pp. 180 *sq.*

[2] R. V. Russell, *op. cit.* iv. 78.

all the cotton scattered behind her in one night.
This is deemed an impossible task, and consequently
her friends at home entertain no fear of the return
of the ghost when once the cotton has been scattered.
To prevent the return of such a ghost, some people
pass underneath the bier the legs of the cot on which
the woman lay in her confinement, while others
drive in an iron nail at the end of the street immediately after the corpse has been carried beyond
the village boundary. In some places the nail is
driven into the threshold of the house. Even after
these ceremonies have been observed to prevent the
return of the ghost of such a woman, other rites
are performed, and a number of Brahman women
feasted on the twelfth and thirteenth day after death
to propitiate her departed soul, for the fear of the
mischief she may do is very strong.[1]   In Travancore
the spirits of women who die in pregnancy are
believed to become demons. Their bodies accordingly are carried away to some distant spot in the
jungle, and there incantations are pronounced over
them to prevent their ghosts from returning and
molesting the survivors.[2]

The Oraons of Chota Nagpur are firmly convinced that every woman who dies in pregnancy or
childbirth becomes an evil and dangerous spirit
(*bhut*), who, if steps are not taken to keep her off,
will come back and tickle to death those whom she
loved best in life. " To prevent her, therefore, from

[1] R. E. Enthoven, *The Folk-Lore of Bombay* (Oxford, 1924), p. 197.   [2] S. Mateer, *Native Life in Travancore* (London, 1883), p. 90.

coming back, they carry her body as far away as they can, but no woman will accompany her to her last resting-place lest similar misfortune should happen to her.   Arrived at the burial-place, they break the feet above the ankle, twist them round, bringing the heels in front, and then drive long thorns into them.   They bury her very deep with her face downwards, and with her they bury the bones of a donkey, and pronounce the *anathema* ' If you come home may you turn into a donkey : ' and the roots of a palm-tree are also buried with her ; and they say, ' May you come home only when the leaves of the palm-tree wither ', and when they retire they spread mustard-seeds all along the road saying, ' When you come home, pick up all these '.   They then feel pretty safe at home from her nocturnal visits, but woe to the man who passes at night near to the place where she has been buried.   She will pounce upon him, twist his neck, and leave him senseless upon the ground, until brought to by the incantations of a sorcerer." [1]

To complete this account of the quaint rites observed in such cases by the Oraons I will subjoin the report of another highly-competent witness, the Indian ethnologist, Mr Sarat Chandra Roy, who has made a special study of the tribe.   " A *Churil* or *Churel* or *Malech* is the ghost of a woman dying in pregnancy or childbirth or within a few days of it.

[1] Rev. P. Dehon, " Religion and Customs of the Uraons ", in *Memoirs of the Asiatic Society of Bengal*, vol. i. No. 9 (Calcutta, 1906), pp. 139 *sq.*

A *Churil* spirit, it is said, carries a load of coal upon its head, imagining it to be its baby. It is believed that if a *Churil* spirit sees any man passing by its. grave it pursues him and takes delight in tickling him under the arms and, if possible, throwing him down senseless and embracing him. If, however, the man perceives the approach of a *Churil* by its spectral figure which is sometimes visible or by the rustling and shaking of the branches of some neighbouring tree, and calls out the *Churil* by the name which it formerly bore in life, and asks—' So-and-so [names], is it you ? ' the spirit forthwith decamps. Or, when the *Churil* attacks him, if the man can take away her load of charcoal, the spirit is said to lose its power and to burst into tears. Drunken wayfarers are naturally easy victims of this spirit. It is with the object of preventing such spirits from moving about, that the feet of women dying in childbed are broken and turned backwards and thorns inserted on the soles of their feet. When a *Churil* is visible, its feet appear, it is said, to be inverted with the heels forward. A person, particularly a drunken man, supposed to have been chased and tormented by a *Churil*, is sometimes so seriously affected that it requires the services of a spirit-doctor (*Mati* or *deonra*) to cure him by exorcising the spirit. When the trouble caused by a *Churil* is not more serious than a griping of the stomach or such other ailment, a few mustard-seeds, two grains and a half of some pulse, a little iron-slag and a bit of charcoal are thrown outside the house in the direction of the spot where the *Churil* was met with." [1]

Among the Birhors, another primitive tribe living in the jungles of Chota Nagpur, the spirit of a woman who has died within twenty-one days of childbirth may never be admitted into the community of ancestor-spirits, because such a spirit is always dangerous. In her case, therefore, a new doorway in the hut is opened through which her corpse is carried out to the grave. Such a corpse is buried in a place apart from the ground where other corpses are interred. Women and not men bury such corpses: the men only dig the grave and go away. Thorns are thrust into the woman's feet to prevent her ghost from leaving the grave. The corpse in the grave is formally made over by the spirit-doctor (*mati*) to the charge of some spirit of a hill or jungle of the neighbourhood. In doing so the spirit-doctor works himself up to a state of supposed possession, and says, " O, Spirit of such-and-such hill or forest! [names] We make over so-and-so [names the deceased] to you. Guard her well and let her remain here." The spirit-doctor, or rather, as is believed, the spirit speaking through the mouth of the spirit-doctor, says, " I do take charge ". If the first spirit asked to take charge does not make such a reply, another spirit is similarly invoked, and so on, until some spirit agrees to take charge of the dangerous corpse. [2]

[1] S. C. Roy: *Oraon Religion and Customs* (Ranchi, 1928), pp. 96-97. Cf. E. T. Dalton, *Descriptive Ethnology of Bengal* (Calcutta, 1872), p. 258.

[2] S. C. Roy, *The Birhors* (Ranchi, 1925), pp. 267 *sq.*

Speaking of the much-dreaded spirits of these unhappy women in Bengal generally, Sir Edward Gait, a high authority on the subject, observes, " But the most malevolent of all spirits is the Churel or Kichin, the spirit of a woman who dies in childbirth. Her feet are turned backwards, she has no mouth, and she haunts filthy places. She is specially feared by women, whom she attacks during the menstrual period, or at the time of parturition. Sometimes she falls in love with young men, before whom she appears in the form of a beautiful girl neatly decked and dressed with ornaments, and whom she eventually kills by a slow process of emaciation. Like other similar spirits, she can only be ejected by exorcism. The fear of the Churel is by no means confined to the Hindus. It is even more dreaded by the aboriginal tribes, and amongst the Bhuiyas of Keonjhar, if a woman should die before delivery, the embryo is extracted from the corpse and the bodies are burnt on the opposite banks of a hill stream. As no spirit can cross water, and the mother cannot become a witch unless united to her child, this precaution is believed to avert all risk of evil to the villagers." [1]

Among the Lushais of North-Eastern India, when a woman dies in childbed, the relatives offer a sacrifice to her departed soul, " but the rest of that village treat that day as a holiday and put a small green branch on the wall of each house on the out-

---

[1] Sir E. A. Gait, in *Census of India*, 1901, vi. Bengal: Part I. (Calcutta, 1902) p. 199.

side near the doorpost to keep out the spirit of the dead woman ".[1] The Lakhers, a tribe of the same region, think that the ghost of a woman who has died in childbed becomes a dangerous spirit, to be classed with the spirits of all who have died an unnatural death. Her corpse may not be carried out of the house by the doorway, but through a hole cut in the back wall. This is done because, as the spirits of women who have died in childbed do not follow the road taken by the spirits of those who have died natural deaths, but have to go by another path to the *Sawvawkhi*, the place reserved in the spirit land for the souls of all who have died an unnatural death, it is thought that the corpse should not leave the house by the ordinary path, but should also take a different path to the grave.[2]

The Kachins of Burma are so afraid of the ghosts of women dying in childbed that no soooner has such a death taken place than the husband, the children, and almost all the people in the house take to flight lest the ghost should bite them. They bandage the eyes of the woman with her own hair to prevent her from seeing anything ; they wrap the corpse in a mat and carry it out of the house, not by the ordinary door, but by an opening made for the purpose either in the wall or in the floor of the room where she breathed her last. Then they convey the body to a deep ravine where foot of man seldom penetrates, and there, having heaped her

[1] Lieut.-Col. H. G. W. Cole, " The Lushais ", in *Census of India*, 1911, vol. iii. Assam : Part I. (Shil- long, 1912) p. 140.

[2] N. E. Parry, *The Lakhers* (London, 1932), pp. 406-408.

clothes, her jewellery, and all her belongings over her, they set fire to the pile and reduce the whole to ashes. "Thus they destroy all the property of the unfortunate woman in order that her soul may not think of coming to fetch it afterwards and to bite the people in the attempt." When this has been done the officiating priest scatters some burnt grain of a climbing plant (*shāmien*), inserts in the earth the pestle which the dead woman used to husk the rice, and winds up the exorcism by cursing and railing at her ghost, saying, "Wait to come back till this grain sprouts and this pestle blossoms, till the fern bears fruit, and the cocks lay eggs". The house in which the woman died is generally pulled down, and the timber may only be used as firewood or to build small hovels in the fields. Till a new house can be built for them, the widower and the orphans receive the hospitality of their nearest relatives, a father or a brother ; their other friends would not dare to receive them from fear of the ghost. Occasionally the dead mother's jewels are spared from the fire and given away to some poor old crones who do not trouble their head about ghosts. If the medicine-man who attended to the woman in life and officiated at the funeral is old, he may consent to accept the jewels as the fee for his services ; but in that case no sooner has he got home than he puts the jewels in the hen-house. If the hens remain quiet, it is a good omen and he can keep the trinkets with an easy mind ; but if the fowls flutter and cackle, it is a sign that the ghost is sticking to the jewels, and in a fright he restores them to the family. The old man or old woman into whose hands the trinkets of the dead woman thus sometimes fall cannot dispose of them to other members of the tribe, for nobody who knows where the things come from would be so rash as to buy them. However, they may find purchasers among the Shans or Chinese, who do not fear Kachin ghosts.[1]

With regard to these customs and beliefs of the Kachins, another writer, who knows the tribe well, tells us that when a woman has died in childbed her body is cremated, and saplings are then procured and rude representations of the male organ of generation are carved at one end of each. These are stuck in the ground, and bending towards the spot where cremation took place. In returning from the grave or cremation ground precautions have to be taken against any assault by the dead woman's dangerous spirit. A long bamboo is procured, and split in half for about half way or more of its length. One half is fixed in the ground, the other half lying loose. Between the two halves a wedge is inserted about three or four inches off the ground, thus forming a triangle with the wedge as base. All who have attended the funeral pass through the triangle, the medicine-man and the butcher bringing up the rear. Either of these two knock away the wedge after passing over it and the two halves of the bamboo close with a snap. Those

<hr>

[1] Ch. Gilhodes, " Naissance et enfance chez les Katchins (Birmanie) ", in *Anthropos*, vi. (1911) pp. 872 *sq.*

who have guns fire as many shots as they can into the bamboo to frighten and drive away the malignant spirit.[1] The passage of the mourners through the split bamboo is no doubt another mode of eluding the pursuit of the ghost; when the two halves of the bamboo have closed with a snap the gate has been shut in her face.

Another writer who travelled in Burma in the second half of the nineteenth century has described somewhat differently the customs and beliefs on this subject observed and held by the Kachins, or Kakhyens, as he calls them. His account runs as follows. " Funeral rites are also denied to those who die of small-pox and to women dying in child-birth. In the latter case the mother and her child are believed to become a fearful compound vampire. All the young people fly in terror from the house, and divination is resorted to, to discover what animal the evil spirit will devour, and another with which it will transmigrate. The first is sacrificed, and some of the flesh placed before the corpse; the second is hanged, and a grave dug in the direction to which the animal's head pointed when dead. Here the corpse is buried, with all the clothes and ornaments worn in life, and a wisp of straw is burned on its face, before the leaves and earth are filled in. All property of the deceased is burned on the grave, and a hut erected over it. The death dance takes place, to drive the spirit from the house, in all cases.

[1] W. J. S. Carrapiett, *The Kachin Tribes of Burma* (Rangoon, 1929), p. 47.

The former custom appears to have been to burn the body itself, with the house and all the clothes and ornaments used by the deceased. This also took place if the mother died during the month succeeding childbirth, and, according to one native statement, the infant also was thrown into the fire, with the address, ' Take away your child ' ; but if previously any one claimed the child, saying, ' Give me your child ' it was spared, and belonged to the adopting parent, the real father being unable at any time to reclaim it." [1]

The Shans of Burma believe that the death of a woman with her unborn child is the greatest misfortune that can befall her own and her husband's family. It is thought that the spirit of the dead woman becomes a malignant ghost, who may return to haunt her husband's home and torment him, unless precautions are taken to keep her away. In the first place, her unborn child is removed by an operation ; then the bodies of mother and child are wrapped in separate mats and buried without coffins. If this be not done, the same mishap may befall the woman in her future life, and the widower will suffer from the attacks of her ghost. When the corpses are being removed from the house, part of the mat wall in the side of the house is taken down, and the dead woman and her baby are lowered to the ground through the opening. The hole through which the bodies have passed is immediately filled with new mats, so that the ghost may not know how

---

[1] J. Anderson, *Mandalay to Momien* (London, 1876), pp. 145 *sq.*

to return. In such a case no guests are invited, and there is no burial ceremony, though a funeral feast may be given on the anniversary of the death.[1]

The Palaungs of Burma regard the spirits of women dying in childbed as the most terrifying of all unhappy spirits. After such a death has taken place in a house, the woman's body is hurriedly washed and dressed in new clothes, and the usual food and other things are placed beside her in a new mat, which is wrapped round her body. The corpse is then lowered through a hole which has been cut in the flooring-boards of the room where she died. And as the desire of every one is to remove her body from the house and the village as quickly as possible for burial, a coffin is not made. The unborn child may be removed by an operation, wrapped in another mat, and buried by itself, but this is seldom done. As soon as the body has been lowered, the floor is washed and the hole is closed with new boards. This, they hope, will prevent the return of the spirits of the unfortunate mother and child. The husband does not attend the funeral, but goes to spend days, or even weeks, at the monastery. It is now the practice to dig a grave of the usual shape in a lonely part of the jungle, and when earth has been heaped above the body, a banana-tree, the emblem of fertility, is sometimes planted beside it. In olden times a grave was made in the shape of a well, and the woman's body was buried in a standing

---

[1] Mrs. Leslie Milne, *The Shans at Home* (London, 1910), p. 96. Cf. *The Fear of the Dead in Primitive Religion*, ii. pp. 102 *sq.*

position, a large terra-cotta pot, inverted, being placed on her head, so as to rest on her shoulders. When a pregnant woman dies, no woman still capable of child-bearing and no girl should go into the house of the dead woman, until the body has been removed. When the funeral has taken place the mourners in the house may be visited by girls and young unmarried women, who should accept no food there until seven days have passed. They fear that if they eat in the house before the spirit of the dead woman has gone to eat of the fruit of forgetfulness, a similar fate may befall them should they marry.[1]

In Cambodia it is believed that the spirits of women who die in childbed become malignant spirits who torment living folk in a variety of ways. They are called *khmoch-preai* (the wicked dead). They cause all kinds of sicknesses, they turn into beasts of prey, they throw stones and sand at the mango-trees in the garden in order to frighten the people in the house. No one is safe from their ravages. The first prince of the blood, the highest authority but one in the land, has been heard to complain bitterly of the depredations committed in his garden by these wicked spirits.[2]

The ghosts of women dying in childbed are much dreaded by the Malays of the peninsula and of the Indian Archipelago; it is supposed that they appear in the form of birds with long claws and are

[1] Mrs. Leslie Milne, *The Home of an Eastern Clan* (Oxford, 1924), pp. 304 *sq.*

[2] J. Moura, *Le Royaume du Cambodge* (Paris, 1883), ii. 178.

exceedingly dangerous to their husbands and also to pregnant women. Such a ghost is called a *pontianak*. She is commonly seen in the form of a huge bird uttering a discordant cry. She haunts forests and burial-grounds, appears to men at midnight, and is said to emasculate them. She afflicts children and pregnant women, causing abortions.[1] A common way of guarding against such dangerous ghosts is to put an egg under each armpit of the corpse, to press the arms close against the body, and to stick needles into the palms of the hands. The people believe that the ghost of the dead woman will be unable to fly and attack people; for she will not spread out her arms for fear of letting the eggs fall, and she will not clutch anyone for fear of driving the needles deeper into her palms. Sometimes, by way of additional precaution, another egg is placed under her chin, thorns are thrust into her fingers and toes, her mouth is stopped with ashes or beads, and her hands, feet, and hair are nailed to the coffin.[2]

[1] T. J. Newbold, *British Settlements in the Straits of Malacca* (London, 1839), ii. 191.

[2] Van Schmidt, " Aanteekeningen nopens de zeden, etc., der bevolking van de eilanden Saparoea, etc.", *Tijdschrift voor Neêrlands Indië*, v. Tweede Deel (Batavia, 1843), pp. 528 *sqq.*; G. Heijmering, " Zeden en gewoonten op het eiland Timor ", *Tijdschrift voor Neêrlands Indië*, vii. Negende Aflevering (Batavia, 1845), pp. 278 *sq.* note; B. F. Matthes, *Bijdragen tot de Ethnologie van Zuid - Celebes* (The Hague, 1875), p. 97; W. E. Maxwell, " Folk-lore of the Malays ", *Journal of the Straits Branch of the Royal Asiatic Society*, No. 7 (June, 1881), p. 28; W. W. Skeat, *Malay Magic* (London, 1900), p. 325; J. G. F. Riedel, *De sluik- en kroesharige Rassen tusschen Selebes en Papua* (The Hague, 1886), p. 81; B. C. A. J. van Dinter, "Eenige geographische en ethnographische aanteekeningen betrefende het eiland Siaoe ", *Tijdschrift voor Indische Taal- Land- en Volkenkunde*, xli. (1899) p. 381; A. C. Kruijt, " Eenige ethnographische Aanteekeningen omtrent de Toboengkoe en de Tomori ", *Mededeelingen van wege het Nederlandsche Zendelinggenootschap*, xliv.

Besides these precautions, which are universal in
the Malay region, the Achinese of Sumatra give the
corpse of such a woman an entangled ball of cotton
and a needle without an eye ; when the ghost wants
to go off, she must first sew trousers from her shroud,
but spends the time in disentangling the cotton and
seeking the eye of the needle.[1]

The fear of these dangerous spirits of women
dying in childbed is deeply felt and widely held
by the natives of Nias, an island lying to the west
of Sumatra.[2] In Lolowaoe, a village in the mountains of Western Nias, the natives say that such a
spirit, named *matianak*, appears like the shadow of
a woman with her hair wound about her head. Only
the priests have the faculty of recognizing such
spirits. The *matianak* lives by choice on the banks
of rivers, and feeds on fish, crabs, and other water
creatures. She has a grudge not only at women, but
also will not leave men in peace. In the evening she
sallies forth and tries to catch some man, whom she
then drags to her abode beside the river. There she

(Rotterdam, 1900) p. 218 ; *id.*, *Het
Animisme in den Indischen Archipel*
(The Hague, 1906), p. 252 ; G. A.
Wilken, *Handleiding voor de ver-
glijkende Volkenkunde van Nederlandsch-Indië* (Leyden, 1893), p.
559 ; J. H. Meerwaldt, " Gebruiken
der Bataks in het maatschapplijk
leven ", *Mededeelingen van wege
het Nederlandsche Zendelinggenootschap*, xlix. (1905) p. 113 ; N.
Adriani and A. C. Kruijt, *De Bare'e-
sprekende Toradjas van Midden-
Celebes* (The Hague, 1912), ii. pp.
113 *sq*. The common name for

these ghosts is *pontianak*. For a full
account of them, see A. C. Kruijt,
*Het Animisme in den Indischen
Archipel*, pp. 245 *sqq*.
[1] A. C. Kruijt, " Indonesians ",
in Hastings' *Encyclopaedia of Religion and Ethics* (Edinburgh, 1914),
vii. 241.
[2] J. W. Thomas and L. N. N. A.
Chatelin, " Godsdienst en bijgeloof
der Niassers ", in *Tijdschrift voor
Indische Taal- Land- en Volkenkunde*, 1881, p. 133, and E.
Modigliani, *Un Viaggio a Nias*
(Milan, 1890), pp. 554, 630.

ducks her victim under the water till he loses con-sciousness. When he comes to himself, she orders him to climb a high coconut palm and fetch her a coconut. In the oil which she extracts from the nut she boils a human head and therewith prepares an ointment, with which the man must smear his body. Then he is fully in the power of the spirit (*matianak*) and ready to comply with her sexual desires. On the other hand, the *matianak* will also be helpful to her victim. The ointment which he gets from her enables him to steal without being perceived. When he comes to a house which he wishes to rob, he has only to measure at the doorway a space equal to that between his little finger and thumb and to smear on it the ointment which he received from the *matianak*. That enables him to enter the house without being observed by the inmates. Also if he has a grudge against anybody, he may give his knife to the *matianak*, and with it she will rip up the belly of the hated person, so that he or she dies.

It is at evening that these evil spirits go about. Hence, to guard oneself against their attacks, it is well, when you are walking at evening, to brandish a knife or a stick from time to time; this keeps them off. Or the wayfarer throws leaves behind him; the demon stops to pick them up in order to make an ointment out of them, and she loses so much time in picking up the leaves that she cannot overtake the wayfarer.

According to the natives of Eastern Nias it is especially against pregnant women that the *mati-anak* has a grudge: she causes them to fall sick or to miscarry. In order to keep the demon from his pregnant wife, a husband will, in the eighth month of her pregnancy, plant a leafy branch of a *damo* tree at a cross-road close to the house. The leaves flutter in the wind, thus showing their white glistening under-sides. That frightens the *matianak* so that she dare not approach the house. Besides that, at the back of the house, close to the woman's chamber, a banana-tree is planted to bar the road against the *matianak*. The people also place idols, with grim faces, at the entrance of the house and beside the woman's bed, the intention of which must be to frighten the *matianak*. If the woman is safely delivered, a thank-offering is made to these idols, but if she dies in childbed the idols which have been made are thrown away. Otherwise they are kept. The natives of Eastern Nias think that the *matianaks* also attack men, wrenching the arms out of their bodies and then inserting them in the reverse way, so that the palms of the hands are turned outwards.[1]

Among the Toradyas of Central Celebes, as additional precautions against the ghost of a woman dying in childbed, an old woman will smear chalk on the cheeks of the corpse, and sometimes the stem of a banana-tree is placed in the coffin with her, to make her think it is her child, and so to soothe and pacify her perturbed spirit.[2]

[1] J. P. Kleiweg de Zwaan, " De 'Pontianak' of Nias ", in *Tijdschrift van het Koninklijk Nederlandsch Aardrikskundig Genootschap*, Tweede Deel, Serie xxix. (1912)

pp. 25 *sqq.*

[2] N. Adriani and A. C. Kruijt, *De Bare'e-sprekende Toradjas van Midden-Celebes*, ii. 114.

We have already seen that a similar mode of contenting the maternal longings of a dead mother is adopted in some parts of Melanesia, including Fiji, and also in the Pelew Islands.[1]

Once more, among the Kayans or Bahaus of Central Borneo, " the corpses of women dying in childbed excite a special horror ; no man and no young woman may touch them ; they are not carried out of the house through the front gallery, but are thrown out of the back wall of the dwelling, some boards having been removed for the purpose." [2] Indeed, so great is the alarm felt by the Kayans at a miscarriage of this sort that when a woman labours hard in childbed, the news quickly spreads through the large communal house in which the people dwell ; and if the attendants begin to fear a fatal issue, the whole household is thrown into consternation. All the men, from the chief down to the boys, will flee from the house, or, if it is night, they will clamber up among the beams of the roof and there remain in terror ; and, if the worst happens, they remain there till the woman's corpse has been removed from the house for burial. In such a case the burial is carried out with the greatest despatch. Old men and women, who are indifferent to death, will undertake the work, and they will extract a large fee for their services. The body, wrapped in a mat, is buried in a grave dug in the earth among the tombs, instead of being laid in a coffin raised on

[1] See above, pages 59, 60, 61   [2] A. W. Nieuwenhuis, *Quer durch Borneo* (Leyden, 1901-1907), i. 91.

a tall post ; for the spirit of the woman who dies in childbirth goes, with the spirits of those who fall in battle, or die by violence of any kind, to Bawang Daha (the lake of blood).[1]

The Kiwai of British New Guinea think that the spirits of women dying in childbed are very dangerous ghosts, threatening in particular their husbands, to whom their misfortune is attributed. The spirit of the dead baby is also feared. Not until long afterwards, when the spirits are thought to have gone away, will the husband venture out hunting.[2]

Among the Ewe-speaking peoples of Togo, in West Africa, when a woman dies in childbed they carry her body into the forest, and remain beside it overnight. During the night they light a fire, discharge shots, beat drums, and sing till morning breaks. Then they wash the corpse, spread banana leaves upon the ground, cover them with a mat, and lay the body on the mat. Then they smear the dead woman's face with white earth. And whoever comes to see her takes white earth in his left hand, and strews it on her body, saying three times " I pity thee ". This they do till the time comes for the burial. If the child is still in her womb a man is charged with the duty of cutting open her body at the edge of the grave, so that the dead mother may see her babe. If the child is barely in life they kill it by dashing its head against a tree. But if they see that the child may live they take it home and

---

[1] C. Hose and W. McDougall, *The Pagan Tribes of Borneo* (London, 1912), i. 155.

[2] G. Landtman, *The Kiwai Papuans of British New Guinea* (London, 1927), p. 284.

rear it.   If the child is a male they call it *Kpeme*.
They say that only male children, and not female,
kill their mothers at birth.   The bodies of women
who have died in childbed are buried in a special
place (*Atsiamanya*).   Nine days after the burial the
funeral rites are performed, the woman's house is
broken up and the materials are burned on the road
outside the town, in order that no evil influence may
attach to the timbers.   The inhabitants of the town
receive a fine of forty *hoca* of cowrie shells from the
relations of the deceased.   Then they take a small
dog and a toad, tie them to the end of a palm
branch, and drag them through the town.   This
ceremony is called '*kplo gbo me* (sweeping the
town, purifying it from evil spirits).   Behind them
a bell is rung all the time, till they have completed
the round of the town.   If this rite were not performed, no solemn purification (*busu*) would thereafter be possible.[1]   From this account we gather
that among these people the death of a woman in
childbed is supposed to affect the whole town
with a pollution which must be effaced before life
can resume its normal course.   The ghost of such
a woman must therefore be deemed particularly
virulent.

The Ibibio of Southern Nigeria regard with fear
and horror the bodies of women who have died in
childbed.   Such corpses are carried out and thrown
away or propped against the foot of a tree in the
Bad Bush.   In the neighbourhood of Awa the mouths

[1] J. Spieth, *Die Ewe-Stämme* (Berlin, 1906), p. 278

of such women are stopped with pitch, while some pitch, mixed with thorns, is also placed at times under the armpits, to prevent them from troubling the living. Otherwise their ghosts, who are thought to hate the whole human race because they have been denied burial, are said to take upon themselves the form of a beautiful woman to lure a man to his destruction. Such a man at his death will find himself surrounded by the ghoul-wife and her demon offspring, and will be prevented from joining his relatives and friends in the ghost town. When the bearers who have carried out the corpse of such a woman and disposed of it in the forest return to the village, they may not enter their own houses, but must wait outside that of the dead woman until the members of her family have brought out and sacrificed a dog, a cock, and some eggs. Magic leaves are ground between stones and rubbed over the bodies of the corpse-bearers, while the kinsmen of the deceased pray that so sad a fate may never again overtake one of their house. The fowl's head is struck off, and its blood is sprinkled over the bearers, who chant meanwhile : " Let not the evil thing pass from me to any woman ". Until the sacrifices have been made and the prayers offered, none who took part in carrying the corpse may touch a woman lest the influence which had proved fatal to the deceased should be communicated by them to the living.[1]

[1] D. Amaury Talbot, *Woman's Mysteries of a Primitive People*, pp. 214 *sq*. P. Amaury Talbot, *The Peoples of Southern Nigeria*, iii. 512.

Among the Ila-speaking peoples of Northern
Rhodesia, when a woman dies in pregnancy, it is
deemed necessary to cut out the child from her
womb, and to bury it separately from the mother,
for otherwise they believe that the mother's ghost
will rise from the grave and kill people.[1]

The ancient Mexicans believed that the spirits
of women who died in childbed were turned into
dangerous and malevolent goddesses, who roamed
about in the air, but descended from time to time
on the earth for their errands of mischief. They
haunted, above all, the cross-roads. On such de-
scents they afflicted children with various maladies,
including paralysis, by penetrating into the bodies
of the sufferers. Hence parents forbade their
children to leave the house on days when they
thought the goddesses descended to earth, lest
their offspring should be harmed by these evil
deities. Paralysis was explained by them as due
to the possession of the sufferer's body by one of
these malignant beings. To appease these dreaded
goddesses the ancient Mexicans held festivals in
their honour, at which they offered them loaves
baked in the shape of butterflies and thunder-
bolts, cakes called *tamalli*, and roasted maize. The
images of these goddesses represented them with
white faces and white hands, arms, and legs, as if
they were smeared with white earth. Their ears
were golden, and the tresses of their hair curled like

[1] Rev. E. W. Smith and Capt. A.
M. Dale, *The Ila-Speaking Peoples*
of Northern Nigeria (London, 1920),
ii. 115.

those of great ladies. Their robes were striped with black, and their petticoats parti-coloured.[1] Oratories of these goddesses were erected in all the wards of the city. In them their images stood, and these were covered with paper on the days when the deities were supposed to descend. Usually the spirits of women dying in childbed were thought to live in the palace of the sun in the western part of the sky, and to accompany the sun daily from midday till his setting in the west. But on certain days of certain months they were believed to descend to earth, and to afflict children with paralysis and other maladies. It was on these days, which were well known from the calendar, accordingly, that parents were careful to keep their children at home, that they might not encounter the dangerous goddesses.[2]

V. *Ghosts of dead Husbands or Wives*

The ghosts of dead husbands and wives are commonly deemed very dangerous to their surviving spouses, whom they are thought to haunt in a variety of ways. This they are thought to do especially when the surviving partner has taken to himself or herself a second wife or husband, for the ghost is naturally jealous of the second wife or husband, and seeks to wreak her spite against the new

---

[1] Bernardino de Sahagun, *Histoire générale des choses de la Nouvelle-Espagne*, traduite et annotée par D. Jourdanet et Remi Simeon (Paris, 1880), pp. 20 *sq.*

[2] Sahagun, *op. cit.* pp. 433-437, 80, 81, 255, 269. Cf. H. H. Bancroft, *The Native Races of the Pacific States of North America*, iii. 362-364.

bride or bridegroom. Hence special precautions are commonly taken to guard the widower or widow against the dangerous spirit of his or her departed spouse.[1]

Thus, for example, among the Nufoors of Dutch New Guinea, when a widow marries for a second time, she walks into the forest with her new husband, followed by a number of widows or married women, who cut branches and twigs from the trees and throw them at the newly wedded pair. This they do for the purpose of driving away the jealous ghost of the widow's late husband, who is supposed to pursue and endanger one or both of them. For the same reason the widow must put off her mourning garb and give it to another widow, because it is believed that the ghost of her late husband adheres to the garments, and that if she did not put them off he might, out of jealousy, visit her or her new husband with sickness. When the couple have ended their walk the female friends who accompanied them and plied them vigorously with branches and twigs receive a present of chopping-knives and petticoats, and that ends the marriage ceremony.[2]

At Issoudun in British New Guinea a French

---

[1] With what follows, compare *Psyche's Task* (*The Devil's Advocate*), pp. 142-149; *Folk-Lore in the Old Testament*, i. 523-529. See also E. S. Hartland, *Ritual and Belief*, chapter "The Haunted Widow", pp. 194 *sqq.*; and E. Westermarck, *The History of Human Marriage* (Fifth Edition, London, 1921), i.

pp. 326 *sqq.*

[2] J. B. van Hasselt, "Die Noerforezen", in *Zeitschrift für Ethnologie*, viii. (1876) p. 182 *sq.*; *id.*, "Eenige aanteekeningen de bewoners der N. Westkust van Nieuw Guinea", in *Tijdschrift voor Indische Taal- Land- en Volkenkunde*, xxi. (1886) p. 585.

missionary has painted a melancholy picture of the
sad lot of a native widower haunted and hag-ridden
by the ghost of his dead wife.   His miseries begin
with the moment of his wife's death.   He is immediately stripped of all his ornaments, abused and
beaten by his wife's relations, his house is pillaged,
his gardens devastated, there is no one to cook for
him.   He sleeps on his wife's grave till the end of
his mourning.   He may never marry again.   By
the death of his wife he loses all his rights.   It is
civil death for him.   Old or young, chief or plebeian,
he is no longer anybody; he does not count.   He may
not hunt or fish with the others ; his presence would
bring misfortune ; the spirit of his dead wife would
frighten the fish or the game.   He is no longer
heard in the discussions.   He has no voice in the
council of elders.   He may not take part in a dance ;
he may not own a garden.   If one of his children
marries, he has no right to interfere in anything or
to receive any present.   If he were dead he could
not be ignored more completely.   He has become
a nocturnal animal.   He is forbidden to show himself in public, to traverse the village, to walk in the
roads and paths.   Like a boar he must go in the
grass or the bushes.   If he hears or sees anyone,
especially a woman, coming from afar, he must hide
himself behind a tree or a thicket.   If he wishes to
go hunting or fishing by himself, he must go at
night.   If he has to consult anyone, even the missionary, he does it in great secrecy, and at night.   He
seems to have lost his voice, and only speaks in a

whisper. He is painted black from head to foot.
The hair of his head is shaved, except two tufts
which flutter on his temples. He wears a skull-cap
which covers his head completely to the ears ; it
ends in a point at the back of his neck. Round his
waist he wears one, two, or three sashes of plaited
grass ; his arms and legs from the knees to the
ankles are covered with armlets and leglets of the
same sort ; and round his neck he wears a similar
ornament. His diet is strictly regulated, but he
does not observe it more than he can help, eating
in secret whatever he is given or he can lay his
hands on. " His tomahawk accompanies him everywhere and always. He needs it to defend himself
against the wild boars and also against the spirit of
his dead wife, who might take a fancy to come and
play him some mischievous prank ; for the souls of
the dead come back often, and their visit is far from
being desired, inasmuch as all the spirits without
exception are bad and have no pleasure but in
harming the living. Happily people can keep them
at bay by a stick, fire, an arrow, or a tomahawk.
The condition of a widower, far from exciting pity
or compassion, only serves to render him the object
of horror and fear. Almost all widowers, in fact,
have the reputation of being more or less sorcerers,
and their mode of life is not fitted to give the lie to
public opinion. They are forced to become idlers
and thieves, since they are forbidden to work : no
work, no gardens : no gardens, no food : steal
then they must, and that is a trade which cannot

be plied without some audacity and knavery at a pinch." [1]

Among the Kiwai Papuans of British New Guinea, when a widow marries again several ceremonies are performed, which appear to be based on a fear of her late husband's ghost. One day just before sundown the pair go to the forest, where they have connexion close to a spider's web spun between them and the village. When the man gets up, he walks home right through the web, breaking it, and at a little distance his wife follows in his tracks. On entering their house they carefully bar the door after them. In the morning when they go back to the bush the spider will have restored its web, and then the past is " shut away ". Another practice is this. The man and widow go to the place where she and her former husband had connexion the last time. There she cooks a little food—a taro root or some sago. They break off the top shoot of a young bamboo, provide themselves each with a little piece of the stem underneath, and replace the shoot. The small pieces of bamboo are put into two portions of the food. They then have connexion, and during the act they put into each other's mouth the two bits of food containing the bamboo. Their intention is to link up their marriage with the first one, at the spot where this had been broken off, and to prevent the new husband from dying as his predecessor had done. The " spirit-smell " still

[1] Father Guis (de la Congrégation du Sacré Cœur d'Issoudun, missionaire en Nouvelle-Guinée), " Les Canaques, mort-deuil ", in *Les Missions Catholiques*, xxxiv. (Lyons, 1902) pp. 208 *sq.*

adheres to the woman, and they want to " wash it away ". As the bamboo grows on, the loose shoot on top, which represents the dead husband, is thrown off, and the stem underneath, symbolizing the new husband, keeps on growing. Before returning home they split the middle part of a certain creeper (*nu-rúde*), leaving the base and top intact, then the man and woman crawl through the opening, which closes behind them, and in this way they " shut the road against the ghost of the dead husband ". These observances are not kept by the bushmen at marrying a widow, hence many of them suffer from shortness of breath, which is supposed to be caused by the first husband's ghost.

If the first husband has been taken by a crocodile, the following rite is observed. The pair go to the place where the accident happened ; there the woman takes off her grass petticoat and breaks her *sógére* (a plaited grass necklace), the last sign of her mourning, throwing them away into the water. After the two have had connexion, the woman stands up astride with her back towards the water, and her husband crawls between her legs from behind. She then puts on a new petticoat and walks home behind her husband. They keep the door of their house carefully closed till next morning. An analogous rite is performed in the case of the first husband having been killed by a snake. The couple have connexion close to the haunt of the snake. Then they fill a coconut bowl with water from some swamp near by, frequented by the creature, and both drink it. A nipa leaflet is partly split in the same way as the creeper in the observance described above, and the two sides are kept apart by means of a transverse stick. The man first crawls through the leaf, knocking down the stick, and after him the woman in the same way, the stick having been replaced. On their return home the door is kept shut after them. There is a third similar rite performed if the widow's first husband has been killed by a wild boar. At a place where the boar has rooted in the ground the woman lies down nude, and the man pours over her genitals some water brought in a coconut-bowl from a hole made by the pig. The woman gets up and drinks the rest of the water in the bowl, the man not drinking any. After a couple of days the pair go back to the same place and have connexion there. On their return to the village the people—men, women, and children—previously summoned by the husband, sit down on the ground, forming a circle, in the middle of which husband and wife seat themselves. The circle of friends round the newly married pair is said to fence or guard them, presumably against the ghost of the deceased husband. The pair remain within the enclosure until sunset, when they go into their house and secure the door.[1]

Among the Toradyas of Central Celebes, a widow, after the death of her husband, may not leave the house until a certain ceremony has been performed over her. A rough fence of umbrellas and cotton is rigged up round about her, and within this

---

[1] G. Landtman, *The Kiwai Papuans of British New Guinea*, pp. 252 *sq.*

circle a priest performs over her certain rites, which
are believed to fasten her soul in her body, and so to
prevent it from following her husband's ghost to
the spirit land.[1] These Toradyas think, or used to
think, that every period of mourning for the dead
must be terminated by a human sacrifice, offered to
the spirit of the dead, either to divert the wrath of
the ghost from the living, or to carry his property to
him in the spirit land. In time of war the scalp of a
slain enemy might be used for the purpose. When
a village in which a death had taken place was not
at war, they tried to obtain a human victim by purchase from a neighbouring tribe and, if they succeeded,
they hacked him or her to death. Sometimes they
employed as victims persons accused of witchcraft.
If all other means failed, as a last resort they under-
took a warlike expedition against hereditary foes at
a distance. A widower must bring back a human
head for his dead wife, even if he had to remain
absent for three years or more before he could procure it. If he came back without it he was put
to public shame by his fellow-villagers.[2] So keen
apparently was the dead woman's ghost to obtain
the bloody trophy.

In India it is, as usual, at the marriage of a widow
or widower that the jealous ghost of the deceased
spouse is particularly dreaded and that, accordingly,

[1] A. C. Kruijt, " Het koppen-
snellen der Toradjás van Midden-
Celebes, en zijne beteekenis ", in
Verslagen en Mededeelingen der
Koninklijk Akademie van Weten-
schappen, Vierde Reeks, Derde Deel.

xxv. (Amsterdam, 1899) p. 188.

[2] N. Adriani and A. C. Kruijt,
De Bare's Sprekende Toradjas van
Midden-Celebes (The Hague, 1912),
pp. 105-107.

special precautions are adopted to guard against his or her unwelcome attentions. Thus among the Barai, a caste of betel-leaf growers and sellers in the Central Provinces, when a man marries a widow he offers a coconut at the shrine of a certain deity called Maroti. The nut is afterwards placed on a plank and kicked away by the widow's new husband, in token of his thus dismissing summarily the ghost of her dead spouse. Later on the coconut is buried in order to lay the spirit of the deceased.[1] Again among the Bhāmta, a caste of thieves and growers of hemp in the Central Provinces, if a man marries a second wife after the death of the first, the new wife wears on her neck an image of the first wife, and offers it the *hom* sacrifice by placing some melted butter (*ghi*) on the fire before taking a meal. In cases of doubt and difficulty she often consults the image by speaking to it, while any chance stir of the image due to the movement of her body is interpreted as a sign of the approval or disapproval of the dead wife.[2] Thus the second wife attempts to appease the jealous spirit of her predecessor in the affections of her husband. Among the Kunbi, the great agricultural caste of the Marathi country, the ceremony of widow-marriage is largely governed by the idea of escaping or placating the wrath of the first husband's ghost. It always takes place in the dark fortnight of the month, and always at night. Sometimes no women are present, and if they do

---

[1] R. V. Russell, *The Tribes and Castes of the Central Provinces of*   *India*, ii. 195.

[2] R. V. Russell, *op. cit.* ii. 237.

attend they must be widows, for it would be a very bad omen for a married woman or an unmarried girl to witness the ceremony. This, it is thought, would shortly lead to her becoming a widow herself. The bridegroom goes to the widow's house with his male friends, and two wooden seats are set side by side. On one of the seats is placed a betel-nut, which represents the deceased husband of the widow. The new bridegroom advances with a small wooden sword, touches the nut with its tip, and then kicks it off the seat with his right toe. The barber picks up the nut and burns it : this is believed to lay the deceased husband's ghost and to prevent his interference with the new union. The bridegroom then takes the seat from which the nut has been displaced and the woman sits on the other side to his left. He puts a necklace of beads round her neck and the couple leave the house and go to the husband's village. It is considered unlucky to see them as they go away, as the second husband is regarded in the light of a robber. Sometimes they stop at a stream on the way home, and, taking off the woman's clothes and bangles, bury them on the bank. An exorcist may also be called in, who will confine the late husband's spirit in a horn by putting in some grains of wheat, and after sealing up the horn deposit it with the clothes. When a widower or widow marries for a second time, and is afterwards attacked by illness, it is ascribed to the ill-will of their former partner's spirit. The metal image of the first husband or wife is then made and worn as an amulet on the arm or round the neck, to protect the wearer against the ghost of the deceased spouse.[1] Among the Mahars, an impure caste of menials, labourers and village watchmen in the Maratha country, when a man marries a widow, and she is proceeding to her new husband's house, she is stripped of her old clothes, necklace and bangles, and these are thrown into a river or stream, and she is given new ones to wear. This is done to lay her first husband's ghost, who may be supposed to hang about the clothes which she formerly wore as his wife, and when they are thrown away or buried the exorcist mutters spells over them in order to lay the spirit of the deceased spouse.[2]

Similarly among the Mana, a Dravidian caste of cultivators and labourers in the Central Provinces, when a widow is to be married again, and is proceeding for that purpose to her new husband's house, she stops by the bank of a stream, and here her clothes are taken off and buried by an exorcist for the sake of laying her first husband's spirit and preventing him from troubling the new household.[3] Among the Mang-Gorari, a criminal subdivision of the Mang caste in the Central Provinces and Berar, if a widow survived two or three husbands and then married again, she had to go through the ceremony holding a fowl under her arm, and the bird was afterwards killed to appease the ghost or ghosts of her late husband or husbands.[4] Among

[1] R. V. Russell, *op. cit.* iii. pp.27 *sq.*

[2] R. V. Russell, *op. cit.* iv. 135.

[3] R. V. Russell, *op. cit.* iv. 175

[4] R. V. Russell, *op. cit.* iv. 193.

the Panwar, a famous Rajput clan, when a widow
marries again the stool on which she sat at the ceremony is afterwards stolen by her new husband's
friends. After the wedding, when she reaches the
boundary of his village the axle of her cart is removed, and a new one made of ebony wood (*tendu*)
is substituted for it. The discarded axle and the
shoes worn by the husband at the ceremony are
thrown away, and the stolen stool is buried in a field.
The wood of the *tendu* or ebony tree is chosen because
it has the valuable property of keeping off spirits and
ghosts. When a child is born a plank of this wood
is laid along the door of the room to keep the spirits
from troubling the mother and the new-born infant.
In the same way, no doubt, this wood keeps the
ghost of the first husband from entering with the
widow into her second husband's village.[1] Among
the primitive Bhils, Mavchis and Konkanis of
India, when a man's wife has died and he marries
again, custom requires him to carry at the ceremony
a large stone engraved with the image of a woman.
After the marriage ceremony this stone is buried in
the cemetery, in such a way that the image of the
woman still shows above the surface. The object
of this rite is to fix the ghost of the deceased wife
and to prevent it from wandering.[2]

Among the Somavansi Kshatriyas in Bombay
" there is a strong belief that when a woman marries
another husband, her first husband becomes a ghost

[1] R. V. Russell, *op. cit.* iv. 345.
[2] J. Abbott, *The Keys of Power* (London, 1932), p. 244.

and troubles her. This fear is so strongly rooted in their minds that whenever a woman of this caste sickens she attributes her sickness to the ghost of her former husband, and consults an exorcist as to how she can get rid of him. The exorcist gives her some charmed rice, flowers and basil leaves, and tells her to enclose them in a small copper box and wear it round her neck. Sometimes the exorcist gives her a charmed coconut which he tells her to worship daily, and in some cases he advises the woman to make a copper or silver image of the dead and worship it every day." [1] So in Northern India when a man marries again after the death of his first wife he wears " what is known as the Saukan Maura, or second wife's crown. This is a little silver amulet, generally with an image of Devî engraved on it. This is hung round the husband's neck, and all presents made to the second wife are first dedicated to it. The idea is that the second wife recognizes the superiority of her predecessor, and thus appeases her malignity. The illness or death of the second wife or of her husband soon after marriage is attributed to the jealousy of the ghost of the first wife, which has not been suitably propitiated." [2]

In the Bombay Presidency most high-caste people, on the death of their first wives, take an impression of their feet on gold leaves or leaf-like tablets of gold

[1] W. Crooke, *The Popular Religion and Folk-Lore of Northern India* (Westminster, 1896), i. 235 *sq.*, quoting J. M. Campbell's *Notes on* the *Spirit Basis of Belief and Custom*, p. 171.

[2] W. Crooke, *op. cit.* i. 236.

and cause their second wives to wear them round the neck. These impresses of feet are called mourning footprints. Among the lower castes the hands or the feet of the second wife are tattooed in the belief that this prevents the deceased wife from causing injury to the second wife.[1] A similar purpose, no doubt, is served by the golden footprints of a first wife which the second wife of a high-caste man wears as an amulet on her neck.

The Bhandari are a caste of toddy-drawers, who are scattered all over the Bombay Presidency. They permit the marriage of widows with the sanction of the *panch* or head man of the caste. " The ceremony is performed at night in an unoccupied outhouse. The details vary in the different localities according to local usages. In the Ratnágiri district, where the caste is most numerous, it is celebrated as follows. The ceremony of *oválani* (waving a platter containing lighted wicks, a pice, a coconut, rice grains and a cock) is first performed by a *Bhagat* (exorcist) in order to free the widow from the dominion of the spirit of her deceased husband, who is supposed to haunt her. The materials of the *oválani*, except the cock, which is taken by the *Bhagat*, are carefully packed together and sent to the house of the widow's deceased husband in order to be lodged at the foot of the *tulsi* (sweet basil) plant in front of the house, as it is supposed that these *oválani* materials collected together carry back with them the spirit of the deceased husband. The *Bhagat* himself is possessed

[1] R. E. Enthoven, *Folk-Lore of Bombay* (Oxford, 1924), p. 196.

of his favouring spirit while he is performing the ceremony. Thus possessed, he promises good to the pair, and conjures the spirit of the widow's deceased husband by means of the *oválani*. Thus freed, the widow is presented to her husband by another widow who acts as her bridesmaid. She applies paste made of flour of *udid* (black gram) to the left knee of the latter, and puts some grains of rice on it. Next, her new husband presents her with a new dress and ornaments which she puts on in the presence of the assembly. This completes the ceremony. A dinner is then held, and a present of Rs. 5 is made to the caste *panch* who sanctioned the marriage. On the following morning before daybreak the widow's new husband, accompanied by his friends and followed by her, leaves the house to return home. The widow takes a cock under her arm. When the procession reaches the boundary of the village the cock is immolated, and its head, together with a lock of hair from the widow's head and a bit of the new robe worn by her are buried under a rock. The body of the cock is taken away and eaten by the *Bhagat*, who accompanies the pair till they reach home. This ceremony is also performed by the *Bhagat* and is intended to be an offering to the guardian spirit of the village resident on the boundary, who is expected to take charge of the spirit of the deceased husband. Not unnaturally the deceased husband is believed to be very jealous of the second husband, and all the efforts of the *Bhagat* are directed towards annihilating his influence, in case he may be hovering near

in the spirit with evil intentions."[1]   Among the
Gabit, a caste of fishers on the Bombay coast, the
marriage of a widow is celebrated in an uninhabited
house on the village boundary, or in a temple of
Vetál or Bhutnáth. At the ceremony "in order to
prevent disturbance from the spirit of the widow's
deceased husband, a cock, a coconut and rice
grains are first offered to him."[2] Among the Mahar,
a tribe of the Bombay Presidency, at the remarriage
of a widow, when the ceremony is over and the newly-
wedded pair are starting for the bridegroom's house,
but before they reach it, a cock is killed and a piece
of the widow's robe is cut off and Rs. 2 with a *ser* of
rice grains and a coconut or five *Nagchampa* leaves
tied in a piece of cloth are sent to the house of the
widow's deceased husband and placed in the basin
of the sweet basil plant in the courtyard. This offering is made to appease the spirit of the widow's deceased husband.[3] Among the Nhavi, the barber caste
of the Bombay Presidency, when a widow has been
remarried, on the night of the marriage day, and
before daybreak, the newly-wedded pair start for the
bridegroom's home, the wife holding a cock under
her arm. At the same time a man of the caste leaves
for the widow's deceased husband's house taking
with him a coconut, some fruit, rice grains and
one rupee. On arriving there, he places these things
either in the house or in the courtyard, unseen by anybody. When the procession of the remarried couple

[1] R. E. Enthoven, *The Tribes and
Castes of Bombay* (Bombay, 1920),
i. 101-102.

[2] R. E. Enthoven, *op. cit.* i. 349.

[3] R. E. Enthoven, *op. cit.* ii. 415.

reaches the boundary of the widow's village, the cock
under the widow's arm is sacrificed and a coconut
is broken. The body of the cock and the coconut
are given to a *virakti* (worshipper of a village deity).
Next, another cock is placed under the widow's arm,
and the procession proceeds on its way. When they
reach the boundary of the bridegroom's village,
another coconut is broken and the cock under the
widow's arm is killed by a *virakti*, and the head of
the cock together with a hair from the widow's head
and a bit of her robe are buried under a rock. The
body of the cock is taken away and eaten by the
virakti, who is also paid some money for his services
by the bridegroom. " All these efforts are directed
to preventing the spirit of the widow's deceased
husband from troubling the second husband. When
the party reach home, a jar filled with water is placed
on the threshold of the door. The widow takes it
on her head and enters the house, thus ending the
ceremony." [1] By this last act the widow may perhaps be supposed to place a barrier of water between
herself and the ghost of her late husband.

Among the Ramoshi, a very numerous caste of
the Bombay Presidency, the remarriage of a widow
is celebrated on a dark night. Only men attend
the ceremony. As it is considered unlucky for
married unwidowed women to hear the service, the
ceremony is celebrated in a deserted place. The
widow and her new husband separate after the ceremony, and do not see each other or any of the caste

[1] R. E. Enthoven, *op. cit.* iii. pp. 132 *sq.*

for a day. " If a woman has lost three husbands and wishes to marry a fourth, she holds a cock under her left arm when the ceremony is being performed. The priest reads the service first in the name of the cock, and then of the man, the object evidently being that, in case the spirits of her former husbands or rather the spirit of her first husband who killed the next two for meddling with his property, be inclined to do any harm, it may fall on the cock and not on the man." [1] Among the Teli, a caste of oilmen in the Bombay Presidency, the marriage of widows is permitted. In the Ratnágiri district, before the marriage of a widow takes place a bundle of cloth containing a rupee, a coconut, and a betelnut is sent to the widow's late husband's house, and a coconut and a cock are waved off her face to free her from molestation by her deceased husband's spirit. [2] Among the Parit, a caste of washermen in the Bombay Presidency, when a widow has been married again she or her new husband sacrifices a cock every year to appease the wrath of her deceased husband's ghost. [3]

Among the Savaras, an important hill-tribe of Southern India, whoever marries a widow must perform a religious ceremony, during which a pig is sacrificed. The flesh, with some liquor, is offered to the ghost of the widow's deceased husband, and prayers are offered by the priest to propitiate the ghost, so that it may not torment the woman and her

[1] R. E. Enthoven, *op. cit.* iii. 301.   [3] R. E. Enthoven, *op. cit.* iii. 176.
[2] R. E. Enthoven, *op. cit.* iii. 374.

second husband. "Oh man!" says the priest, addressing the deceased by name, "here is an animal sacrificed to you, and with this all connexion between this woman and you ceases. She has taken no property belonging to you or your children. So do not torment her within the house or outside the house, in the jungle or on the hill, when she is asleep or when she wakes. Do not send sickness on her children. Her second husband has done no harm to you. She chose him for her husband, and he consented. Oh man! be appeased; oh! unseen ones; oh! ancestors, be you witnesses." The animal sacrificed on this occasion is called *long danda* (inside fine), or fine paid to the spirit of a dead person inside the earth.[1]

Among the Kamchadals or Koryaks of Kamtchatka in north-eastern Asia no man would marry a widow before a ceremony called "removing the sin from her" had been performed. The ceremony consisted in her having sexual intercourse with a stranger, who had to be paid for his services, for his office was considered disgraceful, and until the advent of the Russians it was difficult to find any man who would undertake the duty; but after the coming of the Cossacks there was no lack of men willing to take upon themselves the sin of a handsome young widow.[2] Our authorities for this custom

[1] E. Thurston, *Castes and Tribes of Southern India* (Madras, 1909), vi. 321.
[2] S. Krascheninnikow, *Beschreibung des Landes Kamtschatka* (Lem- go, 1766), p. 259; G. W. Steller, *Beschreibung von dem Lande Kamtschatka* (Frankfurt and Leipzig, 1774), p. 346.

do not explain what the sin of the widow consisted in, but we may conjecture with a fair degree of probability that it was the offence which she gave to the ghost of her late husband by her first act of sexual intercourse after his death. This view is accepted by competent modern authorities who have touched upon the custom.[1]

In Africa the fear of the ghost of a dead husband or a dead wife is strongly pronounced among the Ewe-peoples of Togo. At Agome, in Togoland, a widow is bound to remain for six weeks in the hut where her husband lies buried. She is naked, her hair is shaved off, and she is armed with a stick with which to repel the too pressing familiarities of her husband's ghost; for were she to submit to them she would die on the spot. At night she sleeps with the stick under her, lest the wily ghost should attempt to steal it from her in the hours of slumber. Before she eats or drinks she always puts some coals on the food or in the beverage, to prevent her dead husband from eating or drinking with her; for if he did so she would die. If any one calls to her she may not answer, for her dead husband would hear her, and she would die. She may not eat beans or flesh or fish, nor drink palm-wine or rum, but she is allowed to smoke tobacco. At night a fire is kept up in the hut, and the widow throws powdered peppermint leaves and red pepper on the

[1] W. Jochelson, *The Koryak*, ii. 752 (Jesup North Pacific Expedition, Memoir of the American Museum of Natural History) (Leyden and New York, 1908); E. Westermarck, *The History of Human Marriage* Fifth Edition, London, 1921), i. 327.)

flames to make a stink, which helps to keep the
ghost from the house. Among these people widowers
observe a similar seclusion after the death of their
wives, but only for eight days, and we are not told
that they resort to the same means of repelling the
ghosts of their deceased spouses.[1]

Among the Ibibio of Southern Nigeria, when a
widow begins to contemplate a second marriage she
is terrified lest the ghost of her late husband should
return and seek to draw her after him to the spirit
land. Should she suspect that the ghost is actually
preparing to do so, she consults a member of the
secret society called Idiong, who has a great reputation for second sight. By his advice food is cooked
and placed in a corner of the room. The priest takes
up a position immediately before this, and stands
calling upon the name of the ghost. Close to the
place where the food is laid some member of the
family crouches, holding a strong pot, preferably of
iron, tilted forward ready to invert over the one in
which the food is served. When the ghost is supposed to be partaking of the food in the first pot the
wizard makes a sign and the second pot is inverted and
clapped over the first pot, and the two are bound fast
together, thus entrapping the spirit of the woman's
late husband, and so presumably preventing him
from offering any obstacle to her second marriage.

---

[1] Lieutenant Herold, " Bericht betreffend religiöse Anschauungen und Gebräuche der deutschen Ewe-Neger", *Mitteilungen von For-schungsreisended und Gelehrten aus den deutschen Schutzgebiet*, v. Heft 4 (Berlin, 1892), p. 155 ; H. Klose, *Togo unter deutscher Flagge* (Berlin, 1899), p. 274.

If, on the contrary, a widow loved her late husband very much, she will cook food for him after his death and place it secretly in a corner of her room so that his spirit may be induced to return and enjoy it.[1]   Among the Baganda of Central Africa, when a man wished to marry a widow he first paid the deceased husband a barkcloth and a fowl, which he put into the little shrine at the dead man's grave : in this way he imagined that he could pacify the ghost.[2]

Among the Wajagga of Mount Kilimanjaro in East Africa, when a man marries a widow he purchases the right to do so from her late husband by sacrificing a goat to his ghost, for the dead man is supposed to retain all the rights that he had in life. The sacrifice is offered at evening in the cattle kraal. When the goat has been killed the contents of the stomach are extracted, carried into the hut, and laid upon one of the stones of the hearth.   The bridegroom and the widow crouch beside the hearth, and together draw the hearthstone out of the earth. Thereupon the bridegroom repeats his adjuration to the ghost of the widow's late husband to the following effect : " To-day I take over thy kraal and thy children, in order that I may look after them and bring them up, and that they may bring offerings to thee.   If I know any black or white root that could have killed you, may I perish by this stone.   It was thy fate, I had no share in thy death, let me live and

_____

[1] D. Amaury Talbot, *A Woman's Mysteries of a Primitive People*, pp. 174 *sq.*

[2] J. Roscoe, *The Baganda* (London, 1911), p. 97.

thrive in this place. And if I beget a child by thy wife, let it grow up with its brothers and sisters that they may be a credit to the members of their age-grade."

They think that if this satisfaction were not offered to the spirit of the dead husband his ghost might take offence and kill the widow. In his address to the ghost at offering the sacrifice the new husband is careful to insist that he by no means wishes to intrude upon the rights of his predecessor. He begs to be allowed to purchase and pay for his predecessor's rights. He promises to care for his predecessor's cattle and to rescue them should they fall into the hands of the enemy. In return for the sacrifice of the goat, the ghost is requested to transfer all his rights to the new husband, in order that he may go out and in the kraal in safety, and to help him to rear the dead man's orphan children.[1]

Among the Dinkas of the Upper Nile, before a widow may marry again a sacrifice must be offered to appease the spirit of her late husband. A brother of the deceased (and it may be the very brother who is about to marry her) kills a bull from the dead man's herd and the blood is collected in a gourd. The blood and the meat are boiled and eaten by the widow and her children, the woman's clan taking one hind leg and the clan of the deceased the rest. After this satisfaction has been given to the ghost of her dead husband, the widow is free to marry again.[2]

[1] B. Gutmann, *Das Recht der Dschagga* (Munchen, 1926), pp. 52 sq.
[2] C. G. and B. Z. Seligman, *Pagan Tribes of the Nilotic Sudan* (London, 1932), p. 164.

Speaking of the natives of Congo in West Africa a French writer of the eighteenth century tells us that according to their belief the ghost of a dead husband lights upon the head of his widow. Hence when a husband has breathed his last, his widow rushes to some river or tank with a minister of their sect, whose special function it is to perform the rite. There the widow is tied with cords and flung several times into the river, in the belief that this will drown the soul of her late husband and prevent it from returning to torment her. As soon as she returns from the river she is free to marry again. But if a widow does not thus drown her husband's ghost, she must stay at home clad in old, torn, dirty, dark-coloured robes, doubtless in order to elude the attention of her late husband's ghost.[1] In Loango, a province of West Africa to the south of the Congo, widows fear to be visited at night by the ghosts of their dead husbands. They think that as a consequence of such a visit they would either die or give birth to monsters. To guard against such a visit a wizard will provide a widow with a magic bolt with which to close the door of the hut against the ghost, or with a magic cord to fasten round her bed at night. Or he may shift the door of the house to another side of the dwelling, in order to baffle the ghost. If all these precautions fail to allay the widow's anxiety her friends will remove her secretly by night to another house, taking her by a

[1] J. B. Labat, *Relation historique de l'Éthiopie occidentale* (Paris, 1732), i. 404.

roundabout way which the ghost cannot follow, and effacing her footsteps, in order that the ghost may not track her to her new abode. With a view to leaving no tell-tale footprints behind they will sometimes carry the widow, or put sandals on her feet if she walks, for in this last case the ghost will not be able to recognize the widow's own footprints. In addition to all these precautions a widow is always provided with a magic cudgel which she lays between her legs when she sleeps at night, to be employed in self-defence against the ghost should he succeed in approaching her.[1]

Among the Wabemba or Awemba, a Bantu tribe of the Congo Free State and North-Eastern Rhodesia, before a widower may marry again he must appease the spirit of his dead wife by scraping with his fingers a little hole at the head of her grave and pouring into it a libation of beer, doubtless to slake the thirst of the ghost.[2] Among the Mashona of Southern Rhodesia, when a man's wife has died he may not marry again until after the obsequies for his dead wife have been fully performed. His father-in-law could accuse him of witchcraft if he took another wife while the ghost of his dead wife still hovered about unappeased. It was thought that such wickedness might cause the ghost to strike her own people : she could not strike him or his.[3]

[1] P. Güssfeld, J. Falkenstein, E. Pechuël-Loesche, *Die Loango-Expedition ausgesandt von der deutschen Gesellschaft zur Erforschungen Aquatorial - Africas*, 1873 – 1876 (Stuttgart, 1907), iii. 2, 308 *sq.*

[2] C. Delhaise, *Notes ethnographiques sur quelques peuplades du Tanganyika* (Brussels, 1905), p. 10.

[3] C. Bullock, *The Mashona* (Johannesburg, 1928), p. 261.

The Amazulu of Southern Africa believe that a widow is sometimes visited and troubled by the ghost (*Itongo*) of her dead husband. If such a ghostly visit takes place during her pregnancy, and she afterwards miscarries, the ghost of her dead husband is laid because he has done her an ill turn. Should the ghost trouble her when she has gone to another man without being as yet married, leaving her late husband's children behind, the ghost of her dead husband will follow her and ask, " With whom have you left my children ? What are you going to do here ? Go back to my children. If you do not assent I will kill you." In such a case the vengeful ghost of the dead husband is at once laid in that village because he harasses his widow.[1]

The following is a native account of the method of laying a dead husband's troublesome ghost (*Itongo*) which is practised by the Amazulu. " If a woman has lost her husband, and she is troubled excessively by a dream, and when she is asleep her husband comes home again, and she sees him daily just as if he was alive, and so she at last wastes away, and says, ' I am troubled by the father of So-and-So ; he does not leave me ; it is as though he was not dead ; at night I am always with him, and he vanishes when I awake. At length my bodily health is deranged ; he speaks about his children, his property, and many little matters.' Therefore at last they find a man who knows how to bar out

[1] Rev. C. Calloway, *The Religious System of the Amazulu* (Natal,   Capetown and London, 1868), p. 161.

that dream for her. He gives her medicine and
says, ' There is medicine. When you dream of
him and awake, chew it ; do not waste the spittle
which collects in your mouth while dreaming ; do
not spit it on the ground, but on this medicine, that
we may be able to bar out the dream.' Then the
doctor comes and asks if she has dreamt of her
husband ; she says she has. He asks if she has
done what he told her ; the woman says she has.
He asks whether she has spit on the medicine the
spittle that collected in her mouth while dreaming ;
she says she has. He says, ' Bring it to me then ;
and let us go together to the place where I will shut
him in'. The doctor treats the dream with medicines which cause darkness ; he does not treat it
with white medicines ; for among us black men we
say there are black and white *ubulawo* ; therefore
the doctor churns for the woman black *ubulawo*,
because the dream troubles her. So he goes with
her to a certain place to lay the *Itongo* ; perhaps he
shuts it up in a bulb of *inkomfe*.[1] The bulb has a
little hole made in its side, and the medicine mixed
with the dream-spittle is placed in the hole, and it is
closed with a stopper ; the bulb is dug up, and
placed in another hole, and the earth rammed
round it, that it may grow. He then leaves the
place with the woman, saying to her, ' Take care
that on no account you look back ; but look before
you constantly till you get home. I say the dream

---

[1] " *Inkomfe*, a bulbous plant, the leaves of which contain a strong fibre,
and are used for weaving ropes."

will never return to you, that you may be satisfied I am a doctor. You will be satisfied of that this day. If it returns, you may tell me at once.' And truly the dream, if treated by a doctor who knows how to bar the way against dreams, ceases. And even if the woman dreams of her husband, the dream does not come with daily importunity; she may dream of him occasionally only, but not constantly as at first. The people ask her for a few days after how she is. She replies, ' No, I have seen nothing since. Perhaps it will come again.' They say, ' Formerly was there ever a time when he did not come?' The woman says, ' There was not. There used to be not even one day when he did not come. I am still waiting to know whether he is really barred from returning.' The doctor prevails over the dead man as regards that dream; at length the woman, says ' O! So-and-So is a doctor. See, I no longer know anything of So-and-So's father. He has departed from me for ever.' Such then is the mode in which dreams are stopped."[1]

In America also the ghosts of dead husbands and wives have been much dreaded by the Indian tribes. Thus among the Delaware Indians a widow should not marry within a year of her husband's death, for the Indians say that he does not forsake her before that time, and then his soul goes to the land of spirits. During this year she must live by her own industry. She is not allowed to buy any meat, for the Indians think their guns

[1] Rev. Canon Calloway, *op. cit.* pp. 318 *sqq.*

would fail and shoot no deer if a widow should eat of the game they have killed. After the first year is over, the friends of her deceased husband clothe and provide for her and her children.[1] Among the Ojebway Indians, when a man has died, " it is often the custom for the widow, after the burial is over, to spring or leap over the grave, and then run zig-zag behind the trees, as if she were fleeing from someone. This is called running away from the spirit of her husband, that it may not haunt her. In the evening of the day on which the burial has taken place, when it begins to grow dark, the men fire off their guns through the hole left at the top of the wigwam. As soon as this firing ceases, the old women commence knocking and making such a rattling at the door as would frighten away any spirit that would dare to hover near. The next ceremony is, to cut into narrow strips, like ribbon, thin birch bark. These they fold into shapes, and hang round inside the wigwam, so that the least puff of wind will move them. With such scarecrows as these, what spirit would venture to disturb their slumbers ? "[2] Among the Menomonie Indians, if a widow contemplates a second marriage, she is careful not to look back at the grave of her first husband, but returns to her lodge by some devious and circuitous road. This she does, the Indians say, to prevent the ghost of her dead

[1] G. H. Loskiel, *History of the Mission of the United Brethren among the Indians of North America* (London, 1794), pp. 64 *sq.*

[2] Rev. Peter Jones, *History of the Ojebway Indians* (London, N.D.), pp. 99 *sq.*

husband following her. Sometimes the widow is accompanied by a person, who, walking behind her, flourishes a bundle of twigs over the widow's head, as if driving away flies. This is done, no doubt, to drive away the dead husband's ghost.[1]

Among many tribes of British Columbia the conduct of a widow and widower for a long time after the death of their spouse is regulated by a code of minute and burdensome restrictions, all of which appear to be based on the notion that these persons, being haunted by the ghost, are not only themselves in peril, but are also a source of danger to others. Thus among the Shushwap Indians of British Columbia widows and widowers fence their beds with thorn bushes to keep off the ghost of the deceased ; indeed they lie on such bushes, in order that the ghost may be under little temptation to share their bed of thorns. They must build a sweat-house on a creek, sweat there all night, and bathe regularly in the creek, after which they must rub their bodies with spruce branches. These branches may be used only once for this purpose; afterwards they are stuck in the ground all round about the hut, probably to fence off the ghost. The mourners must also use cups and cooking-vessels of their own, and they may not touch their own heads or bodies. Hunters may not go near them, and any person on whom their shadow were to fall would at once be ill.[2] Again among the Tsetsaut

---

[1] *Narrative of the Captivity and Adventures of John Tanner, during Thirty Years' Residence among the* *Indians* (London, 1830), p. 292.

[2] Franz Boas, in *Sixth Report on the North-Western Tribes of Canada,*

Indians, when a man dies his brother is bound to marry the widow, but he may not do so before the lapse of a certain time, because it is believed that the dead man's ghost haunts his widow and would do a mischief to his living rival. During the time of her mourning the widow eats out of a stone dish, carries a pebble in her mouth, and a crab-apple stick up the back of her jacket. She sits upright day and night. Any person who crosses the hut in front of her is a dead man. The restrictions laid on a widower are similar.[1] Among the Lkuñgen or Songish Indians, in Vancouver Island, widow or widower, after the death of husband or wife, are forbidden to cut their hair, as otherwise it is believed that they would gain too great power over the souls and welfare of others. They must remain alone at their fire for a long time, and are forbidden to mingle with other people. When they eat, nobody may see them. They must keep their faces covered for ten days. For two days after the burial they fast and are not allowed to speak. After that they may speak a little, but before addressing anyone they must go into the woods and clean themselves in ponds and with cedar branches. If they wish to harm an enemy they call out his name when they first break their fast, and they bite very hard in eating. That is believed to kill their enemy, probably (though this is not said) by directing the

p. 92 (*Report of the British Association for the Advancement of Science*, Leeds, 1890, separate reprint).

[1] Franz Boas, in *Tenth Report on the North-Western Tribes of Canada*, p. 45 (*Report of the British Association for the Advancement of Science*, Ipswich, 1895, separate reprint).

attention of the ghost to him. They may not go near the water or eat fresh salmon lest the fish might be driven away. They may not eat warm food, else their teeth would fall out.[1] Among the Bella Coola Indians the bed of a mourner is protected against the ghost of the deceased by thorn-bushes stuck into the ground at each corner. He rises early in the morning and goes out into the woods, where he makes a square with thorn-bushes, and inside of this square, where he is probably supposed to be safe from the intrusion of the ghost, he cleanses himself by rubbing his body with cedar-branches. He also swims in ponds, and after swimming he cleaves four small trees and creeps through the clefts, following the course of the sun. This he does on four subsequent mornings, cleaving new trees every day. We may surmise that the intention in creeping through the cleft trees is to give the slip to the ghost. The mourner also cuts his hair short, and the cut hair is burnt. If he did not observe these regulations, it is believed that he would dream of the deceased, which to the savage mind is another way of saying that he would be visited in sleep by his ghost. Amongst these Indians the rules of mourning for a widower or a widow are especially strict. For four days he or she must fast, and may not speak a word, else the dead wife or husband would come and lay a cold hand on the mouth of the offender, who would die. They may not go

[1] Franz Boas, in *Sixth Report on the North-Western Tribes of Canada,* pp. 23 *sq.* (*Report of the British* *Association for the Advancement of Science,* Leeds, 1890, separate reprint).

near water, and are forbidden to catch or eat salmon
for a whole year.   During that time also they may
not eat fresh herring or candle-fish (*olachen*).   Their
shadows are deemed unlucky, and may not fall on
any person.[1]

Among the Thompson Indians of British Columbia, widows or widowers, on the death of the
husbands or wives, went out at once and passed
through a patch of rose-bushes four times.   The
intention of this ceremony is not reported, but we
may conjecture that it was supposed to deter the
ghost from following for fear of scratching himself
or herself on the thorns.   For four days after the
death widows and widowers had to wander about at
evening or break of day wiping their eyes with fir-
twigs, which they hung up in the branches of trees,
praying to the Dawn.   They also rubbed their eyes
with a small stone taken from under running water,
then threw it away, while they prayed that they
might not become blind.   The first four days they
might not touch their food, but ate with sharp-
pointed sticks, and spat out the first four mouthfuls
of each meal, and the first four of water, into the fire.
For a year they had to sleep on a bed made of fir-
branches on which rose-bush sticks were also spread
at the foot, head and middle.   Many also wore a
few small twigs of rose-bush on their persons.   The
use of the rose-bush was no doubt to keep off
the ghost, through fear of the prickles.   They were

---

[1] Franz Boas, in *Seventh Report on the North-Western Tribes of Canada*, p. 13 (*Report of the British Association for the Advancement of Science*, Cardiff, 1891, separate re-print).

forbidden to eat fresh fish and flesh of any kind for a year. A widower might not fish at another man's fishing-place or with another man's net. If he did, it would make the station and the net useless for the season. If a widower transplanted a trout into another lake, before releasing it he blew on the head of the fish, and after chewing deer-fat he spat some of the grease out on its head, so as to remove the baneful effect of his touch. Then he let it go, bidding the fish farewell, and asking it to propagate its kind. Any grass or branches upon which a widow or widower sat or lay down withered up. If a widow were to break any sticks or branches, her own hands or arms would break. She might not cook food nor fetch water for her children, nor let them lie down on her bed, nor should she lie or sit where they slept. Some widows wore a breech-cloth made of dry bunch-grass for several days, lest the ghost of her dead husband should have connexion with her. A widower might not hunt or fish, because it was un-lucky both for him and for other hunters. He did not allow his shadow to pass in front of another widower or of any person who was supposed to be gifted with more knowledge or magic than ordinary.[1] Among the Lillooet Indians of British Columbia the rules enjoined on widows and widowers were somewhat similar. But a widower had to observe a singular custom in eating. He ate his food with the right hand passed underneath his right leg, the knee

[1] James Teit, "The Thompson Indians of British Columbia", pp. 332 sq. (The Jesup North Pacific Expedition, Memoir of the American Museum of Natural History, 1900).

of which was raised.[1] The motive for conveying
food to his mouth in this roundabout fashion is not
mentioned : we may conjecture that it was to baffle
the hungry ghost, who might be supposed to watch
every mouthful swallowed by the mourner, but who
could hardly suspect that food passed under the knee
was intended to reach the mouth.

Among the Kwakiutl Indians of British Columbia,
we are told, " the regulations referring to the mourning period are very severe. In case of the death of
husband or wife, the survivor has to observe the
following rule : for four days after the death the
survivor must sit motionless, the knees drawn up
toward the chin. On the third day all the inhabitants of the village, including children, must take a
bath. On the fourth day some water is heated in a
wooden kettle, and the widow or widower drips it
upon his head. When he becomes tired of sitting
motionless, and must move, he thinks of his enemy,
stretches his legs slowly four times, and draws them
up again. Then his enemy must die. During the
following sixteen days he must remain on the same
spot, but he may stretch out his legs. He is not
allowed, however, to move his hands. Nobody must
speak to him, and whosoever disobeys this command
will be punished by the death of one of his relatives.
Every fourth day he takes a bath. He is fed twice
a day by an old woman at the time of low water,
with salmon caught in the preceding year, and given

[1] James Teit, " The Lillooet
Indians " (Leyden and New York,
1906), p. 271 (The Jesup North   Pacific Expedition, Memoir of the
American Museum of Natural His-
tory).

to him in the dishes and spoons of the deceased. While sitting so, his mind is wandering to and fro. He sees his house and his friends as though far, far away. If in his visions he sees a man near by, the latter is sure to die at no distant day ; if he sees him very far away, he will continue to live long. After the sixteen days have passed he may lie down, but not stretch out. He takes a bath every eighth day. At the end of the first month he takes off his clothing, and dresses the stump of a tree with it. After another month has passed he may sit in a corner of the house, but for four months he must not mingle with others. He must not use the house door, but a separate door is cut for his use. Before he leaves the house for the first time he must three times approach the door and return, then he may leave the house. After ten months his hair is cut short, and after a year the mourning is at an end." [1]

Though the reasons for the elaborate restrictions thus imposed on widows and widowers by the Indians of British Columbia are not always stated, we may safely infer that, one and all, they are dictated by fear of the ghost of the deceased, who, haunting the surviving spouse, surrounds him or her with a dangerous atmosphere, a contagion of death, which necessitates his seclusion both from the people themselves and from the principal sources of their food supply, especially the fisheries, lest the infected person should poison them by his malignant presence.

[1] Franz Boas, in *Fifth Report on the North-Western Tribes of Canada*, pp. 43 *sq*. (*Report of the British Association for the Advancement of Science*, Newcastle-on-Tyne, 1889, separate reprint).

In Australia also the ghost of a dead husband is
sometimes said to haunt his widow for a certain
time after his death. Thus in the Unmatjera and
Kaitish tribes of Central Australia a widow's hair
is burnt off and she covers her body with ashes from
the camp fire, and keeps renewing them through the
whole time of her mourning. If she does not do this
the ghost (*atnirinja*) of her late husband, who constantly follows her about, will kill her and strip all
the flesh off her bones. In addition, her late husband's younger brother would be justified by tribal
custom in severely thrashing, or even killing her, if
during her period of mourning he were to meet
her without tokens of respect for her late husband's
spirit.[1]

VI. *Ghosts of the Unmarried and Childless Dead*

In primitive society adults who die unmarried
are regarded as unfortunate because they have
missed what is generally esteemed the crowning
blessing of life. It is thought that their ghosts are
therefore very unhappy in the spirit land : they
repine at their solitary lot, and may seek to repair
it either by finding a mate for themselves among the
living, or by appealing to their surviving friends to
furnish them with one. Thus in one way or another
the spirits of the unmarried dead may become very

---

[1] (Sir) Baldwin Spencer and F. J.   *Central Australia* (London, 1914),
Gillen, *The Northern Tribes of*   pp. 507 *sq.*

troublesome to the kinsfolk whom they have left on earth. To appease their importunate desires many peoples have resorted to a ceremony of posthumous marriage, either of the dead to the dead, or of the dead to the living, or of the dead to some substitute for a living mate.

The Fijians, for example, were strongly impressed with the notion of the unhappiness of the unmarried dead in the spirit land ; hence when a man died they used to strangle his widow in order that her spirit should attend him to the spirit land. " An excuse for the practice of widow-strangling may be found in the fact that, according to Fijian belief, it is a needful precautionary measure ; for at a certain place on the way to Mbulu (Hades) there lies in wait a terrible god called Nangga-nangga, who is utterly implacable towards the ghosts of the unmarried. He is especially ruthless towards bachelors, among whom he persists in classing all male ghosts who come to him unaccompanied by their wives. Turning a deaf ear to their protestations, he seizes them, lifts them above his head, and breaks them in two by dashing them down on a projecting rock. Hence it is absolutely necessary for a man to have at least one of his wives, or at all events a female ghost of some sort, following him.

" Women are let off more easily. If the wife die before her husband, the desolate widower cuts off his beard, and puts it under her left armpit. This serves as her certificate of marriage, and on her producing it to Nangga-nangga he allows her to pass."[1]

In Savoe, an island of the Indian Archipelago, the people marry very young, often when they are mere children. These early marriages are connected with the religious ideas of the people. For they think that the souls of those who die unmarried do not go to the spirit land, which is in Soemba. The Savoenese Charon, by name Ama Piga Laga, refuses to ferry unmarried persons over to the place where the dead live. Hence the souls of the unwedded dead are doomed to roam about Savoe. They run along the shore lamenting : rest and peace they never find.[2]

In Africa the Bavenda, a Bantu tribe of the Northern Transvaal, have a curious mode of providing the unhappy ghost of a dead bachelor with a substitute for a wife. The method has been described as follows : " There is one interesting rite in connexion with the spirit world that is still occasionally performed. There is a Tshivenda expression—'u lubumbukavha ? '—which has the same meaning as the English ' Are you daft ? ' or ' Are you all there ? ' This word lubumbukavha (simpleton), is also used to describe any young man above the age of puberty who dies before he has been given a wife ; he is a poor foolish fellow, having left the

[1] L. Fison, " Notes on Fijian Burial Customs ", in Journal of the Royal Anthropological Institute, x. (1881) p. 139.
[2] J. K. Wijngaarden, " De zede-lijke toestanden op Savoe ", in Mededeelingen van wege het Nederlandsche Zendelinggenootschap, xxxvi. (1892) p. 407.

world ignorant of the all-important subject of sex and parenthood, and dying before he has fulfilled the purpose for which he was born. If he is not pacified he may become a source of endless trouble to his lineage. So he is given an old used hoe-handle (*gulelwa*), with a cotton string tied near the hole, to symbolize a wife, the string being her waist-band and the hole the female genitalia. A girl, never the deceased man's sister, fixes this symbol at a fork in the path in a well-cleared open space where the young man's spirit can clearly see it, with the handle pointing towards him as he faces his old village. The handle is fixed with four pegs made of the *tshiralala* tree (from *uralala*, to wander about), or of the *tshilivhalo* (from *ulivhala*, to forget). Two are knocked into the ground on each side of the head and tied to it with a string made of wild cotton which has been treated with a mixture made from the roots of the *vhulivhadza* (from *u livhadza*, to make forget), and the *mpeta* (to dissolve or tie up), with powder from the hedgehog quill, *thoni* (bashfulness). These preparations, as can be seen by their names, are used to confuse the young man's spirit so that it will forget its anger, become bashful and ashamed, and run away before reaching the village. When the handle is properly fixed, a woman of the dead man's lineage, generally the *makhadzi* (father's sister), pours beer into the hole of the hoe, saying : ' To-day we have found you a wife ; the wife is here. Do not worry us any more. If you are annoyed with us, come here.' This ends the

ceremony, and the spirit of the young man is supposed to be satisfied for ever. A similar rite is, very
rarely, performed after the death of a girl dying
unmarried, having reached the age of puberty.
Such a girl is called *luphofu*, the blind one, as she
has died without any knowledge of sexual life. A
peg is driven through the hole in the hoe handle that
is provided for the comfort of her spirit, to symbolize
the male organ. The two rites are identical in all
else." [1]

Among the Wajagga of Mount Kilimanjaro in
East Africa, when an adult man dies unmarried
his family looks out for a woman whom they may
marry to his ghost in the spirit land. His father
goes to a man whose daughter has died unmarried,
and says to him, " Give me your dead daughter for
my dead son, who is alone ". The father of the
unmarried girl kills a goat, and brings the animal's
head to the father of the unmarried youth. The
father buries the animal's head as a symbol of the
maiden's head under the sepulchral monument, and
sets over it the three stones which are usually placed
on a woman's grave in reference to the stones of her
domestic hearth, at which the woman used to be
busied in her lifetime. In doing so he says to his
dead son, " To-day you have your marriage ". In
addition, the usual offerings are made to the dead.
If the father of the dead youth is poor, he pays only

[1] H. A. Stayt, *The Bavenda* (London, 1931), pp. 241 *sq.* Cf. Rev. E.
Gottschling, " The Bavenda, a
Sketch of their History and Customs ", in the *Journal of the Royal
Anthropological Institute*, xxxv.
(1905) p. 381.

a symbolical bride-price to the girl's father, by handing him a piece of wood, instead of the usual beer and the goat. After this marriage of the dead the father of the dead bride says, " Now I must help my daughter to cook ". He then brings small portions of food to the parents of the dead bridegroom, who are now deemed the parents-in-law of his dead daughter, and they eat the food which he brings them. Among rich people it sometimes happens that the father of the dead bachelor himself marries a living woman as a wife for his deceased son. The marriage is celebrated in the ordinary way, but without any mention of the dead man. But the wife is called the wife of the dead man. For example, if the father were called *Muro*, and the son were called *Nsau*, the bride is called the wife of *Nsau*, and any children she may have are called the children of *Nsau*. The first male child born to her is known by the name of his living father, as if the father were the grandfather of the infant, and the first-born female child is known by the name of her mother, as if she were her grandmother, in accordance with the custom of the Wajagga, who name first-born children after their grandparents and not after their parents. The present case is only an apparent exception to the rule that the name of a father has never been borne by his son.[1]

Among the Akamba, a Bantu tribe of Kenya, if a young unmarried man is killed away from his

[1] B. Gutmann, *Dichten und Denken der Dschagganeger* (Leipzig, 1909), pp. 81 *sq.* Cf. Hon. Chas. Dundas, *Kilimanjaro and its People* (London, 1924), pp. 249 *sq.*

village, his spirit (*muimu*) will return there and speak to the people through the medium of an old woman in a dance, and say, "I am So-and-So speaking, and I want a wife". The youth's father will then make arrangements to buy a girl from another village and bring her to his, and she will be called the wife of the deceased, speaking of him by name. She will presently be married to a brother of the dead man, but she must continue to live in the village where the deceased had his home. If at any time her living husband beats or ill-treats her, and she in consequence runs away to her father, the spirit of her dead husband will come and pester the people of the village and they will have bad luck. The ghost will probably ask, through the usual medium, why his wife has been ill-treated and driven away. The head of the family will then take steps to induce the girl to return for fear of the wrath of the spirit of his deceased son.[1]   Among the Shilluk, a tribe of the Upper Nile, if a chief or other distinguished man dies, after betrothal but before marriage, so that his relations might fear the vengeance of his dissatisfied ghost, the father of the betrothed girl takes her to the grave and marries her to the dead man. He says to the dead man, " Herewith I bring you my daughter, that you may marry her ". The bride is then considered to be related to all her dead husband's kinsfolk, but the relationship is not so strict as to exclude her subsequent marriage to a

[1] C. W. Hobley, " Further Researches into Kikuyu and Kamba Religious Beliefs and Customs ", in *Journal of the Royal Anthropological Institute*, xli. (1911) p. 422.

living man.   At her marriage to her dead husband
offerings are made to the spirits of many of her great
ancestors now deceased, just as they would be
entitled to receive them if they were still in life.
That is a right of the kinsfolk which they do not lose
even by death.[1]   Among the Dinkas, another tribe
of the Upper Nile, when an unmarried man dies his
brother must marry a woman especially to raise up
seed to the deceased.   Should he fail to do so his
dead brother's spirit would cause his living brother's
children to die, or prevent the birth of children if
none had been born already.   If a man has several
dead unmarried brothers he must take a wife for
each before he may take one for himself.[2]   A
similar custom prevails among the Nuer, another
tribe of the same region.   If an unmarried man dies
a wife must be found who will bear children to him
lest his spirit should be angry.[3]

The Baigas, a primitive Dravidian tribe of the
Central Provinces in India, think that the souls of
unmarried persons become malignant spirits (*bhuts*)
after death, and in that form haunt trees, while the
souls of the married dead dwell in streams.[4]   The
Bhats, another caste of the Central Provinces in
India, think that the spirit of a Brahman boy who
died unmarried will haunt any person who steps
over his grave in an impure condition or otherwise

[1] W. Hofmayr, *Die Shilluk* (St.
Gabriel bei Wien, 1925), p. 293.   Cf.
C. G. and B. Z. Seligman, *The Pagan
Tribes of the Nilotic Sudan* (London,
1932), pp. 68 *sq.*

[2] Seligman, *op. cit.* p. 164.
[3] Seligman, *op. cit.* p. 220.
[4] R. V. Russell, *The Tribes and
Castes of the Central Provinces of
India*, ii. 86.

defiles it, and when a man is haunted in such a manner it is called *Brahm laga*. Then an exorcist is called, who sprinkles water over the possessed man, and this burns the Brahm Deo or spirit inside him as if it were burning oil. The spirit cries out, and the exorcist orders him to leave the man. Then the spirit tells him how he has been injured by the man, and refuses to leave him. The exorcist asks the spirit what he requires on condition of leaving the man, and the spirit asks for some good food or something else, and is given it. Then the exorcist takes a nail and goes to a *pīpal* tree, and orders the spirit to go into the tree. The spirit obeys, and the exorcist drives the nail into the tree. After that the spirit remains imprisoned in the tree until somebody takes the nail out, whereupon he will come out of the tree and haunt the man who drew out the nail.[1] The Kirs, another caste of the Central Provinces in India, are of opinion that the souls of persons who die unmarried, or without children, are always prone to trouble their living kinsfolk.

To appease these unquiet spirits songs are sung in their praise on important festivals, the members of the family staying awake all night and wearing the images of the dead on silver pieces round their necks. When they eat and drink they first touch the food with the image by way of offering it to the dead, so that their spirits may be appeased and refrain from harassing the living.[2] We have already seen

[1] R. V. Russell, *op. cit.* ii. pp 266   [2] R. V. Russell, *op. cit.* iii. 483.
sq.

that, before the Sansia—another caste of the Central Provinces—sacrifice to the beneficent spirits of ancestors, they offer sacrifice to the spirits of the unmarried dead, lest these malignant beings should seize and defile the offerings made to the beneficent ancestors.[1] Among the Savars, a primitive tribe of the Central Provinces, if a person dies without a child a hole is made in a stone and his soul is conjured into it by a sorcerer (*gunia*). A few grains of rice are placed in the hole, and it is then closed with melted lead to imprison the ghost, and the stone is thrown into a stream, so that it may never be able to get out and trouble the family.[2] Among the Segidi, the Telugu caste of toddy-drawers and distillers in India, if an adult man dies unmarried, a ceremony of marriage is performed between the corpse and a plantain tree, and if an unmarried woman dies she is married to a sword.[3]

This custom of performing a marriage ceremony for the benefit of persons who died unmarried appears to be not uncommon in India, the intention being to satisfy and pacify the ghost of the deceased, and to prevent him from troubling the survivors with his importunate attentions. On this subject Mr. Abbott writes as follows : " One more form of mock marriage is the marriage of a dead person to a ruī-tree or branch. Brahmins do this when a *Brahmacari* " (a boy who has taken his thread ceremony) " dies before marriage ; *Lingāyats* perform

---

[1] See above, page 168.

[2] R. V. Russell, *op. cit.* iv. 507.

[3] *Central Provinces, Ethnographic* *Survey,* iv., Draft Articles on Tamil and Telugu Castes (Allahabad, 1907), p. 67.

this marriage both when a girl dies a virgin and when a man dies unmarried. When the deceased is a girl a male ruī is used, and a female tree when the deceased is a man. Sometimes the body is taken to a standing ruī-tree in the cremation ground; sometimes a twig of the tree is brought to the house where the dead body lies. The twig and the corpse are smeared with turmeric powder and covered with yellow clothes; the two are tied together with thread, *aksat* (unbroken rice) is thrown on them and sacrificial *hom* (fires) are performed. The tree after being uprooted or the twig is burnt and the obsequies for thirteen days are performed in the usual way. The basis of this form of mock marriage is the belief that anyone dying with unsatisfied desires returns to this world as a ghost in a vain attempt to satisfy his desires. This fear has created in India quite a number of dreaded ghosts." The dreaded ghost of a Brahman boy who has died unmarried is called *Munjā*.[1]

These ceremonies of mock marriage performed for the satisfaction of the ghosts of persons who have died unmarried appear to be particularly common in the south of India. Thus among the Gānigas, an oil-pressing class of the Canarese people, if a young man dies a bachelor, the corpse is married to an arka plant (*Calotropis gigantea*), and decorated with a wreath made of the flowers thereof.[2] Again among the Siviyar, when an adult person dies

---

[1] J. Abbott, *The Keys of Power* (London, 1932), pp. 291 *sq.*

[2] E. Thurston, *Castes and Tribes of Southern India* (Madras, 1909), ii. 267.

unmarried, the corpse is made to go through a mock
marriage with a human figure cut out of a palm leaf.[1]
So among the Vāniyan, oil-pressers among the
Tamils, if a man dies a bachelor, a mock ceremony
of marriage is performed for his benefit. The
corpse is wedded to the arka plant (*Calotropis
gigantea*), and decorated with a wreath made of the
flowers thereof.[2] Among the Kōmatis, the great
trading caste of the Madras Presidency, if a man
and woman have been living together and the man
dies unmarried his corpse is formally married to the
living woman. When the death has been announced
a priest is summoned and the ceremony proceeds.
It has been described as follows by an eye-witness :
" The dead body of the man was placed against the
outer wall of the verandah of the house in a sitting
posture, attired like a bridegroom, and the face and
hands besmeared with turmeric. The woman was
clothed like a bride, and adorned with the usual
tinsel ornament over the face, which, as well as
the arms, was daubed over with yellow. She sat
opposite the dead body, and spoke to it in light
unmeaning words, and then chewed bits of cocoanut
and squirted them on the face of the dead man.
This continued for hours, and not till near sunset
was the ceremony brought to a close. Then the
head of the corpse was bathed, and covered with a
cloth of silk, the face rubbed over with some red
powder, and betel leaves placed in the mouth. Now
she might consider herself married, and the funeral

<hr/>

[1] Thurston, *op. cit.* vi. 391.   [2] Thurston, vii. 315.

procession started." [1] Again among the Todas,
a primitive pastoral people of the Nīlgiri Hills in
Southern India, ceremonies of marriage are performed for the benefit of the ghosts of the unmarried
dead.   One such ceremony was witnessed by Mr.
Edgar Thurston, one of our best authorities on the
ethnology of Southern India.   He writes as follows :
" At the funeral of an unmarried Toda girl, which
I witnessed, the corpse was made to go through a
form of marriage ceremony.   A small boy, three
years old, was selected from among the relatives of
the dead girl, and taken by his father in search of a
grass and the twig of a shrub (*Sophora glauca*),
which were brought to the spot where the corpse
was lying.   The mother of the dead child then
withdrew one of its hands from the putkūli (cloth)
in which it was wrapped, and the boy placed the
grass and the twig in the hand, and limes, plantains,
rice, jaggery, honey-comb and butter in the pocket
of the putkūli, which was then stitched with needle
and thread.   The boy's father then took off his
son's putkūli, and covered him with it from head to
foot.   Thus covered, the boy remained outside the
hut till the morning of the morrow, watched through
the night by near relatives of himself and his
dead bride." [2]   Once more, among the Maravars, a
Dravidian tribe in the extreme south of India, if a
man and woman are too poor to afford the cost of
the complete marriage rites, they content themselves

[1] E.   Thurston, *Ethnographic Notes in Southern India* (Madras, 1906), p. 105.

[2] Thurston, *op. cit.* pp. 105 *sq.* Cf. W. H. R. Rivers, *The Todas* (London, 1906), pp. 391 *sqq*

with tying the *tāli* or marriage knot, and then
begin to cohabit. But the other ceremonies must be
performed at some time, or, as the phrase goes,
" the defect must be cured ". Should the husband
happen to die before he can afford to cure the defect,
his friends and kinsfolk will at once borrow money,
and the marriage will be duly completed in the
presence and on behalf of the corpse, which must be
placed on one seat with the woman, and made to
represent a bridegroom. The *tāli* is then taken off,
and the widow is free to marry again.[1]

Among the Chinese settled in Siam, if a young
man is betrothed to a girl and dies before marriage,
his betrothed may claim to be married to him, or
rather to the ancestral tablet which represents him
in the domestic shrine at his father's house. In such
a case the ceremony of marriage is the same as that
performed for a living bride and bridegroom.[2] In
China itself the marriage of the dead to each other
was practised by the Hak-ka, a native Chinese race
in the province of Canton. Among them if a boy
dies before his parents have had time to choose a
bride for him, they seek, among their neighbours
and friends, someone who has lost a daughter of the
same age. When they find what they want the
parents of both families meet and contract a solemn
matrimonial engagement in the name of their dead
children. The marriage ceremony is celebrated in
exactly the same way as it would be if the bride and

[1] Thurston, *op. cit.* p. 106.
[2] Mgr. Bruguière, in *Annales de*
l'Association de la Propagation de
la Foi, v. (1831) 185.

bridegroom were living and not dead. They think that thus they unite the spirits of the two children in a spiritual wedlock.[1]

But indeed this custom of marrying the dead to the dead, or the living to the dead, has been a national institution in China from antiquity down to modern times. It is entirely in harmony with that system of ancestor worship which forms the theoretical basis of Chinese society, for they think that the spirit of a man who has died unmarried and childless is not only unhappy in itself, but involves his family in the deepest misfortune and degradation by depriving them of anyone who can offer to their shades the things which they need for their happiness and welfare in the world beyond the grave.[2]

Evidence of the great antiquity of the custom in China has been adduced by the late J. J. M. De Groot in his classical work on the religious system of China. He writes: " The books of the Empire literally abound with passages which show that re-uniting women with their pre-deceased husbands in the grave has constantly prevailed in China as a regular custom. . . . Human immolations at burials naturally imply the prevalence of a conception that it is urgently necessary to be accompanied into the next life by a wife or concubines, to prevent one's being doomed there to the dreary life of a solitary widower. Consequently, it is only natural that in ancient China there existed the curious custom of

[1] Dr. Eitel, " Les Hak-Ka ", trans. by M. G. Dumoutier, in *L'Anthropologie*, v. (1893) 175.

[2] E. Westermarck, *The Origin and Development of the Moral Ideas*, ii. 400.

placing deceased females in the tombs of lads who had died before they were married. The prevalence in those times of such *post-mortem* weddings for the next world is revealed to us by the following passage in the *Cheu li* : ' The Officer charged with the Preparation of Marriages is to prevent women already buried from being transferred to other tombs, to be thus given in marriage to deceased minor youths '. The legislators of the time, disliking the sacrilegious removal of women from their graves, deemed themselves in duty bound to forbid the practice in question ; but they do not appear to have included in their veto such marrying of deceased women at the time of their burial. The latter weddings may *a fortiori* be supposed to have been very common ; and that they were firmly rooted in the then customs and manners of the people may be inferred from the fact that they have prevailed ever since, being frequently mentioned in the books of all ages. This point is of sufficient interest to deserve illustration by a short series of quotations.

" In the Memoirs of the Three Kingdoms we read : ' The daughter of Ping Yuen died when still young, at the same time as Ts'ang-shu, the favourite son of the Emperor T'ai Tsu (A.D. 220–227), breathed his last. The Emperor tried to have them buried in the same grave, but Yuen refused his consent, saying that such burials were not recognized by the laws of morals. Therefore the deceased prince was betrothed to a deceased daughter of the family Chen, and she was placed with him in the same grave.

And when Shuh, the young daughter of the emperor
Ming of the same dynasty (A.D. 227–239), had died,
he buried together with her one Hwang, a grandson
of the brother of the empress Chen, conferred the
posthumous title of Imperial Prince upon him, and
appointed for him a Continuator with the hereditary
rank of a noble.' This event becomes all the more
curious when we are told that this Hwang was a
mere baby. It is in fact stated in the Standard
Annals of that time that the magnate Ch'en Khiün
rebuked the emperor for having the obsequies of
this child, though not a year old, conducted with
the same ceremonies as appertained to up-grown
people. *Post-mortem* marriages in those times being
concluded even in the Imperial family, and between
infants so very young, we may safely draw the conclusion that they were the order of the day between
adults among the people.

" To convince our readers that such marriages
were of frequent occurrence in ensuing ages, we
need not make a large number of quotations. A
couple of instances, drawn from the Imperial court-
life, will suffice. ' P'ing Ch'ing, son of Muh Ch'ung,
died when he was still young. During the reign
of Hiao Wen (A.D. 471–499), the Imperial princess
Shi-p'ing died in the Palace. The posthumous
dignity of Prince Consort was then conferred upon
P'ing-Ch'ing, and he was united with the Princess
in marriage for the World of Shades.' Three
centuries afterwards ' the Imperial concubine Wei
caused her deceased younger brother Siün, after the

dignity of Prince of Jü-nan had been conferred upon
him, to be united in marriage for the next life with
a deceased daughter of (Siao) Chi-chung, and she
had them buried together in one grave. But after
this lady Wei had been defeated (in an attempt to
usurp the throne), Chi-chung opened the grave,
took his daughter's coffin out of it and brought it
home ', thus showing that the ties of relationship
with a traitress to the cause of lawful government
were cut off by him.

" An interesting account of the manner in which
such *post-mortem* marriages were concluded at a
period when the Sung dynasty governed the Empire,
is given by a contemporary work in the following
words : ' In the northern parts of the Realm it is
customary, when an unmarried youth and an unmarried girl breathe their last, that the two families
each charge a match-maker to demand the other
party in marriage. Such go-betweens are called :
match-makers for disembodied souls. They ac-
quaint the two families with each other's circumstances, and then cast lots for the marriage by order
of the parents on both sides. If they augur that
the union will be a happy one, (wedding) garments
for the next world are cut out and the match-makers
repair to the grave of the lad, there to set out wine
and fruit for the consummation of the marriage.
Two seats are placed side by side, and a small
streamer is set up near each seat. If these streamers
move a little after the libation has been performed,
the souls are believed to approach each other ; but

if one of them does not move, the party represented
thereby is considered to disapprove of the marriage.
Each family has to reward its match-maker with a
present of woven stuffs. Such go-betweens make
a regular livelihood out of these proceedings. . . .'
    " The following instance of a marriage between
deceased persons, which occurred in the fourteenth
century, must not be passed unnoticed, because it
proves more clearly than any other case on record
that in times relatively modern the old conception
still obtained that a wife's place is at the side of her
deceased husband in the life hereafter, and that she
may not suffer another woman to occupy her place
there. ' Madam Yang was a native of Sü-ch'ing in
Tung-p'ing (province of Shantung). Her husband
Kwoh San marched off from Siang Yang with the
army, and she, being left behind, served her parents-
in-law so perfectly that she obtained a great repute
for filial devotion. In the sixth year of the period
Chiyuen (A.D. 1340) her husband died in his garrison.
Then her own mother laid schemes for taking her
home and marrying her again, but, bitterly wailing,
she took such an oath that these schemes were not
carried out. After some time, when the mortal
remains of her husband were brought home, her
father-in-law said : ' She, having been married to
him only a short time, and being still young, will
certainly marry again in the end ; ought I to leave
my son under the ground in a state of loneliness ? '
But when he was on the point of requesting a fellow
villager to give him the bones of his deceased

daughter, that he might bury them in the same grave with his son, Madam Yang being informed of his project became still more overwhelmed by grief, and refused all food. Five days afterwards she hung herself, upon which she was buried with her husband in the same grave. . . .

" Yang Yung-siu, an author who lived under the Ming dynasty, asserts that the custom of uniting dead persons in marriage was prevalent in his time. ' Nowadays ', he writes, ' it is still practised among the people, and it is not forbidden by anybody or anything. Consequently such marriages must have prevailed under former dynasties.' Whether the custom still exists at the present time we are not able to say, as no case has come under our notice whilst in China. But, considering that it has flourished for so many ages, we can scarcely believe it has entirely died out even now." [1]

That the custom of marrying the dead to the dead in China persisted in full blast down to the second half of the nineteenth century we know from the evidence of the Rev. J. H. Gray, Archdeacon of Hongkong, who personally witnessed the ceremony and described it as follows : " One other marriage custom, as absurd as it is wicked, remains to be noted. In China, not merely the living are married, but the dead also. Thus the spirits of all males who die in infancy or in boyhood are in due course of time married to the spirits of females who have been

---

[1] J. J. M. De Groot, *The Religious System of China* (Leyden, 1894), vol. ii. Book I., pp. 802-806.

cut off at a like early age. If a youth of twelve years
dies, it is customary when he has been dead six or
seven years for his parents to seek to unite his spirit
in wedlock with that of a girl whose birth and death
corresponded in point of time with those of their son.
For this purpose application is made to a go-between,
and when a selection has been made from this func-
tionary's list of deceased maidens, an astrologer is
consulted. When the astrologer, having cast the
horoscopes of the two departed spirits, has pronounced the selection judicious, a lucky night is set
apart for the solemnization of the marriage. On
that night, a paper figure representing a bridegroom
in full marriage costume is placed in the ceremonial
hall of his parents' house ; and at nine o'clock, or
in some instances later, a bridal chair, which is
sometimes made of a rattan-frame covered with
paper, is despatched in the name of the spirit of the
youth to the house of the parents of the deceased
girl, with a request that they will be so good as to
allow the spirit of their daughter to seat itself therein
for the purpose of being conveyed to her new home.
As one of the three souls of which the body of a
Chinese is supposed to be possessed, is said after
death to remain with the ancestral tablet, the tablet
bearing the name of the girl is removed from the
ancestral altar and placed in the bridal chair, where
it is supplemented by a paper figure meant to represent the bride. The bridal procession is headed
by two musicians, one of whom plays upon a lute
and the other upon a tom-tom, and sometimes the

wearing apparel which belonged to the deceased girl, and which for the future is to be in the keeping of the parents of the departed youth, is carried in it. On the arrival of the procession, the tablet and the effigy are removed from the bridal chair, and placed, the former on the ancestral altar, and the latter on a chair close to that occupied by the effigy of the bridegroom. A table covered with various kinds of viands is placed before the effigies, while five or six priests of Taou are engaged in chanting prayers to the spirits, calling upon them to receive one another as husband and wife, and to partake of the wedding repast. At the close of this ceremony the effigies are burned, together with a great quantity of paper clothes, paper money, paper man-servants and maid-servants, fans, tobacco-pipes, and sedan chairs. I was once present at such a ceremony. It took place at the house of a China friend named Cha Kum-hoi, who resided in the Kwong-ga-lee street of the western suburb of Canton. The immediate occasion of this marriage was, it so happened, the illness of this gentleman's wife, which was attributed by the geomancer or fortune-teller to the angry spirit of her son, who was importunate to be married. A matrimonial engagement was therefore immediately entered into on behalf of the deceased son, and was solemnized as I have described it." [1]

The latest notice of a marriage of the dead in China which I have met with dates from 1891. It runs as follows: " A writer in the *North China*

[1] J. H. Gray, *China* (London, 1878), i. pp. 216 *sqq.*

Daily News records a case of something like a *post-mortem* marriage, in which a Chinese girl, recently deceased, was married to a dead boy in another village. ' It not unfrequently happens ', he explains, ' that the son in the family dies before he is married, and that it is desirable to adopt a grandson. The family cast about for some young girl who has also died recently, and a proposition is made for the union of the two corpses in the bonds of matrimony. If it is accepted, there is a combination of a wedding and a funeral, in the process of which the deceased bride is taken by a large number of bearers to the cemetery of the other family and laid beside her husband.' "[1]

A similar custom of marrying the dead to the dead prevailed among the Tartars, and has been described by Marco Polo as follows : " If any man have a daughter who dies before marriage, and another man have had a son also die before marriage, the parents of the two arrange a grand wedding between the dead lad and lass. And marry them they do, making a regular contract ! And when the contract papers are made out they put them in the fire, in order (as they will have it) that the parties in the other world will know the fact, and look on each other as man and wife. And the parents thenceforward consider themselves sib to each other just as if their children had lived and married. Whatever may be agreed on between the parties as dowry, those who have to pay it cause to be painted on pieces of paper and then put these in the fire, saying that in that way the dead person will get all the real articles in the other world." [1]   The same custom is also vouched for the Tartars by Alexander Guagninus.[2]

Among the Ingush of the Caucasus when a man's son dies another man whose daughter is dead will go to him and say, " Your son may need a wife in the other world, I will give him my daughter.   Pay me the price of the bride."   Such an obliging offer is never refused, though the price of a bride is some- times as much as thirty cows.[3]

A similar custom of marriages contracted for the benefit of the dead has been known, and to a limited extent appears still to survive, among some Slav peoples.   On this subject Mr. Ralston writes as follows :   " Strongly impressed with the idea that those whom the nuptial bond had united in this world were destined also to live together in the world to come, they so sincerely pitied the lot of the un- married dead, that, before committing their bodies to the grave, they were in the habit of finding them partners for eternity.   The fact that, among some Slavonian peoples, if a man died a bachelor a wife

---

[1] Marco Polo, translated by Col. H. Yule, Second Edition (London, 1875), i. 259 *sq.*

[2] " De Religione Muscovitarum omniumque Ruthenorum ", printed in *De Russorum, Muscovitarum, et Tartarorum religione, sacrificiis, nuptiarum, funerum ritu* (Spirae

libera civitate, 1582), p. 253.

[3] J. von Klaproth, *Reise in den Kaukasus und nach Gorgien,* i. 616 *sq* ; Potocki, *Voyage dans les Steps d'Astrakhan et du Caucase* (Paris, 1829), i. 127 (who, however, merely copies Klaproth).

was allotted to him after his death rests on the
authority of several witnesses, and in a modified
form the practice has been retained in some places
up to the present day. In Little Russia, for instance, a dead maiden is dressed in nuptial attire,
and friends come to her funeral as to a wedding,
and a similar custom is observed on the death of a
lad. In Podolia, also, a young girl's funeral is
conducted after the fashion of a wedding, a youth
being chosen as the bridegroom who attends her to
the grave, with the nuptial kerchief twined around
his arm. From that time her family consider him
their relative, and the rest of the community look
upon him as a widower. In some parts of Servia,
when a lad dies, a girl dressed as a bride follows him
to the tomb, carrying two crowns ; one of these is
thrown to the corpse, and the other she keeps, at
least for a time.[1]

It was an ancient Greek custom to place on the
tombs of all unmarried persons, whether male or
female, a pitcher of a peculiar shape called the "bath-
bearer " (*loutrophoros*). Examples of such pitchers
have been found. In shape they are tall and
slender, with a high neck and high handles on either
side. Some of the ancient interpreters, who wrote
after the custom had fallen into disuse, supposed
that the " bath-bearers " placed on the tombs of
the unmarried were figures of boys or girls carrying
such pitchers ;[2] but archaeological discoveries have

[1] W. R. S. Ralston, *The Songs of the Russian People* (London, 1872), pp. 309 *sq*.

[2] Harpocration and Suidas, *s.v.* " λουτρόφορος " : Pollux, viii. 66.

confirmed the view of Eustathius in his great commentary on Homer [1] that it was the pitcher itself,
or at all events a representation of it carved in relief,
which was thus used to mark the graves of maids
and bachelors. The intention was, according to
Eustathius, to intimate that the person on whose
grave one of these pitchers stood had never enjoyed
the bath which a Greek bride and bridegroom took
on their wedding day, and for which the water was
fetched from a special spring by a boy who was a
near kinsman. [2] It may be suggested that the
custom of placing such a pitcher, so intimately connected with marriage, on the grave of an unmarried
person, was originally part of a ceremony designed
to provide his or her spirit with a spouse in the spirit
land, by means of a marriage ceremony, like that
which we have seen celebrated for the same purpose
by so many peoples in so many lands. [3]

VII. *Ghosts of the Unburied Dead*

In primitive society it is generally believed that
the soul of a recently deceased person is much concerned with the disposal of his mortal remains. He
desires that his surviving relatives should treat
them with all due respect, by interring or otherwise
disposing of them in the traditional manner, includ-

[1] Eustathius, *Commentary on Homer*, *Iliad*, p. 1293, referring to *Iliad* xxiii. 141.

[2] Harpocration and Suidas, *loc. cit.*, Photius, *Lexicon, s.v.* " λουτρά ": Pollux, iii. 43, who may be wrong in saying that the water was fetched by a girl.

[3] Cf. my commentary on Pausanias, Book X. chapter xxxi. 9 (vol. v. pp. 388 *sqq.*).

ing the performance of rites intended to please and
satisfy the ghost.   If this satisfaction is not accorded
to him his spirit is perturbed and dissatisfied, and
may visit his displeasure on his undutiful kinsfolk.
Every effort therefore is made by the survivors to
find the mortal remains and to lay them to rest with
every mark of reverence and honour.   But sometimes the body cannot be found, as for example
when a person has been drowned at sea, or devoured
by wild beasts in the forest, or has furnished the
materials of a cannibal feast to his enemies in war.
In all such cases the ghost is supposed still to claim
his satisfaction, and to meet his imperious desires
his friends have recourse to a simple device : they
make an effigy of him, or try to find some personal
relic of his, and over the one or the other they perform all the funeral rites just as if the substitute were
the real body of the deceased.   This is thought fully
to satisfy the desires of the ghost, who accordingly
leaves the survivors in peace.

Thus among the Maoris of New Zealand, when
a chief was killed in battle, and his body eaten by
his foes, his spirit was supposed to enter the stones
of the oven with which his body had been cooked,
which retained their heat so long as it remained in
them.   His friends repeated their most powerful
spells to draw his spirit out of the stones, and bring
it within the sacred grove (*wahi tapu*), for it was
thought that otherwise it could not rest, but would
wander about inflicting injury upon the living, all
spirits being considered maliciously inclined towards

the survivors. So when any were slain in battle, if the body could not be obtained, the friends endeavoured to procure some of the blood, or fragments of their garments, over which they uttered their spells (*karakia*), and thus brought the wandering soul within this spiritual fold. These places are still looked upon with much fear, as the spirits are thought occasionally to wander from them and cause sickness.[1]

Of the natives of Samoa we are told that the unburied dead caused great concern. " No Roman was ever more grieved at the thought of his unburied friend wandering a hundred years along the banks of the Styx than were the Samoans while they thought of the spirit of one who had been drowned, or of another who had fallen in war, wandering about neglected and comfortless. They supposed the spirit haunted them everywhere, night and day, and imagined they heard it calling upon them in a most pitiful tone, and saying, ' Oh, how cold ! oh, how cold ! ' Nor were the Samoans, like the ancient Romans, satisfied with a mere *tumulus inanis* at which to observe the usual solemnities ; they thought it was possible to obtain the soul of the departed in some tangible transmigrated form. On the beach, near where a person had been drowned, and whose body was supposed to have become a porpoise, or on the battlefield, where another fell, might have been seen, sitting in silence, a group of

[1] Rev. R. Taylor, *New Zealand and its Inhabitants* (London. 1870), p. 221.

five or six, and one a few yards before them with a sheet of native cloth spread out on the ground in front of him. Addressing some god of the family he said, ' Oh, be kind to us ; let us obtain without difficulty the spirit of the young man ! ' The first thing that happened to light upon the sheet was supposed to be the spirit. If nothing came it was supposed that the spirit had some ill-will to the person praying. That person after a time retired, and another stepped forward, addressed some other god, and awaited the result. By and by something came ; grasshopper, butterfly, ant or whatever else it might be, it was carefully wrapped up, taken to the family, the friends assembled, and the bundle buried with all due ceremony, as if it contained the real spirit of the departed." [1]

The Nufoors of Dutch New Guinea make wooden images (*korwar*) of their dead, conjure the spirits of the deceased into them, and then preserve the images in their houses, and consult the inspired images from time to time as oracles. In general they make images only of persons who have died at home. But in the island of Ron such images are also made of persons who have died away from home or have fallen in battle. In such cases the difficulty is to compel the soul to quit its mortal remains far away and come to animate the image. However, the natives of Ron have found means to

---

[1] G. Turner, *Samoa a Hundred Years Ago and Long Before* (London, 1884), 150 *sq.* Cf. Rev. S. Ella, " Samoa ", in *Report of the* *Australasian Association for the Advancement of Science*, Hobart (1892), p. 641, who substantially repeats Turner's account.

overcome this difficulty. They first carve the
wooden image of the dead person and then call his
soul back to the village by setting a great tree on
fire, while the family assemble round it, and one of
them, holding the image in his hand, acts the part
of medium, shivering and shaking and falling into
a trance after the approved fashion of mediums in
many lands. After this ceremony the image is
supposed to be animated by the soul of the deceased,
and it is kept in the house with as much confidence
as any other.[1]

Among the Galelareese of Halmahera, an island
to the west of New Guinea, when some one dies away
from home, in a foreign land, as soon as the relations
get news of the death they shear their hair and bathe
as soon as possible, undertaking at the same time
all the obligations incidental to mourning. They
now consult whether to celebrate the death-feast at
once, or to wait until the bones of the deceased have
been brought back from the foreign land. If they
decide to celebrate it at once, they make ready and
decorate a mourning chamber in the house, and
there on the sleeping bench they lay, instead of
the corpse, a puppet (*gari*) into which the soul of
the deceased has been temporarily conjured by the
seers. After that the usual death-feast takes place.
The ceremony of decorating the grave is usually
deferred until the bones have been brought back

[1] F. S. A. de Clercq, " De Wes-
ten Noordkust van Nederlandsch
Nieuw-Guinea ", in *Tijdschrift van
het Kon. Nederlandsch Aardrijks-*
kundig Genootschap, 2de Serie, x.
(1893), p. 621. As to these images
of the dead (*korwar*), see *Belief in*
Immortality, i. pp. 309 *sqq.*

from abroad.[1] In the district of Tobelo in North
Halmahera, when men who are famous for their
bravery die elsewhere and it is desired to secure
their souls for the village, a symbolical burial takes
place for the purpose of making the soul to stay in
the neighbourhood of the dwelling. For this purpose a puppet is made with a peeled coconut for
a head, a pillow for a body, and long rolled-up leaves
for limbs. This puppet is placed either on a hurdle
in the chief house of the village or in the little soul-
house (*goma ma-taoe*), and a funeral banquet is held
for four days. Then the puppet is wrapped in a
mat and buried. That the soothsayer conjures the
soul into the puppet is not expressly stated by our
authority, but is highly probable.[2] The Alfoors of
Poso in Central Celebes make offerings for the
spirits of persons who have been drowned or devoured by crocodiles, and whose bodies consequently
have not been found. In such cases the Tolage of
the same region make a wooden image (*pemia*) of the
missing person, which serves as a substitute for the
body. The Popebats do not make such images :
they only think of the missing person at the festival.
As to persons whose heads have been carried off by
enemies in a raid, some tribes replace the missing
articles with coconuts, others celebrate the festival
over the headless bodies.[3]

[1] M. J. van Baarda, " Een apo-
logie voor de Dooden ", in *Bijdragen
tot de Taal- Land- en Volkenkunde
van Nederlandsch-Indië*, lxix. (The
Hague, 1914), pp. 86 *sq.*
[2] F. S. A. de Clercq, " Dodadi

Ma-Taoe en Goma Ma-Taoe, of
Zielenhuisjes in het district Tobelo
op Noord-halmahera ", in *Internationales Archiv für Ethnographie*,
ii. (1889), p. 211.
[3] A. C. Kruit, " Een en ander

Among the Ibans or Dyaks of Sarawak in Borneo, in the case of persons who die far away from home, as soon as the news of the death arrives at the village the clothes, ornaments, and other articles of the deceased are heaped together in the *Ruai* (common room) and covered over with a blanket so as to represent a corpse laid out. This is called the *Rapoh* and all the usual mortuary rites are performed for the simulated corpse, just as if it were the body of the deceased. In the early morning this simulated corpse is taken to the burial ground, and the articles of dress are hung about among the trees.[1] In Bali, a small island to the north of Java, when the body of a deceased person cannot be found his friends make an image of him out of wood or the leaves of a certain tree, and celebrate the mortuary rites over it, instead of over the actual corpse.[2]

The Annamites believe that when a tiger has taken a man, the soul of the deceased rides on the animal's back and guides him back to his house, where he hopes to find offerings. To prevent this the people are very careful, as soon as anybody has been carried off by a tiger, to go in search of his remains. When they find any part of the corpse, or merely his turban or tobacco pouch, they make paper effigies of the tiger and the man, burn them,

aangaande het geestelijk en maatschappelijk leven van den Poso Alfoer ", in *Mededeelingen van wege het Nederlandsche Zendelinggenootschap*, xxxix. (1895), p. 32.

[1] L. Nyuak, " Religious Rites and Customs of the Iban or Dyaks of Sarawak ", translated by Rev. E. Dunn in *Anthropos*, i. (1906), p. 171.

[2] G. A. Wilken, " Het Animisme bij de Volken van den Indischen Archipel ", in *De Verspreide Geschriften van G. A. Wilken* (The Hague, 1912), iii. pp. 61 *sq.*

and carefully bury all the remains they have discovered.   The soul of the deceased, which had been
supposed to inhabit the tiger, now passes into the
grave, and his family sleeps quiet.[1]

Among the Black Taï, a tribe of mountaineers in
Tonkin, when the body of a deceased relative cannot
be found, as may happen after a battle, they collect
some articles that belonged to him, and with these as
representatives of the dead man they proceed to the
ceremony of cremation, and to the erection of a tomb,
just as if they were in possession of the corpse.[2]

Among the Red Karens of Burma, when a man
dies far from home and the body cannot be found,
the funeral cannot take place until the spirit of the deceased has been recalled and has given his consent.
The usual feast is held at home, and in the centre
of the room hangs a bullock bell suspended from the
roof.   Dancing and beating of gongs goes on until
the spirit announces his arrival and approval by
tinkling the bullock-bell.   If the spirit delays his
coming guns are fired to hasten and guide him on
his way.   He never fails to arrive sooner or later.
At the man's house the whole ceremony of funeral
is gone through.   An effigy made of straw and cloth
is placed in the coffin to represent the body of the
deceased and the usual rites are performed as if this
were the actual corpse.[3]

[1] R. P. Cadière, " Croyances et
Dictons populaires de la Vallée du
Nguôn-son, Province de Quang-binh
(Annam) ", in *Bulletin de l'École
Française d'Extrême-Orient*, i. (1901,
Hanoi), pp. 135 *sq.*

[2] Col. E. Diguet, *Les Monta-
gnards du Tonkin* (Paris, 1908), p. 89.
[3] J. G. Scott and J. P. Hardiman,
*Gazetteer of Upper Burma and the
Shan States* (Rangoon, 1900), Part
I, vol. i. p. 528.   In this passage the

Among the Khasis of North-Eastern India, if a man dies far from home, for example in a foreign country, whose body has not been burnt in accordance with custom, and whose bones have not been collected, the members of his clan, or his children, take three or five seeds or cowries (*sbai*) to a place where three roads meet. Here they summon the spirit of the departed in a loud voice, and throw up the seeds or cowries into the air, and when they fall to the ground they say, " Come, now, we will collect you " (the idea being that the seeds represent the bones of the deceased). Having collected the seeds, they place them on a bier and perform the service for the dead just in the same way as if a real corpse were to hand. If possible a portion of the dead person's clothes should be burned with the seeds in the bier, and it is for this reason that the coats or cloths of Khasi coolies, who die when employed as porters on military expeditions at a distance from their homes, are brought back by their friends to give to the relatives.[1]   According to another account in such a case the Khasis look in the direction of the place in which the dead man died, and call upon his spirit to come back and enter a shell, which is then burned instead of the body, or if they know exactly the place where the man died they go thither, and on their return they scatter leaves on the path to guide the spirit of the deceased back to his home, and they stretch strings over streams to help the

writers speak of " The guardian spirit of the deceased ", but the real reference seems to be to the dead man's spirit or ghost.

[1] Lt.-Col. P. R. T. Gurdon, *The Khasis* (London, 1914), pp. 136 *sq.*

returning soul to cross the water.[1]   In other parts
of India the custom of burning or burying an effigy
to represent a deceased person when his body cannot
be found appears to be both ancient and widespread.
Thus, for example, "the Garuḍa-purāṇa directs that
if a man dies in a remote place, or is killed by
robbers in a forest and his body is not found, his son
should make an effigy of the deceased with Kuśa
grass and then burn it on a funeral pile with similar
ceremonies ".[2]   According to another account in
such a case the effigy should be made of 360 leaves
of the *Butea frondosa* and as many threads, to represent the members of the body, and having been
smeared with meal it was burned on a pyre.[3]   An
ancient Indian book of ritual, the *Grihya Sûtra*,
ordained that when the corpse could not be found,
360 stems of *Palâsa* should be wrapped up in a black
goat-skin, such as was regularly spread under the
corpse on the pyre, and the rest of the funeral ceremonies performed as if the corpse were present.[4]
Other ancient Indian texts direct that when the body
of a long-deceased person could not be found, but
the place of his death was known, some dust should
be gathered from the spot, or a garment should be
spread out on the bank of a stream, and the name

[1] A. Bastian, " Hügelstämme As-
sams ", in *Verhandlungen der Berliner Gesellschaft für Anthropologie*
(1881), p. 150.
[2] Monier Williams, *Religious
Thought and Life in India* (London,
1883), p. 300.
[3] A. Bastian, *Die Völker des oest-*

lichen Asien, vi. 12 n. referring to
Colebrooke.

[4] Max Müller, " Die Todten-
bestattung bei den Brahmanen ", in
*Zeitschrift der deutschen morgen-
ländischen Gesellschaft*, ix. Abhang,
p. xxxvi.

of the deceased called out. After such an invocation any animal or insect that lighted on the garment was to be treated as if it were the corpse itself.[1] This ancient Indian rite closely resembles the custom which, as we have seen, the Samoans were wont to observe in similar cases. In modern India, when a person is drowned and his body cannot be found, a rite known as Palasvidhi is performed. An effigy of the deceased is made, in which twigs of the Palâsa tree represent the bones, a coconut or Bel fruit the head, pearls or cowrie shells the eyes, and a piece of birch bark or the skin of a deer the cuticle. It is then filled up with Urad pulse instead of flesh and blood, and a presiding priest recites a spell to bring life into the image, which is symbolized by putting a lighted lamp close to the head. When the light goes out, life is believed to be extinct and the funeral rites are performed in the regular way, the only exception being that the period of impurity for the mourners lasts for three instead of ten days.[2] Among the Sunār, a caste of goldsmiths and silversmiths in the Central Provinces of India, when a man has died a violent death and his body cannot be found, they construct a small image of him and burn it with all the ceremonies usually observed at a regular cremation.[3] In the Himalayan districts of the North-West Provinces of India, when a father dies in a strange land and his relatives cannot find

[1] H. Oldenberg, *Die Religion des Veda* (Berlin, 1894), p. 581.
[2] W. Crooke, *The Popular Religion and Folklore of Northern India*, ii. 114.
[3] R. V. Russell, *The Tribes and Castes of the Central Provinces of India*, iv. 521.

his body to perform the usual rites, a ceremony called *náráyana-bali* is observed. A figure of the deceased is made of the reed *kans* and placed on a funeral pyre and burned with the dedication that the deceased may not be without funeral rites.[1]

In China the custom of burying an effigy instead of the corpse when the body cannot be found is ancient and apparently universal. " During the reign of the emperor Chan-tuk, in the first century of the Christian era, it was enacted that if the bodies of soldiers who fall in battle, or those of sailors who fall in naval engagements, cannot be recovered, the spirits of such men shall be called back by prayers and incantations, and that figures shall be made either of paper or of wood for their reception, and be buried with all the ordinary rites.   It is recorded in the annals of China, that the first persons who conformed to this singular enactment were the sons of an officer named Lee Hoo, who fell in battle and whose body could not be recovered. The custom is now universally observed."[2]   " In case the corpse is not brought home to be buried, a letter, or some of the clothing recently worn by the deceased, or his shoes, or part of his baggage, is often sent home instead. The white cock and the mourners go forth to meet the departed just as they would go to

---

[1] E. T. Atkinson, *The Himalayan Districts of the North-Western Provinces of India* (Allahabad, 1884), ii. 932.   For a fuller account of the rite, see E. T. Atkinson, " Notes on the History of Religion in the Himalaya of the N.W. Provinces ", in *Journal of the Asiatic Society of Bengal*, liv. (1885), p. 14.

[2] J. H. Gray, *China*, i. pp. 295 *sq.* On this custom, with the evidence for its antiquity, see J. J. M. De Groot, *The Religious System of China*, vol. iii. Book I, pp. 847 *sqq.*

meet the corpse.   On meeting the letter or the relic, the spirit passes as readily into the fowl as it would pass into it were the corpse itself met, and the spirit is conducted home just as surely." [1]   Archdeacon Gray witnessed one of these ceremonies of burial in effigy, and he has described it as follows.   " On the occasion of a visit which I paid to Tai-laak, the capital of the ninety-six villages, I had the opportunity of seeing so singular a ceremony.   An effigy of the missing man, clad in robes of the most costly kind, was placed on the ground, and a number of men and women, dressed in deep mourning, knelt round it.   In the centre of the circle a Taouist priest invoked the spirit to come to the body prepared for it, and accompany it to the tomb.   Lest the souls of the deceased should be imprisoned in one of the ten kingdoms of the Buddhist hades, miniature representations of the infernal prisons were made by means of small clay flags or tiles.   They reminded one of dolls' houses.   Prayers in which the kings of the infernal regions were in turn evoked were then offered, and at the conclusion of each invocation the priest with a short magic wand dashed to the ground one of the miniature prisons.   The effigy was eventually, with the usual observances, put into a coffin and conveyed to the grave by the sorrowing relatives." [2]

In Japan it is customary to preserve the navel-strings of the family in the old home, and should a

[1] Rev. J. Doolittle, *Social Life of the Chinese* (London, 1868), 164.

[2] J. H. Gray, *op. cit.* i. 296.

member of the family die in a foreign land, or be drowned at sea, and his body be not recovered, his navel-string is buried instead of his corpse.[1]

Among the Orotchi, a Tartar tribe of Tungussic origin in north-eastern Asia, if a person has been drowned and his body has not been found within two years, it is customary to carve a wooden image in the likeness of the deceased, and placing it in a coffin to bury it under a small conical hut.[2]

In Madagascar there are cenotaphs for the reception of the souls of persons whose bodies have not been found. These cenotaphs generally consist of a low wall built on three sides of a square. They are intended to be the last resting-place for the souls of those who have died in battle, and whose mortal remains have not been recovered. Their ghosts, it is thought, are allured to repose in the sacred spots thus reared for them by the hands of friends, and thereby find that rest which otherwise they would have sought in vain, while wandering with the owls and animals of ill omen in the forests, or paying unwelcome visits to their former dwellings, and disturbing their surviving friends.[3] On this subject Alfred Grandidier, our great authority on the ethnography of Madagascar, tells us that when the Malagasy cannot recover the body of a deceased relative, they bury his pillow and mat instead of his

---

[1] L. Hearn, *Glimpses of Unfamiliar Japan* (London, 1894), i. 507.

[2] E. H. Fraser, " The Fish Skin Tartars ", in *Journal of the China*

Branch of the Royal Asiatic Society, xxvi. (1891–1892), pp. 31 *sq.*

[3] Rev. W. Ellis, *History of Madagascar* (London and Paris, N.D.). i. 255 *sq.*

corpse, and set up a sepulchral monument to his memory.[1]

Among the Tschi-speaking peoples of the Gold Coast in Africa a ceremony called *Toh-fo* is performed when a person has died and his body has been either destroyed or cannot be found, for example, when a man has been burned to death and the body reduced to ashes, or when one has been drowned and the body cannot be recovered. A miniature coffin is made, covered with white cloth, and in the case of the drowned man is carried to the sea-shore. Rum is poured out on the waves, and the name of the deceased is called out three times, the mourners crying at the same time in a plaintive chant, "We have sought for you but cannot find you". Some sand from the beach is then placed in the coffin, some sea-water poured into it, and, with the usual lamentations, the coffin is buried, commonly on the beach. In the case of a man destroyed by fire, some of the ashes of the body, or of the house in which it was consumed, are placed in the coffin, with similar ceremonies. In this ceremony a fragment of the corpse is always interred if possible, but, if no portion of it can be found, some earth, water, or other substance from the place where the death occurred is buried in the grave. This custom appears to owe its origin to the belief that if respect be not shown to the deceased, by showing him the usual funeral honours, his ghost will come into the dwellings of

---

[1] A. Grandidier, "Des rites funéraires chez les Malgaches", in *Revue d'Ethnographie*, v. (1886), p. 214.

the neglectful relatives, cause sickness, and disturb them by night. Consequently, no body being forthcoming they perform the funeral rites over a substitute, taking care, however, to announce to the spirit of the deceased that they have sought for the body in vain.[1]

Among the Ewe-speaking peoples of the Slave Coast, when a person dies abroad the family try to obtain something that belonged to him, such as locks of his hair or parings of his nails, and over these they perform the funeral ceremonies, for the general belief is that until these rites have been carried out the ghost lingers near the remains, and either cannot or will not depart for Dead-land before this satisfaction has been accorded him.[2] Similarly among the Yoruba-speaking peoples of the Slave Coast, when a man dies abroad his family makes the greatest exertions to obtain something belonging to him, over which the usual funeral rites may be held. Locks of hair or parings of the nails are most sought for this purpose, but if these cannot be obtained a portion of the clothing worn by the deceased suffices. Such relics are called *eta*: they are supposed to bring back the soul of the deceased to the place where the funeral ceremonies are being performed.[3] Among the Ibo-speaking people of Southern Nigeria

[1] A. B. Ellis, *The Tschi-Speaking Peoples of the Gold Coast of West Africa* (London, 1887), pp. 222 *sq.*

[2] A. B. Ellis, *The Ewe-Speaking Peoples of the Slave Coast of West Africa* (London, 1890), p. 159.

[3] A. B. Ellis, *The Yoruba-Speaking Peoples of the Slave Coast of West Africa* (London, 1894), p. 163, and Father Baudin, " Le Fétichisme ou la religion des Nègres de la Guinée", in *Les Missions Catholiques*, xvi. (Lyons, 1884), pp. 258 *sq.*

if a man dies far away and his body cannot be re-covered they take a palm-leaf and a chicken and go to the "bad bush." Holding the palm-leaf in the hand, they kill the chicken, throw it into the "bad bush," knock the leaf on the ground, take it on the left arm and go back, saying, " Dead man follow me home ". If it is a man who has died they put the leaf outside the yam store, if it is a woman they leave it outside the door of her house.   In the case of a man a goat and a cock are sacrificed, and blood is put upon the leaf exactly as it would be upon the dead man's eyes, the leaf is wrapped in cloth as if for a body ; in the case of a woman the goat's heart is put upon a spot to represent the chest.[1]   Concerning these Ibo people we are told elsewhere by the same authority that when the body of a deceased person cannot be found, as for example in the case of a drowned man, the leaf of a certain palm (*omu ojuku*) is struck four times on the bank of the stream where the accident took place and the dead man's name is called out four times.   The palm-leaf is then covered with a cloth and laid on a board, and ceremonies are per-formed for it as for a corpse.[2]

The Giagues are a tribe or nation of conquerors who, coming from the interior of Africa invaded the kingdoms of Matamba and Congo about two cen-turies ago.   Among them, as we learn from an old writer, if anyone dreams of a deceased relation, he fancies that it is the soul of the dead who suffers for

[1] N. W. Thomas, " Some Ibo Burial Customs ", in *Journal of the Royal Anthropological Institute,* xlvii. (1917), p. 167.

[2] N. W. Thomas, *op. cit.* pp. 184 *sq.*

lack of food and drink, and therefore appears to demand help, and reproach his kinsman for his neglect. So the man has recourse to the Ganga-ga-Zumbi, the protector or guardian of the dead, or medicine man, as we may call him. It is chiefly with the sick that this guardian of the dead has to do, for they attribute disease to the anger of the neglected dead. The most difficult case with which the protector of the dead has to deal is that of the ghost of a dead person whose body has not been buried, because he has been killed and eaten by his enemies or by wild beasts. In that case the medicine man spreads nets round the house of the sick man and even into the forest, in order that the soul of the dead man may be caught in the net when he comes to annoy the patient. When a bird, rat, lizard, ape, or other animal is caught in the net, it is taken to be the incarnation of the dead man's soul. The medicine man takes it to the sick man and says, " Rejoice: we've got him. He shan't escape." But before he kills the animal he demands a new fee. When this is agreed to, he kills the animal, to the sick man's joy. But to prevent the soul returning the animal must be ground to powder and swallowed by the sick man. For this grinding to powder, the medicine man must be paid again. When the man has swallowed the powder, digested it, and voided it in his excrement, then he is rid of the tormenting spirit finally.[1] In this case the tormenting spirit

---

[1] J. B. Labat, *Relation historique de l' Éthiopie Occidentale* (Paris, 1732), ii. 209 *sqq.*

of the unburied dead is not recalled and propitiated, as in the preceding cases, but is ground to powder and apparently laid to its last rest in the stomach of the person whom he had been persecuting.

Among the Wajagga of Mount Kilimanjaro, if a man has died in a foreign land, and his body has not been recovered, his friends go to the boundary of the land where he died, and from there bring back a skull-shaped stone, over which they perform the usual mourning ceremonies and raise the customary lamentations for the dead, just as if it were the corpse of the deceased.[1] Among the Basoga, a Bantu tribe of Uganda, " a curious custom still remains in connexion with a man who dies at some distance from his home, and whose body therefore cannot be transported back to be buried in his own house. The relatives of the deceased will march for two or three hours into the bush, and come away with a branch or a long reed. The straight branch or reed stem is then thrown on the ground, and one of the relations calls out the dead man's name and says : ' We have come to bring you home for burial '. After this the reed or stick is covered up with bark-cloth, and the relations march back to the dead man's home carrying with them this substitute for burial. As they get near the village one of their number runs on ahead to apprise the neighbours that the dead

<hr>

[1] B. Gutmann, " Trauer und Be-gräbnissitten der Wadschagga ", in *Globus*, lxxxiv. (1906), p. 198 ; *id.*, *Dichten und Denken der Dschagga-Neger*, p. 137. Cf. M. Merker, " Rechtsverhältnisse und Sitten der Wadschagga ", in *Petermanns Mitteilungen*, Ergänzungsheft, No. 138 (1902), 18 *sq.*

man's body is being brought to his last home. The women then start wailing for the dead, and continue screaming and shouting until the long stick wrapped up in a bundle of bark-cloth is deposited in the grave. The rest of the ceremony is identical with that which follows the actual deposit of a corpse in its grave under the house."[1]

Among the Bavenda, a Bantu tribe of the Northern Transvaal, if a man has died far from home and his body cannot be recovered, if his spirit becomes troublesome and requires to be propitiated by a sacrifice at the grave, his friends proceed to hold a fictitious burial ceremony. They kill a sheep and use its head to symbolize the corpse of the deceased. A grave is dug and the sheep's head is buried with due reverence in the usual way, together with some of the dead man's clothing or possessions. This grave is afterwards considered to be that of the dead man.[2] Among the Ovaherero, a Bantu tribe of South-West Africa, if a man has died far from home, as in war, and his body has not been brought back, the people of his village select for him at home a place at which they erect for him a monument of stones put together in a peculiar manner, and at these stones they perform the same ceremonies as they would have performed at the grave, if the dead man's body had been brought back and buried.[3]

In America the Eskimo about Bering Strait in

[1] Sir H. Johnstone, *The Uganda Protectorate*, ii. 717 *sq*.
[2] H. A. Stayt, *The Bavenda* (London, 1931), p. 163.
[3] Rev. G. Viehe, "Some Customs of the Ovaherero", in *South African Folk-lore Journal*, i. (Capetown, 1879), p. 57.

Alaska are wont to erect memorial wooden posts, carved in human shape, for such persons as have died but have remained unburied because their bodies have not been found. At Tununuk village, near Cape Vancouver, Mr. E. W. Nelson saw three such large wooden posts, representing human figures, and several subordinate posts. One of them represented a woman who had been buried in a landslide, while others of them represented men who had been drowned at sea. Mr. Nelson was told " that among the people of this and the neighbouring villages, as well as of the villages about Big Lake, in the interior from this point, it is the custom to erect memorial posts for all people who die in such a manner that their bodies are not recovered. Each year for five years a new fur coat or cloth shirt is put on the figure at the time of invitation to the festival of the dead, and offerings are made to it as though the body were in its grave box there. When the shade comes about the village to attend the festival of the dead, or at other times, these posts are supposed to afford it a resting-place, and it sees that it has not been forgotten or left unhonoured by its relatives." [1] The Tlingit Indians of Alaska used to dispose of their dead by burning them, but towards the close of last century they were persuaded by a missionary to adopt the practice of burying instead of burning. The innovation was followed by a period of storms and bad weather, which the

<hr>

[1] E. W. Nelson, " The Eskimo about Bering Strait ", in the *Eight-* *eenth Report of the Bureau of Ethnology* (Washington, 1899), i. 317 *sq.*

Indians attributed to the wrath of the spirits of their deceased friends at being deprived of the time-honoured ceremony of cremation.   So on the beach they kindled great fires, in which they burnt puppets to represent their dead friends, hoping thus to appease their angry spirits.   As the ceremony was followed by no improvement in the weather the Indians, not without difficulty, discovered the graves of their dead under the snow, and dug up the bodies, presumably that their spirits might have the satisfaction of witnessing the cremation of the puppets, and so might cease to afflict their surviving kinsfolk with a continuance of bad weather.[1]

Among the Aht Indians of Vancouver Island we read of a bereaved father whose son was drowned at sea and his body not recovered.   In default of the corpse the father took two cedar boards, one of which bore the roughly traced representation of a man, while the other supported a small porpoise.   These he carried to a resting-place in the forest, where he celebrated funeral rites for the peace of his drowned son's soul.   After it he distributed all his own property among the mourners present.[2]

In Ancient Mexico, if a travelling merchant died on a journey or was killed by his enemies and his body had not been brought back, his friends at home used to make an effigy of him of pine-wood, and dressed it in paper garments, such as were usually placed on a corpse.   This effigy they carried

[1] A. Krause, *Die Tlinkit-Indianer* (Jena, 1885), p. 231.
[2] G. M. Sproat, *Scenes and Studies of Savage Life* (London, 1868), p. 263.

to a temple, where it was left for a whole day, and mourned by the relatives. At midnight it was carried out into the courtyard of the temple and there burned, after which the ashes were buried in the usual fashion.[1]

In modern Greece, when a man dies abroad, a puppet is made in his likeness, and dressed in his clothes ; it is laid on the bed, and mourning is made over it.[2] Mr. T. H. Bent witnessed at Mykonos a formal lamentation for an absent dead man, but where the bier would have stood there was an empty space.[3] A similar custom of mourning over an effigy is observed in some parts of Calabria.[4] In Albania, when a man dies abroad all the usual lamentations are made at home as if the body were present ; the funeral procession goes to the church, but in place of the bier a boy walks carrying a dish on which a cracknel is placed over some boiled wheat. This dish is set in the middle of the church, and the funeral service is held over it ; it is not, however, buried, but the women go and weep at the grave of the relation who died last.[5] Among the Rumanians of Transylvania, when any one dies abroad, his clothes are carried to the churchyard of

[1] B. de Sahagun, *Histoire générale des choses de la Nouvelle-Espagne* (Paris, 1880), p. 264 ; Abbé Clavigero, *The History of Mexico*, trans. by Cullen, i. 387 ; Abbé Brasseur de Bourbourg, *Histoire des nations civilisées du Mexique* (Paris, 1858), iii. 621 *sq.* ; H. H. Bancroft, *Native Races of the Pacific States of North America*, ii. 616.

[2] C. Wachsmuth, *Das alte Griechenland im neuen* (Bonn, 1864), p. 113.

[3] T. H. Bent, *The Cyclades* (London, 1885), pp. 222 *sq.*

[4] V. Dorsa, *La Tradizione Greco-latina . . . della Calabria* (Cosenza, 1884), p. 93.

[5] J. G. von Hahn, *Albanesische Studien* (Jena, 1854), i. 152.

his home with all the usual formalities of a regular burial. A plain wooden cross is set up to his memory in the churchyard, with his name and the place of his death carved on it.[1]

VIII. *Ghosts of Animals*

The strictly logical character of primitive thought has sometimes been doubted or denied, but in one respect at least primitive man is more consistently logical than his civilized brother, for he commonly extends to the lower animals that theory of the survival of the soul after death which civilized peoples usually restrict to human beings. Hence primitive hunters or fishermen stand in awe of the spirits or ghosts of the animals and fish which they kill and eat, fearing lest their angry ghosts should seek to take vengeance on their killers, or by giving warning to their fellows should prevent them from coming to be caught and killed in like manner, and so diminish or cut off entirely a principal source of the food supply. Accordingly the primitive hunter or fisherman attempts to propitiate the ghosts of the animals which he kills by sacrificing to them or addressing them in complimentary and persuasive language, and certain precautions are taken to guard him against their dangerous attacks. In a work dealing with the fear of the spirits of the human dead in primitive religion we should not omit to

---

[1] R. Prexl, "Geburts- und Todten-gebräuche bei Rumänen in Sie- benbürgen", in *Globus*, lvii. (1890), p. 30.

notice that parallel fear of the spirits of dead
animals which many primitive peoples are reported to entertain. Elsewhere I have discussed
this curious side of primitive thought at some
length : [1] here I will content myself by illustrating
it with some fresh and typical instances.

Thus, for example, with regard to the Bachama,
a tribe of Northern Nigeria, we are told that " there
are special hunting and head-hunting rites. In
every village may be seen a large collection of standing stones surrounded with the heads of the larger
game. When a Bachama kills a lion, leopard,
rhinoceros, buffalo, elephant, hippopotamus, or
wart-hog, the fame of his exploit is soon made
known, and on returning he is saluted on the out-
skirts of the town by everyone who owns a horse.
He is escorted to the hunting shrine, before which
he sits down. The chief or some senior man takes
the tail of the dead animal and, speaking words of
congratulation, touches the arm of the hunter with
the tail. He then smears some flour over the head
and body of the hunter, with the intention, it was
stated, of protecting him from pursuit by the ghost
of the dead animal." [2] Again with regard to the
Bolewa, Ngamo, Ngizim, and Kare-Kare tribes of
the Bornu Province of Northern Nigeria, we are
told that the leopard seems to be feared by them
more than any other animal. " To kill a leopard
or even look on its dead body is to expose oneself

[1] *The Golden Bough : Spirits of*   *Northern Nigeria* (London, 1931),
the Corn and of the Wild, ii. 204 *sqq.*   i. 45.
[2] C. K. Meek, *Tribal Studies in*

to the assault of the leopard's ghost, the first sign
of which is a violent fit of coughing.   The afflicted
person is swathed in a white cloth resembling the
shroud used for the dead.   A hunter attends with
his company of fiddlers, playing and singing praises
to the leopard : ' If your head is shaven there is no
blood (*i.e.* you cannot be scalped by your enemy) ;
behold the cloth is becoming covered with spots '.
The characteristic spots of the leopard are said to
appear on the cloth, and are immediately plucked
out by the hunter.   In this way the man's life is
saved.   But if the spots do not appear he is doomed
to die.   No one would eat leopard's flesh without
first providing himself with some protective medicine." [1]   Among the Yungur-speaking peoples of
Northern Nigeria, after a man has killed a dangerous
animal he is treated with the same rites as were
formerly accorded to a human being.   An official
known as Kpana smears the hunter's shoulders with
mahogany oil to prevent the dead animal's ghost
from pursuing him.[2]   The Jen, a small group of
people in Northern Nigeria, believe that the hare
has a powerful pursuing spirit, and for that reason
women and children are not allowed to eat hare's
flesh.   If a hare is killed by a dog, a small boy is
formally charged with the deed, in order to prevent
the dog being killed by the pursuing spirit of the
hare.[3]

   With regard to beliefs and practices of this sort

[1] C. K. Meek, *op. cit.* ii. 274.   [3] C. K. Meek, *op. cit.* ii. 523.
[2] C. K. Meek, *op. cit.* ii. 458.

among the peoples of Northern Nigeria in general, a competent authority well acquainted with the province writes as follows : " Lions, leopards, and all the larger wild animals are universally feared by members of both their own and other clans on account of the supposed powerful spiritual influence which, in the same manner as powerful men, they are held to possess. This fear is in fact at the basis of all hunting and fishing magic, whereby it is sought to propitiate the souls of animals slain, whether members of a totem species or not. The practice of such propitiatory or expiatory rites is as a rule confined to the larger or more important animals, such as, among non-totem animals, hyenas, buffaloes, the larger antelopes and ant-eater. The object is both to protect the individual from future pursuit by the vengeful ' pattern ' soul (*ekiti*) of the slain and to purge him from his existing state of ' saturation ' with the spiritual influence or ' matter soul ' (*kofi*) of his victim.

" I was given the following account by a hunter of the procedure stated to be adopted at the present day where a Kwotto hunter kills a lion at a place within the political jurisdiction of the chief of the lion clan. After slaying the lion, the hunter, before taking any steps to remove it, reports the matter to the chief. At the same time he seeks to obtain the forgiveness of the latter, for having slain his kinsman, by the offer of presents, including a white cock and beer.

" The chief, on his part, rewards the successful

hunter for his valour by gifts, usually including a
gown and turban.   These, incidentally, are among
the traditional items of apparel with which a senior
chief invests a junior on appointment, so that the
gift may conceivably in origin be connected with
the idea of hailing the hunter as ' chiefly ', owing
to his having become impregnated with the royal
spiritual influence of the lion.   The chief then
arranges for a bearer party to go and fetch the lion
in order that it may be given ceremonial burial.
The lion is wrapped round with a red winding-
cloth and carried on a bier in procession through
the town into the presence of the chief, to the accom-
paniment of the beating of drums and the joyful
shrill cry (' *Kururua* ') of women.   The people
salute the corpse gravely as it passes, addressing it
as ' lion ' and ' grandfather '.   Later the animal is
flayed, only certain privileged persons of the royal
household, such as the Edibo, Shifornu and Audigwa,
being allowed to touch the corpse ; and the skin is
presented to the chief to adorn his couch.   It is in
fact a general rule among the Kwottos—not confined to the members of particular clans—that no one
but a chief or his relatives may possess, much less
wear or sit on, the skins of any of the larger wild
beasts, especially those of the lion or leopard.
Similar regulations apply also among all the surrounding tribes with which I am acquainted.

" The skull of the dead lion is given to the hunter
who killed it, to deposit on the lion-clan chief's grave,
where he offers up sacrifices and prays before it.

He beseeches the ghost (*ekiti*) of the lion not to harm him for his presumption in killing it, saying : ' O Lion, I give you refreshment to-day, lest your spiritual power (*kofi*) cause me to die '.

" After burying the lion and before returning to live in his village, the hunter retires to the bush for two days, where he performs certain further pro-pitiatory and purificatory rites. These include the eating of a mixture containing atcha-millet, white beans, rice, seven ears of corn and seven ears of maize. To this is added palm-wine and the whole boiled. Were the hunter to neglect to perform these rites it is believed he would go mad. His fellow-villagers will at any rate refuse to receive him into the village until he has purified himself from the *kofi* of the slain animal, conceived as still attaching to him. They fear that if they do so their houses, food, and all their belongings will become contaminated, and the remaining lions come and avenge their comrades by ' eating up ' the village." [1]

The Ewe peoples of Togoland in West Africa think that leopards are animated by the souls of dead men, and therefore ought not to be killed. Whoever kills a leopard must submit to an elaborate ceremony of expiation and purification. Some of the people believe that a leopard is possessed, not by the spirit of a dead man, but by a son of a God, which naturally deepens the crime of killing a leopard. When the news of the killing of a leopard

[1] Capt. J. R. Wilson-Haffenden, *The Red Men of Nigeria* (London, 1930), pp. 167 *sqq.*

reaches a village men who have already killed a leopard go to the spot and bring back the body and the hunter, carrying both on their backs. On arriving at the village they are greeted with cries of joy by the women, and shooting of guns and beating of gongs by the men. At the entrance to the village the body of the leopard is covered with palm-branches, because no one may look on it, for they think that if that rule were not observed a great drought would follow. Then the leopard and its killer are carried to the market-place, followed by the people dancing, singing and drumming. On their arrival at the market-place priests come forward and cover the body of the leopard with palm-branches, and pour libations of water mixed with meal upon the ground, while they express their sympathy with the dead animal by saying, " I pity thee, I pity thee ". If the priests of the leopard-god omitted to perform this ceremony, it is believed that they would die. Afterwards the body of the leopard and the hunter who killed it are taken up and carried by bearers on their shoulders all round the town. Next the leopard's body is carried to a place called *holutime* ; there, as we are told, every one can convince himself that a son of God has really been killed. Thither then comes the oldest man or chieftain of the town, carrying a bush-knife and some palm-wine. He offers a prayer, and pours a libation of the palm-wine to the dead god. With a loud lamentation one of the men present unties the cord which fastened the palm-branches round the leopard's body. Then the leopard's body is placed on a new mat and allowed to lie on the spot till next morning. Then begins the process of skinning and cutting up the carcase, which may only be done by men who have themselves killed leopards. They send parts of the flesh first of all to the oldest people of the town. While they are cutting up and dividing the flesh they cry out continually, " So-and-so [naming the leopard killer] and his helpers are dead ". The reason for this cry is not given by our authority, but we may conjecture that its intention is to assure the soul of the dead animal that his death has been avenged by the death of his slayers.

The leopard's skin goes to the king or chief of the town, who may keep or sell it. After this the man who killed the leopard, and any one who helped him at the killing, must undergo a ceremony of expiation and purification for a period of twenty-one days. A special hut is erected for their accommodation during this time. So long as he remains in this hut the killer of the leopard may not speak : he must behave like a leopard, imitating the voice of the animal, sleeping on palm-branches, and has his body painted or smeared with black and white pigments to imitate the skin of a leopard. From time to time a roar like that of a leopard is heard to proceed from the hut, and after that the mock leopard issues forth to seek his prey. While he is on his raid every one avoids him, for they think that if they were to meet him they would die. Since the leopard eats flesh the mock leopard seeks to imitate the real animal by

procuring some flesh to devour. For this purpose
he goes about armed with a bow and arrows, and
shoots any dog that may cross his path. The dog's
flesh, when he gets it, may not be laid on a plate,
and the water which he drinks may not be quaffed
from a vessel, but must be lapped by him from a
stream. Thus he imitates his prototype the leopard,
both in his eating and drinking. By midday he
must return to his hut, because the leopard only
prowls for prey at morning and evening. Any one
who were to eat or drink of the leopard-killer's food
and water would go mad.

The last of the twenty-one days' seclusion is the
day of the purification of the leopard-killer. From
every side friends flock to him to testify their sympathy and respect, each of them bringing a present
of a piece of cloth and a little money. The cloths
are fastened to each other and used as a garment
with which they clothe the leopard-killer. Women
make strings of cowries with which the body of the
leopard-killer is decked before he is carried to the
place of his purification outside the town. Before
he is carried forth some magical medicine is poured
into his nose, and the same thing is done to several
of the bystanders. After receiving the medicine in
his nose the leopard-killer makes a vibratory or
trembling motion to right and left, but the meaning
of this part of the ceremony was not ascertained
by our authority. Thereupon the leopard-killer,
stripped of clothing, as he had been during his
seclusion, is taken by bearers on their shoulders and

carried in great haste to the place of purification, followed by a crowd from the town. While the ceremony of purification is proceeding the people who remain behind gather in an open space of the town, where they dance, brandish knives with wild gesticulations, sing special hunting songs and beat the hunters' drums. Meantime women have cleaned the hut in which the leopard-killer dwelt during his seclusion, throwing away the palm-branches and the rubbish in the forest. After that the hut itself is pulled down. At the place of purification the body of the leopard-killer is washed thoroughly by certain people. Then they all go back dancing, singing and beating drums to the place in the town where the other people are assembled. The procession is headed by men who have themselves slain men, or are the parents of twins, or are famous hunters. The leopard-killer, dressed in a new robe, has now made his peace with the God whose son he has killed, and he may now go about among his fellows as of old.[1]

Among the Kassounas-Bouras, a tribe of the French Sudan, if a man has killed a lion, or a panther, or a buffalo, or an antelope of a special species, or a hyena, a seer will sometimes tell him that evil will befall him. On receiving this warning the killer of the animal will build a miniature house in front of his hut to lodge the spirit of the animal he has killed, and there he sacrifices to the creature's

[1] C. Spiess, " Beiträge zur Kennt-niss der Religion und der Kultus-formen in Sud-Togo ", in *Baessler Archiv*, ii. (1912) pp. 70 *sqq.*

soul. Another creature, the killing of which requires to be expiated by a sacrifice, is a species of
bird called by the natives *kouma* or *koumvava*. It
is perhaps the crested crane. If a man has killed a
bird of this sort he makes a miniature house for it,
and there offers sacrifice to the bird's ghost. The
plumage of birds of this sort is used to decorate garments of chiefs and wealthy people. Again, if a man
kills a red ape or a boar he will build a miniature
house for the animal's soul, and there offer sacrifice
to it, should the seer direct him to do so.[1]

Again, among the Gouros, a tribe inhabiting the
interior of the Ivory Coast, if a man has killed a deer
of a special species he hastens to take the animal's
skull, on which he offers a sacrifice to the animal's
vengeful ghost in order that it may not pursue him,
and he resorts to a similar mode of appeasing the
vengeful ghost of an elephant or a leopard which he
has killed. Even if he does not consider himself to
be related to these animals through his clan, he still
sacrifices to them, lest their ghosts should haunt him
in his sleep.[2] The Gouros who inhabit the northern
part of the Ivory Coast similarly fear the vengeful
ghosts of certain animals which they kill. Hunters
who are in the habit of killing such animals obtain
from old people charms to protect them from these
dangerous ghosts. They particularly dread the
ghosts of a certain species of deer or antelope,
and if they have killed one of them they take the

[1] L. Tauxier, *Le Noir de Soudan*
(Paris, 1912), p. 327.

[2] L. Tauxier, *Nègres Gouro et
Gagou* (Paris, 1924). p. 204.

animal's skull and on it offer a little sacrifice to the ghost.[1]

The Lango, a Nilotic tribe of Uganda, believe that some species of animals, but not all, possess a shade or soul (*tipo*), which survives the death of its body and may prove dangerous to its slayer. Animals which are credited with the possession of such a soul are the wart-hog, rhinoceros, elephant, roan, giraffe and bushbuck. Some animals, including, curiously enough, the lion and the leopard, are not supposed to possess such dangerous souls. The ghost of the roan is thought to be particularly vengeful and vicious. When a man has killed an animal of that species he must at once return to his village and consult a seer, according to whose advice an offering is made and special rites are observed to pacify the ghost of the animal. The ceremonies vary according to the directions of the seer, but in all cases a black ram must be sacrificed at the door of the slayer's house. The carcase is dragged whole into the bush and left near a river, but the old men of the village may go and eat it there, after which they burn the skin and bones and throw the ashes into the water. Having thus appeased the animal's ghost, the slayer may return and cut up the animal's body, but the horns of the roan may not be brought into the village, on account of the peculiarly vicious and dangerous character of that animal's ghost. For a similar reason it was formerly forbidden to bring into the village the horns of a slain rhinoceros.

[1] L. Tauxier, *op. cit.* p. 255.

A like ceremony of expiation has to be performed for the killing of any one of those species of animals which are supposed to possess a vengeful shade or spirit.[1]

Among the Wajagga of Mount Kilimanjaro, boys amuse themselves by shooting birds with a bow and arrows. For every bird that he kills the boy makes a notch in the wood of his bow. When a boy has shot a hundred or a hundred and fifty birds he sacrifices a goat to expiate the bow and himself, and thereafter shoots at no bird, lest he should expose himself to the vengeance of the dead bird's ghost.[2] Among the Wandamba of Tanganyika, when the hunters have killed an elephant, the chief medicineman, or in his absence the first man who drew the animal's blood, cuts off the tail and the tip of the trunk, burying the latter as ugly and unfit to be seen by women. Then he mounts the carcase and dances, singing, "He is dead, the rumbling one, he is stone dead". After that the others climb up and dance on the carcase, but a man who has not previously assisted at the killing of an elephant may not do so until he has been invited by the chief medicineman, who first binds a couple of hairs from the animal's tail round the man's neck and washes him. This necklace of hair the man wears until the morning after the return home, when it is handed back to the head medicine-man, and put by him in his bag. If these precautions were not observed the man

---

[1] J. H. Driberg, *The Lango* (London, 1923), pp. 229 *sq.*

[2] B. Gutmann, *Dichten und Denken der Dschagganeger*, p. 106.

would be haunted by the spirit of the dead elephant
and would be subject to fits of madness in which he
would suffer from the illusion that the beast was
pursuing him.[1] The Nanzela, a people of Northern
Rhodesia, observe a similar ceremony at the killing
of an elephant for the purpose of appeasing the
animal's ghost. The ceremony has been described
as follows, by Messrs. Smith and Dale. " We have
never had the opportunity of watching the cutting-
up of an elephant, but, sitting once in company with
some old Nanzela hunters, we asked and obtained
the following description of the process. The
motive underlying the rites is to prevent the ghost
of the deceased elephant from taking vengeance
upon the hunters, and to induce it to assist them in
bringing the same fate upon other elephants. When
the elephant is dead the hunter runs off and is chased
in mock resentment by his companions. Then he
comes back and climbs upon the carcase, his companions surrounding the elephant and clapping
their hands in greeting and congratulation. They
then proceed to cut up the carcase. A beginning
is made by cutting out the fat in the hollows of the
temples : from its quantity and quality they judge
the condition of the animal. They then open the
abdomen and remove the intestines. The linings
of the cavity are carefully separated and spread out
to dry ; they are called *ingubo* (' blankets '), and
are intended for presentation to the *bodi*, the ladies

[1] A. G. O. Hodgson, " Some
Notes on the Hunting Customs of
the Wandamba ", in *Journal of the* *Royal Anthropological Institute*, lvi.
(1926) p. 63.

of the community. They then cut through the
diaphragm : through the opening the hunter puts
his head, seizes the heart in his mouth, and drags it
out. He does not eat it, but the biting is to give him
strength in future hunting. Having removed the
contents of the thorax, they attack the head. There
is some special significance attached to the nerve of
the tusk, called *kamwale* ('the maiden'). It is
carefully abstracted and buried under the site of
the camp-fire. It is not to be looked upon by the
tiros in hunting—they are called *bana* ('children') ;
all the time it is being handled they must turn away
their heads, for were they to see it they would meet
with misfortune. Having now completed their work
they return to the village, beating their axes together
and singing. The people on hearing the noise flock
to meet them, and a great feast, with plenty of beer,
is made. But first an offering is made to Leza ('the
Supreme Being'), to the *mizhimo* ('the ancestral
spirits') and to the ghost (*muzhimo*) of the deceased
elephant which has accompanied them to the village.
Addressing this last they say : ' O spirit, have you
no brothers and fathers who will come to be killed ?
Go and fetch them.' The ghost of the elephant then
returns and joins the herd as the guardian of the
elephant who has ' eaten its name '. Observe that
they regard the elephants as acting as men act : one
dies and another inherits his position, ' eats his
name ', as they say. Before a man can be admitted
into the brotherhood of elephant hunters he must
undergo a process of being doctored. Gashes are

cut in his right arm and ' medicine ' is rubbed in to give him pluck; and other ' medicines ' are administered to enable him to approach his quarry without being seen." [1]   With reference to the Ila-speaking peoples generally of Northern Rhodesia the same writers have described for us the parallel ceremony observed by them at the killing of an eland for the purpose of disarming the vengeful ghost of the animal.   They say : " We have described the ceremonies following the death of an elephant.   When a man kills an eland he must also go through certain rites to avert the retaliating power in the animal. After killing an eland the hunter chews leaves of the Mukono or Munto bush, together with a piece of *kaumbuswa* (ant-heap), holding, meanwhile, a lump of the latter under his foot.   Some of the chewed leaves he rubs on his forehead and some on the eland's forehead.   Having done this he throws at the eland's head the piece of ant-heap that was under his foot.   He also cuts and splits a stick and jumps through the cleft, as the killer of a man does.   He then goes off to the village to get people to help him in carrying home the meat.   On their arrival at the eland he sits apart while they open the carcase.   He must not join them at first, but once it is opened he may help them to skin and cut up the animal.   Were these rites omitted, the eland would trouble him— would come at night and horn him, or in any case cause his death.   But the power in the eland can be

[1] Rev. E. W. Smith and Capt. A. M. Dale, *The Ila-speaking Peoples*   *of Northern Rhodesia* (London, 1920), i. 167 *sq.*

put to use. Medicine put into its horn derives therefrom a more potent efficacy." [1]

Among the Gonds and Korkus in the Central Provinces of India, when a tiger has been killed the hunters singe off the animal's whiskers, because they think that this will prevent the tiger's ghost from haunting them. They often object to touch a man who has been injured or mauled by a tiger, as they believe that to do so would bring down the vengeance of the tiger's ghost upon them. And in some places any Gond or Korku who touches a man mauled by a tiger is put temporarily out of caste and has to be purified and give a feast on being readmitted to the caste.[2] Among the Lushais, a tribe of North-Eastern India, when a man has killed either an enemy or an animal, it is necessary for him to perform a certain ceremony called "Ai" for the purpose of giving him power to control the spirit or ghost of the man or animal. The ceremony consists in the sacrifice of a mithan, goat or pig. After this, before the skull can be placed in the front verandah, a religious ceremony must be performed by a priest or medicine-man. A small white fowl is given to him, and the skull of the animal is placed in front of him. He then takes some rice-beer (*zu*) in his mouth and spits it out over the skull, and, after muttering a charm in so low a tone that no one can hear him, he strikes the skull with the head of the chicken. If some of the feathers stick on the

---

[1] Smith and Dale, *op. cit.* ii. 88.   *of the Central Provinces of India,*

[2] R. V. Russell, *Tribes and Castes*   iii. 564.

skull it is very lucky. After this the skull can be put up. The reason for the performance of this ceremony (*Ai*) is that if it be omitted the soul of the slain animal or man cannot pass to the spirit land, to be there under the mastery of the slayer ; in other words, the aim of the ceremony is to give the slayer full power over his victim's ghost in the world beyond the grave. No such ceremony has to be performed for tame animals when they are killed, presumably because they are already under the control of their killer. Thus we see that the Lushais treat the souls of killed men and killed animals on exactly parallel lines : they do not substantially distinguish between them. The following is a translation of a native account of the ceremony observed by the Lushai after the killing of a tiger. " When Bengkhawia's village was at Thenzawl, a tiger beset the village and in one day killed a mithan and two goats. The crier called on the people to surround the village, and they did so. Thangbawnga shot it, and performed the Ai ceremony ; the night before he must not sleep. A young man cut off its tail ; he also must keep awake all night. The next day he performed the Ai ceremony, sacrificing a mithan. Thangbawnga, who was performing the Ai, dressed himself up as a woman, smoked a woman's pipe, wore a woman's petticoat and cloth, carried a small basket, spun a cotton spindle, wore ivory earrings, let his hair down and wrapped a mottled cloth, which was said to be of an ancient pattern, round his head as a turban. A crowd watched him and

elled with laughter, but it would have been 'thianglo'
unlucky) for him to laugh. Presently he took off
his turban and carried it in the basket. Then he
ook off his woman's disguise and dressed himself
s a man, and strapped on a fighting dah (knife or
lagger) and carried a gun. He also took 'sailungvar'
white flints) and put them into the tiger's mouth,
while he ate eggs. 'You eat the sailungvar', he
aid ; ' who will swallow them the quicker ? I have
ut-swallowed you, you have not swallowed yours ;
have swallowed mine. You will go by the lower
oad ; I will go by the upper. You will be like
he lower southern hills ; I shall be like the high
northern ones. You are the brave man of the south ;
am the brave man of the north ', he said, and cut
he tiger's head three times with his dah. Then the
nen buried the body of the tiger outside the village."
f the tiger has killed men, his eyes are gouged out
with skewers or needles and thrown away, probably
n order to blind the animal's ghost : it is unlucky
thianglo) for the performer to laugh, so he holds
porcupine in his arms, and if he laughs by accident
hey say the porcupine laughed. The idea of the
erformer disguising himself as a woman is that the
pirit of the dead tiger may be humbled, thinking
hat it has been shot by a woman ; and the giving of
he flints while the performer eats eggs is to show the
ower of the performer over the tiger, as he eats the
ggs easily, while the tiger is unable to chew the flints.[1]

[1] Lt.-Col. J. Shakespear, *The Lushei Kuki Clans* (London, 1912), pp.
3 *sqq.*

Among the Lakhers, another tribe of Nortl
Eastern India, when a hunter has killed any of tl
larger animals, on his return home he performs
sacrifice called *Salupakia*, the object of which is *
give him power in the next world over the spir
of the animal he has killed, to please the dea
animal's soul, and so also to help him to kill man
more animals in future. Either a fowl or a pig ma
be sacrificed. If a fowl is used, the sacrifice is pe:
formed as soon as the hunter returns home ; if a pi{
the sacrifice is postponed till the next mornin{
When a fowl is killed, the women may not eat an
part of it, but if the sacrifice is a pig, women ma
eat any part of it except the head, which may b
eaten only by men. The sacrifice is performe
inside the house near a rice-beer (*sahma*) pot, clos
to which is placed the head of the wild animal fc
which the sacrifice is being performed. Before pe
forming the sacrifice the hunter sucks a little rice-bee
out of each rice-beer pot and spits it out into a gourc
He rubs flour all over the animal's head, takes int
his mouth again the rice-beer he has spat into th
gourd, and blows it over the animal's head six time:
The hunter next intones a hunting-song, and kil
the fowl or pig as the case may be. If a fowl i
sacrificed, its tongue is pulled out and placed on th
animal's head, and some feathers are placed in th
nostrils. If the victim is a pig, the animal's hea
is anointed with the blood, and after the pig ha
been cooked and eaten its head is placed on the hea
of the slain animal. The animal's head is then hun{

up in the verandah, and all the old heads already hanging up there are anointed with flour and beer to make them look beautiful and as though they had been freshly shot. This attention is thought to be pleasing to the souls of the dead animals, who will praise the sacrificer to living animals and so induce them to approach him next time he goes out hunting. For the day and night of the sacrifice the sacrificer and his family are taboo (*pana*), and the women of the house may not weave. That night it is forbidden (*ana*) for the sacrificer to sleep with his wife or any other woman ; he must sleep on the place where the sacrifice was made. The Lakhers believe that on the night of this sacrifice the spirit of the animal shot comes and watches the man who has killed it, and if it saw him sleeping with his wife, would say, "Ah, this man prefers women to me", and would go and inform all the other animals that the man who had shot him was unworthy to be allowed to shoot any more animals, as he was fonder of women than of the chase. A man who broke the prohibition on sexual intercourse on the night of the ceremony would therefore be unable to kill any more animals. The next morning the sacrificer takes his gun and goes outside the village and shoots a bird ; if he cannot shoot a bird he must in any case fire his gun off. Having done this, he returns to the village, the taboo (*pana*) ends, and he may have intercourse with women again. If he has shot a bird it means that the sacrifice has taken effect and that the sacrificer will soon shoot more game.

If a man has wounded an animal and returned home without bagging it and intends to follow it up next day, he must sleep alone that night. It is forbidden (*ana*) for a man in these circumstances to sleep either with his wife or with any other woman as it is believed that in that case the wounded animal would escape him. Hunters must remain chaste in these circumstances.[1]

Lakhers have a superstitious fear of tigers, as tigers are believed to have a *saw*, that is, a power of causing sickness or misfortune. Leopards also are believed to possess a similar power for mischief (*saw*), and the ceremony performed over a dead tiger or leopard is intended mainly to render the *saw* harmless. So when a tiger has been shot a special ceremony called *Chakei Ia* has to be performed. This ceremony is similar in some respects to that performed over the head of an enemy slain in war. If any one shoots a tiger and leaves it in the jungle no sacrifice is necessary, but if he brings the head into the village he must perform the *Ia* ceremony, because the dead tiger is *saw*—that is to say, has the capacity of causing sickness and harm to any one touching it, and the *Ia* ceremony both makes the tiger' powerful mischief (*saw*) innocuous, and enables the hunter to retain the tiger for his own use in the next world. Most Lakhers dislike tigers, because they fear the *saw* and are not at all keen on shooting them, and if a man who has shot a tiger says he is going to perform the *Ia* ceremony, and asks his

[1] N. E. Parry, *The Lakhers* (London, 1932), pp. 139 *sq.*

friends to come and help him skin the carcase, and then fails to perform the ceremony, he must give each of the skinners a dog and a fowl to sacrifice, to save themselves from the evil effects of the *saw*. The dog and fowl are killed and then thrown away outside the village, and none of their meat is eaten. They believe that the *saw* is thrown out of the village in the same way as the bodies of the dogs and the fowls. Not only the skinners, but any one touching the skin of a dead tiger over which the ceremony (*Ia*) has not been performed must offer this sacrifice. After the tiger has been skinned, the head is brought up and kept outside the village. Two pigs must be killed for the ceremony (*Ia*). In the morning a pig is killed outside the village. The meat of this pig may be eaten only by men. After this pig has been sacrificed, the tiger's head is brought into the village and put down in front of the house of the man who shot it. A tiger's head, like a man's, is never taken inside a house. The second pig is killed near the tiger's head and the *Ia* ceremony is performed. The man who shot the tiger dresses up in woman's clothes, lets down his hair like a woman, and smokes a woman's pipe. He carries a spindle and thread in his hand, and while winding the thread dances round the tiger's head, finally running the spindle through the tiger's nostrils. One of the assistants then picks up the tiger's head and runs through the village with it, pursued by the man who shot it, jabbing at the tiger's nostrils with the spindle. The head is thrown away outside the village. Tigers' heads are never hung up in the verandah like other trophies. In Chapi and Savang tigers' heads are hung outside the village in the same way as human heads, and the head of the animal sacrificed as *Ia* is hung up near by. During the ceremony it is forbidden (*ana*) to laugh. The origin of this ceremony is said to be that once upon a time a woman went to the land cleared for cultivation (*jhums*), and a tiger came to eat her. The tiger knocked her down, but as he did so the spindle she was carrying entered his nostrils and killed him, and so the woman escaped. Ever since then it has been customary for the killer of a tiger to wear woman's clothes when he performs the ceremony of expiation (*Ia*). During the ceremony the dead tiger's brother is said to watch the proceedings from a high hill, and when he sees, as he thinks, a woman dancing round the tiger, he does not get angry, because he imagines it is only a woman who has killed his brother, and if his brother was fool enough to get killed by a woman he had only himself to blame. So, as it is not worth while punishing a woman, he goes away without taking any revenge.[1] The quaint ceremony just described has for its object to lay the ghost of the tiger that has been killed. During the night which follows it the women may neither spin nor weave for fear of the tiger's ghost.[2]

Again, among these same Lakhers, when any one kills a mithan or bullock, the village is taboo (*pana*) on the day the animal is killed. No work may be

[1] Parry, *op. cit.* pp. 141 *sqq.*   [2] Parry, *op. cit.* pp. 375 *sq.*

done in the fields, and the women may not weave. The same taboo is observed if a mithan is killed by a tiger and the villagers bring the meat into the village to eat.   If the meat is not brought in, there is no taboo.   It is believed that if this taboo is not observed the houses will be blown down by a hurricane, and that the rice will be blown down or will dry up.   Mithan and cows are the largest and most valuable animals kept by men, and have the loudest voice, and when they breathe their breath is like the wind ; hence, when one of these animals is killed, the wind will punish the village where it has been killed unless a taboo (*pana*) is held to appease the mithan's soul and prevent it from calling the wind.[1]

The Moïs, a primitive people inhabiting the mountains of Indo-China, stand in great fear of tigers which infest the surrounding jungle and carry off many victims.   But if they stand in fear of the living tiger, they stand in much greater fear of the tiger's ghost, as will appear from the following account of an incident witnessed by a French official. We read : " Of course it is very unusual to meet this ferocious creature by daylight, even in regions where its ravages are the most frequent.   Every traveller will pass by its lair in the bamboo groves, but it is quite exceptional to see the beast itself, except at night-fall, when it comes forth to seek its prey.   Once a tiger has tasted human flesh it prefers it to all other food.   Accordingly, the natives live in a state of chronic fear of the man-eater, and will willingly

[1] Parry, *op. cit.* pp. 451.

abandon their villages rather than make the least effort to rid themselves of the pest.   As I shall show later, they endow their enemy with human qualities and frequently refuse to destroy it when at their mercy for fear of arousing the vengeance of the whole species.   One of our party once witnessed the following scene.   A tiger had fallen into a pit which had been laid for some deer.   It was not wounded, but the space was so cramped that it was quite unable to move.   The natives were terrified lest it should die, in which case its spirit would never cease to molest them ; so they decided to set it free. They made a cage without a floor, lowered it into the pit, and then raised it up again by means of ropes passed under the creature.   Perched on the neighbouring trees they pulled away the prison and let the captive go, offering their humble apologies for having already detained it so long.   Our representative had been compelled to promise his acquiescence, and, lest he should repent and show fight, his rifle was carefully left behind in the village."[1] Thus these primitive people, far from wishing to kill the trapped tiger, took great pains to save its life, because they feared the dead tiger's ghost much more than the living animal.   A stronger proof they could hardly have given of their belief in the reality and the danger of a tiger's ghost.

Far from the tiger-infested jungles of Indo-China our next and last scene opens on the ice and snow

---

[1] Commandant Baudesson, *Au pays des superstitions et des rites,*   pp. 25 *sq.* ; *id., Indo-China and its Primitive People,* pp. 41 *sq.*

of the Arctic north. The Eskimo are at great pains not to offend the ghosts of the animals which they kill and eat. On this subject Mr. Stefansson, who lived among the Eskimo, tells us as follows : " I learned also why it is that animals allow themselves to be killed by men. The animals are much wiser than men, and know everything in the world—including the thoughts of men ; but there are certain things which the animals need, and which they can only get from men. The seals and whales live in the salt water, and are therefore continually thirsty. They have no means of getting fresh water, except to come to men for it. A seal will therefore allow himself to be killed by a hunter who will give him a drink of water in return ; that is why a dipperful of water is always poured into the mouth of a seal when he is brought ashore. If a hunter neglects to do this, all the other seals know about it, and no other seal will ever allow himself to be killed by that hunter, because he knows he is not going to get a drink. Every man who gives a seal a drink of water, and keeps this implied promise, is known by the other seals as a dependable person, and they will prefer to be killed by him. There are other things which a seal would like to have done for it when it is dead, and some men are so careful to do everything that seals want that seals tumble over themselves in their eagerness to be killed by that particular man. The polar bear does not suffer from thirst as much as the seal, for he can eat the fresh snow on the top of the ice. But polar bears are unable to make for themselves certain tools which they need. What the male bears especially value are crooked knives and bow-drills, and the female bears are especially eager to get women's knives, skin-scrapers, and needle cases; consequently when a polar bear has been killed his soul (*tatkok*) accompanies the skin into the man's house and stays with the skin several days (among most tribes, for four days if it is a male bear, and for five days if it is a female). The skin during this time is hung up at the rear end of the house, and with the skin are hung up the tools which the bear desires, according to the sex of the animal killed. At the end of the fourth or fifth day the soul of the bear is by a magic formula driven out of the house; and when it goes away it takes away with it the souls of the tools which have been suspended with it and uses them thereafter. There are certain manners and customs of humanity which are displeasing to polar bears, and for that reason those customs are carefully abjured during the period when the soul of the bear is in the man's house. The bear, in other words, is treated as an honoured guest who must not be offended. If the bear's soul had been properly treated during his stay with the man, and if he has received the souls (*tatkoit*) of implements of good quality, then he will report those things in the land of polar bears to which he returns, and other bears will be anxious to be killed by so reliable a man. If the wives of certain hunters are careless about treating the souls of the bears properly while they are in their houses, this will offend the bears quite as much as if the man who had killed them had done it, and this may cause an excellent hunter to get no bears at all.   Certain women are known in their communities for this very undesirable quality, and if a woman becomes a widow, her reputation for carelessness in treating the souls of animals may prevent her from getting a good second husband." [1]

Our survey of the facts, imperfect as it necessarily is, must here end ; but enough perhaps has been said to convince us that fear of the spirits of the dead, whether men or animals, has haunted the mind of primitive man from time immemorial all over the world, from the Equator to the Poles, and we may surmise that the same fear has gone far to shape the moulds into which religious thought has run ever since feeble man began to meditate on the great mysteries by which our little life on earth is encompassed.

[1] V. Stefansson, *My Life with the Eskimo* (London, 1913), pp. 56 *sqq.*

INDEX

Abbott, J., cited, 244

Achinese of Sumatra, block openings in head of corpse, 36 ; treatment of woman dying in childbed, 191

Adair, James, cited, 136

Aht Indians, funeral rites in absence of body, 281

Ainus of Japan, custom of destroying a house after death, 7

Akamba of Kenya, marriage after death, 240

A-Kôa of West Africa bury dead man in stream, 24

Alaric the Goth buried in bed of stream, 28

Albania, mourning rites in absence of body, 282

Aleutian Islanders mask the faces of their dead, 35

Alfoors of Celebes sacrifice to their unburied dead, 265

Algonquin Indians burn stinking substances to repel ghosts, 22

Amazulu of South Africa fear ghost of dead husband, 224

Anabali of Orinoco abandon their crops at a death, 18

Andaman Islanders, desert a camp after a death, 6 ; do not name the dead during mourning, 44 ; fear the spirits of those they kill, 114

Andrawilla tribe of Australia do not name the dead, 43

Angoni of Central Africa, women shave their heads in sorrow, 56

—— of Nyassaland remove corpse from house by special opening, 93

Angoni of Zambesi fear the ghosts of the slain, 131

Annam, corpses removed by special opening, 82 ; mourning over relics of unburied dead, 266

Antimerina of Madagascar remove dead king by breach made in wall, 89

Apache-Yumas, an Indian tribe, burn a hut in which one has died, 17

Arosi (Solomon Islands), method of misleading ghost, 62

Arunta of Australia, fear the ghosts of the slain, 104 ; lacerate themselves in mourning, 58

Ashanti of Africa remove dead by special opening, 90

Asisi or spirit of slain man driven away by Orokaiva of British New Guinea, 110

Assam, houses pulled down in which death has taken place, 9

Astrakhan and Caucasus, nurses of dead prince put in hole in ground, 48

Atlas Mountains tribes desert the house of a dead cadi, 15

Atnirinja or ghost of a dead person in Australia, 235

Atonga of Nyassaland remove dead from hut by special opening, 93

Atua or avenging spirit feared by the Maori, 106

Australian natives, bandage the eyes of the dead, 32 ; carry a dead body in circles, 74 ; do not pronounce

Mehtar, a caste of the Punjab, bury dead face down, 30

Melanesians of Bismarck Archipelago fear a victim's ghost, 106
—— of South-East Solomon Islands substitute coconut for dead twin, 63

Menomonie Indians fear ghost of dead husband, 227

Mexicans, ancient, feared ghosts of women dying in childbed, 198

Mexico, ancient, effigy of man dying from home, 281; faces of dead kings masked in, 35

Milne, Mrs. Leslie, cited, 71

Minahassa, Celebes, peculiar funeral custom in, 79

Misol, natives of, in East Indies, abandon a house in which a death took place, 5

Moïs of Indo-China, fear a tiger's ghost, 307; remove their dead by special opening, 82

Mosquito Indians disguise themselves at a funeral, 53

Mossi of Sudan remove corpse by special opening, 91

Mpongwés of Western Africa, costume in mourning, 52

Muimu or ghost among the Akamba, 241

Mukden in Mongolia, at, the body of a dead child removed by special opening, 83

Munjā or dreaded ghost of unmarried dead, 244

Mycenae, golden masks discovered at, 34

Myoro custom in Africa in mourning for dead child, 54

Nairs of Southern India do not shave or cut the hair while in mourning, 56

Naman (British New Guinea), natives of, fear vengeful ghost of slain foe, 108

Name of dead taboo, 42

Nanzela of Rhodesia, ceremony at killing an elephant, 296

Natchez Indians of Mississippi fear souls of slain men, 137

Navahos of United States pull down and burn a hut in which some one has died, 18

Nelson, E. N., cited, 280

New Caledonia, natives of, allow hair to grow after burying a corpse, 57

New Guinea, natives of, costumes in mourning, 52

Nhavi of Bombay Presidency, ceremony at remarriage of widow, 214

Nias, burial customs in, 70; fear of ghosts of women dying in childbed in, 191-3

Nicobar Islands, mourning costume as a disguise from ghost in, 49
—— Islanders close the eyes of corpse, 32

Nigeria, fear of slain animals in, 285

Nishinam widows of California observe silence, 41

Norse rule that corpse may not be removed from house by ordinary door, 101

Nufoors of Dutch New Guinea, ceremony when widow remarries, 200; make images of unburied dead, 263

Nuru or spirit of the slain feared by Thonga of South Africa, 132

Obongo of West Africa bury dead in hollow tree or running stream, 24-25

Ogowe, people of, abandon a site when a chief dies, 13

Oigób of East Africa do not cut their hair for two months after a death, 57

Ojebway Indians, drive off the ghost of a dead husband, 227; remove dead by special opening, 98; repel ghosts by smells, 22

Omaha Indians of United States fear ghost of murdered man, 135

Onas of Tierra del Fuego do not mention the name of a dead man, 47

Oraons of Chota Nagpur, fear ghosts of women dying in childbed, 178; fear the spirits of men killed by tigers, 169 ; propitiate the angry spirit of a murdered man, 120

Oraons of Orissa peg down ghost of dead man, 28, 29

Orestes in Arcadia, legend of, 140-41

Orokaiva of British New Guinea drive away the spirit of a slain man, 109

Orotchi of North-Eastern Asia bury image of unburied dead, 273

Ottawa Indians fear ghosts of slain foes, 135

Ovaherero of South-West Africa, adopt costume as disguise from ghost, 50 ; mourning rites in absence of body, 279

Palaungs of Burma, adopt curious mode of deceiving the ghost of a dead child, 71 ; fear the ghosts of those dying violently, 171 ; their treatment of women dying in childbed, 188

Pampa del Sacramento Indians repel ghosts by stinks, 23

Panwar of India, fear of dead husband's ghost among, 210 ; fear the spirit of a man killed by a tiger, 168

Parit of Bombay Presidency sacrifice - at remarriage of widow, 216

Pehuenches of Central Chile carry dead out feet foremost, 31

Pelew Islanders, bury banana-tree with woman dying in childbed, 60 ; fear ghost of slain foe, 106

Perche, France, removal of still-born children in, 102

Persians, ancient, mourning customs, 55

—— removed dead by hole in wall, 89

Plutarch, as the Father of Folklore, 51

Polo, Marco, cited, 257

Pomerania, suicides in, 157

Prussia, West, suicides in, 157

Ramoshi of Bombay Presidency, ceremony at remarriage of widow, 215

Rumanians mourn over effigy of man dying abroad, 282

Russell, R. V., cited, 150

Russia, coins placed on eyes of corpse in, 34 ; marriage of the dead in, 259

Sacae of antiquity put mourners in pits, 48

Sakai of Perak (Malay Peninsula) burn down a house in which some one has died, 6

Sakalava of Madagascar, practise suicide as form of revenge, 148 ; remove dead king by breach made in wall, 89

Sakalavas of Madagascar do not use words which formed parts of the names of dead kings, 45

Saleijer, Indonesia, special window for corpses, 86

Samoa, treatment of unburied dead in, 262

Samoyeds of Siberia carry out dead by special opening, 84

San Cristoval, natives of, their custom of misleading the ghost, 62

Sansia of India offer sacrifices to those dying violently, 168

Sardinia, men of, do not shave after death of wives, 57

Savars of Central Provinces fear ghost of childless dead, 244

—— of India propitiate soul of man dying violently, 169

Savaras, an Indian tribe, burn down houses in which death has occurred, 9

—— of Southern India, ceremony at remarriage of widow, 216

Savoe (Indian Archipelago), early marriages in, 237

Saw, or spirit of dead animal, 304

Schliemann, Dr., 34

Serbia, coins placed on eyes of corpse in, 34

Scotland, in, coin placed on eyes of corpse if open, 33 ; treatment of suicides in, 158-61

——, Highlands of, corpses of suicides, 102

THE END

Printed in Great Britain by R. & R. CLARK, LIMITED, *Edinburgh.*

THE LITERATURE OF
DEATH AND DYING

Abrahamsson, Hans. **The Origin of Death:** Studies in African Mythology. 1951

Alden, Timothy. **A Collection of American Epitaphs and Inscriptions with Occasional Notes.** Five vols. in two. 1814

Austin, Mary. **Experiences Facing Death.** 1931

Bacon, Francis. **The Historie of Life and Death with Observations Naturall and Experimentall for the Prolongation of Life.** 1638

Barth, Karl. **The Resurrection of the Dead.** 1933

Bataille, Georges. **Death and Sensuality:** A Study of Eroticism and the Taboo. 1962

Bichat, [Marie François] Xavier. **Physiological Researches on Life and Death.** 1827

Browne, Thomas. **Hydriotaphia.** 1927

Carrington, Hereward. **Death:** Its Causes and Phenomena with Special Reference to Immortality. 1921

Comper, Frances M. M., editor. **The Book of the Craft of Dying and Other Early English Tracts Concerning Death.** 1917

Death and the Visual Arts. 1976

Death as a Speculative Theme in Religious, Scientific, and Social Thought. 1976

Donne, John. **Biathanatos.** 1930

Farber, Maurice L. **Theory of Suicide.** 1968

Fechner, Gustav Theodor. **The Little Book of Life After Death.** 1904

Frazer, James George. **The Fear of the Dead in Primitive Religion.** Three vols. in one. 1933/1934/1936

Fulton, Robert. **A Bibliography on Death, Grief and Bereavement:** 1845-1975. 1976

Gorer, Geoffrey. **Death, Grief, and Mourning.** 1965

Gruman, Gerald J. **A History of Ideas About the Prolongation of Life.** 1966

Henry, Andrew F. and James F. Short, Jr. **Suicide and Homicide.** 1954

Howells, W[illiam] D[ean], et al. **In After Days;** Thoughts on the Future Life. 1910

Irion, Paul E. **The Funeral:** Vestige or Value? 1966

Landsberg, Paul-Louis. **The Experience of Death:** The Moral Problem of Suicide. 1953

Maeterlinck, Maurice. **Before the Great Silence.** 1937

Maeterlinck, Maurice. **Death.** 1912

Metchnikoff, Élie. **The Nature of Man:** Studies in Optimistic Philosophy. 1910

Metchnikoff, Élie. **The Prolongation of Life:** Optimistic Studies. 1908

Munk, William. **Euthanasia.** 1887

Osler, William. **Science and Immortality.** 1904

Return to Life: Two Imaginings of the Lazarus Theme. 1976

Stephens, C[harles] A[sbury]. **Natural Salvation:** The Message of Science. 1905

Sulzberger, Cyrus. **My Brother Death.** 1961

Taylor, Jeremy. **The Rule and Exercises of Holy Dying.** 1819

Walker, G[eorge] A[lfred]. **Gatherings from Graveyards.** 1839

Warthin, Aldred Scott. **The Physician of the Dance of Death.** 1931

Whiter, Walter. **Dissertation on the Disorder of Death.** 1819

Whyte, Florence. **The Dance of Death in Spain and Catalonia.** 1931

Wolfenstein, Martha. **Disaster:** A Psychological Essay. 1957

Worcester, Alfred. **The Care of the Aged, the Dying, and the Dead.** 1950

Zandee, J[an]. **Death as an Enemy According to Ancient Egyptian Conceptions.** 1960